Information Resources Management

Management in our knowledge-based society and economy

John R Beaumont

and

Ewan Sutherland

BUTTERWORTH
HEINEMANN

Butterworth-Heinemann Ltd
Linacre House, Jordan Hill, Oxford OX2 8DP

℞ A member of the Reed Elsevier plc group

OXFORD   LONDON   BOSTON
MUNICH   NEW DELHI   SINGAPORE   SYDNEY
TOKYO   TORONTO   WELLINGTON

First published 1992
Reprinted 1994

British Library Cataloguing in Publication Data
Beaumont, John R (1957–)
Sutherland, Ewan (1956–)
    Information resources management: management in our knowledge-based society and
    economy
    – (Contemporary business series)
    I. Title   II. Series
    658.04

ISBN 0 7506 0485 9

Typeset by the authors.
Printed and bound in Great Britain by M & A Thomson Litho Ltd, East Kilbride, Scotland.

Information Resources Management

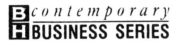

BH **contemporary** **BUSINESS SERIES**

Series Editor: Professor Andrew Lock
Manchester Polytechnic

The Contemporary Business Series is designed with the needs of business studies undergraduates and MBA students in mind, and each title is written in a straightforward, student friendly style. Though all of the books in the series reflect the individuality of their authors, you will find that you can count on certain key features in each text which maintain high standards of structure and approach:

- excellent coverage of core and option subject
- UK/international examples or case studies throughout
- full references and further reading suggestions
- written in direct, easily acessible style, for ease of use by full, part-time and self-study students

Contents

Contents

Preface

This is a book for managers and students — business, management and MBA students, rather than specialists in information technology or information systems. It addresses the growing need for managers to understand the critical issues and strategic questions which we face as our society and economy become increasingly knowledge-based. It is no longer possible to avoid the full implications of how the use of information and communications technologies (ICTs) affect an organisation, in the way it conducts business and the way in which it competes. As competition has intensified in most if not all industries, with more and better competitors, with changing regulatory environments and with heightened customer expectations, managers cannot afford to be complacent or even to be seen to be so. Ultimately, the factor which distinguishes an organisation is the people, it is first-class managers which are the most scarce resource, rather than information and communications technologies.

There must not be a technological imperative. All the evidence demonstrates that information and communications technologies cannot be a source of sustainable competitive advantage, but are instead a competitive necessity. Increasingly organisations recognise that ICTs are a strategic business investment, rather than an administrative cost. Given that information permeates all aspects of an organisation, responsibility must go beyond the data processing or information systems department and must be viewed as a corporate, rather than a functional, activity. The potential of information and communications technologies can only be realised through appropriate management and the recognition of organisational and cultural constraints. There are no automatic benefits from investments, management is essential to exploit the full potential.

There is a need to put the I (the information) back into IT, with more attention to the management, organisation and delivery of information. The underlying perspective of this book is that information is a resource that must be managed continuously, if an organisation is to be planned and controlled effectively. Over the last two decades, organisations have learned how to manage other resources: financial, human and raw materials. The changes associated with managing these resources have been dependent on access to and the manipulation and communication of information.

An information systems strategy must be aligned with the business strategy and driven by the corporate vision, while ensuring the provision of the information required for day-to-day management decision-making. While it is simple to state that there should be improved information resources management, it is not straightforward to achieve. Prescription is neither possible nor desirable, but a structured and flexible approach is feasible, one which managers can and should 'own'.

The real potential of information and communications technologies is not being realised. The business benefits of existing investments are not being achieved and possible new applications are being missed. Managers have been unable to forget the unfulfilled promises, the hype and the jargon of IT vendors, the delays to systems implementation, the difficulties of recruiting qualified technical staff, the cost overruns and the many other problems. Notwithstanding the attribution of blame, the failure to use, or the ineffective use of, information and communications technologies can be a significant cause of competitive vulnerability. More positively, there is a sufficient number of organisations that are achieving business benefits and indeed competitive advantage from their ICT investments. Such firms provide useful and relevant signposts to others.

In the field of information resources management, books have had major deficiencies:

- the technical emphasis on the information and communications technologies;
- the failure to capture real-world business problems and to understand some of the opportunities for information and communications technologies (probably because their authors have confined their experiences to the 'ivory towers' of academia).

This book is the outcome of:

- our recent teaching experiences (undergraduate, MBA, postgraduate and post-experience) and our research, consultancy and management backgrounds in the UK, USA and Europe;
- our frustrations with much of the existing management literature;
- our belief that:
  - an information systems strategy must be an integral and fully aligned component of the corporate business strategy;
  - information flows are the 'life-blood' of an organisation's decision-making.

Following from this, we hope to make the reader think about:

- how to understand the strategic information links of an organisation;
- how to develop the 'information culture' in an organisation;
- how to specify the information requirements for management decision-making;
- how to forecast potential investment payoffs;
- how to design and implement information systems;
- how to diagnose problems.

The real difficulty with writing a book such as this is knowing when to stop. The nature of the subject means that there is a constant flow of additional material from technological developments to new applications and from new strategic alliances to new thinking on management practices. Moreover, each chapter could be a book in its own right. A halt was called, as demonstrated by the book's publication.

As with all books from the perspective of general management and business strategy, we do not attempt to offer either an in-depth discussion of substantive topics or a detailed set of tools and procedures. The coverage is broad, though, inevitably, there are gaps. The balance and the admittedly unequal treatment of the topics reflects the authors' views on the perspective necessary for the 1990s. A 'management' rather than a 'technical' outlook is offered and sufficient issues are raised and discussed to cause readers to think and to want to find out more. The orientation is towards managers as individuals rather than their organisations, in the belief that it is the people in an organisation who ultimately determine whether opportunities are identified and taken up. Our experiences indicate that the more 'information literate' managers (recent graduates and MBAs) have already begun to raise challenges for their senior colleagues.

Both authors are equally responsible for the contents of this book. It is the outcome of our last five year's work during which we have been influenced by many people. The experiences of advising and working in various organisations ('big' and 'small', 'good' and 'bad') and learning from students, managers and colleagues are all very important and much appreciated (although it is difficult to identify all the individuals).

In particular our thinking has been shaped by recent involvement in the development of executive courses and research related to the findings from the 'Management in the 1990s' Program undertaken by the Sloan School of Management at the Massachussetts Institute of Technology, described by Alan Cane in the *Financial Times* (30 April 1990) as:

> ... there has never been such a profound analysis of the ways in which information technology can affect business performance for good or ill, nor such a complete prescription of the measures companies must adopt if they are to stay afloat in the uncharted waters of today's fiercely competitive global marketplace.

Our thanks go to our 'teacher', Hugh Macdonald, who forced us to confront difficult issues and to communicate them in straightforward terms. The abilities of Kathleen Murray and Paddy Yerburgh to find order in chaos was a fundamental force behind one of the authors doing anything. As usual, any errors and omissions remain the responsibility of the authors.

At the end of each chapter we have provided review questions to help readers test their understanding of the material covered. We have also devised study questions which require further work and reading. To help in further reading, we have provided annotated reading lists for each chapter and a complete bibliography at the end of the book.

A set of master copies for overhead projector slides is available for academic staff who adopt this book for teaching.

Our changing business world

Learning objectives:

- to be aware of the effects and potential of information and communications technologies at different levels, from society as a whole to the single individual;

- to appreciate the importance of knowledge in business.

1.1 Introduction

The world of business is both complex and competitive. Looking to the future, it can only become more complicated and the competition more severe. The excitement of management comes from creating opportunities and from challenging others to respond:

> Some of the most famous battles of business and war have been won not by doing things correctly but by breaking the rules, by *creating* the categories. (Mintzberg, 1990, page 135.)

While the 'management of change' has been with us for nearly twenty years, it is becoming ever clearer that managers must have the vision to transform their organisations if they are to ensure that the organisations survive, let alone prosper. Managers must become agents of change, rather than its grudging acceptors. While change is not new, the scale and frequency with which we must transform organisations certainly is. Tom Peters (1987) gave us 'thriving on chaos', as the battlecry for a management revolution, while Charles Handy (1989) writes about the world turned 'upside down'. No longer is it a matter of unfreeze-change-refreeze, it is continuous and large-scale change. It will not be sufficient merely to perform today's activities more quickly and more efficiently than in the past, the business processes must be transformed. As we approach a new millenium, Alfred North Whitehead's observation, made in 1925, is even more appropriate:

> The rate of progress is such that an individual ... will be called upon to face novel situations which find no parallel in his past. The fixed person of the fixed duties, who in older societies was such a godsend, in the future will be a public danger.

In considering the dynamics of the business world, the most pressing need is for managers to have a positive desire to seek out and encourage change. This outlook does not come naturally; it is only human to be reticent about change. Moreover, senior managers have vested interests in maintaining the *status quo*; they are the products of the existing system. Having achieved their successes and having been rewarded by the system, they have no reason to seek to overthrow it. Tomorrow's successful managers will be those who are positive about change and who are attuned to the future, rather than to the present or, worse still, who linger in the past. It is all too easy to say that managers should relish change, it is much more difficult to carry it into practice. Too often we find organisations that alter their strategies (and even their structures), while the managers continue to work in the same old way:

> I'm not here to predict the world. I'm here to be sure I've got a company that is strong enough to respond to whatever happens. (Jack Welch, Chairman and CEO of General Electric.)

Although the focus of this book is on Information Resources Management (IRM), it must be stressed at the outset that we cannot justify a technological imperative. Managers must ask about the business opportunities and the benefits offered through the use of information and communications technologies (ICTs), rather than focus on their technological capabilities or their functionality. It should be emphasised that there is no evidence to demonstrate that information and communications technologies can be a source of sustainable competitive advantage; there are no 'magic bullets' in business.

As the term 'information resources management' tries to indicate, the success or failure of information and communications technologies is dependent directly on the quality of its management, rather than the quantity of the investment. The gap between the 'gee-whizz' of science and technology and the realities of business operations is a reflection of the limited achievements of managers and the impractical nature of many scientists and technologists. Nonetheless, the potential provided by ICTs is immense:

> Telecommunications — and computers — will continue to drive change, just as manufacturing did during the industrial period. We are laying the foundations for an international information highway system. In telecommunications we are moving to a single worldwide information network, just as economically we are becoming one global marketplace. We are moving toward the capability to communicate anything to anyone anywhere, by any form — voice, data, text, or image — at the speed of light. (Naisbitt and Aburdene, 1990, page 14.)

References to the so-called 'information society' and 'information economy' have been around for over twenty years. In this chapter, we explore a number of important themes about doing business in a society and economy which will be based on knowledge. This perspective extends beyond earlier views of a 'post-industrial society', with its emphasis on the growing significance of the service sector at the expense of manufacturing. It provides a focus on the information and communications technologies (ICTs) sector, its increasing range of products and services and the growing numbers employed in it. Figure 1.1 illustrates the changing significance of the composition of employment in the economy.

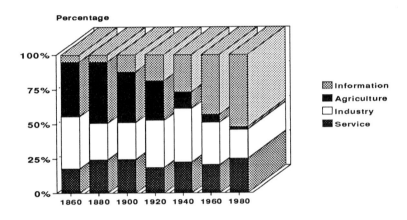

Figure 1.1 *Employment patterns in the United States of America* (Adapted from Porat)

While the only thing certain about the future is its uncertainty, there are some important socio-economic and political trends that we can be confident will affect managers and their organisations. Exaggerated claims about the potential of information and communications technologies must be avoided; the 'paperless office' and the 'factory of the future' did considerable harm. No attempt is made here to identify the next great technological breakthrough; too many authors have been caught out at unnecessary and unjustified futurology. Existing, and indeed old, technologies are neither used effectively nor efficiently. For most managers in most organisations, it is quite adequate to look at the capabilities of the existing technology and the developments known to be coming to the market. It is dangerous and unnecessarily foolhardy to rely on anything other than 'proven technology' to build a platform for business. Instead of always looking to new technologies, we should make greater efforts to exploit the existing technologies more fully.

In order to explore how the use of ICTs has developed and how the growing dependence on knowledge will have significant implications, we need to look on several levels and from different perspectives, each closely inter-related (see figure 1.2). The individual operates in society, in the economy and in the organisation for which he or she works, and is therefore affected by a number of inter-locking effects.

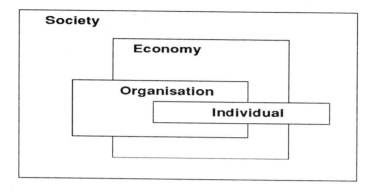

Figure 1.2 *Framework to discuss the effects of ICTs*

Knowledge-based

The term 'knowledge-based' is used to stress the increasing significance of knowledge as organisations become more dependent on brain power or 'intellectual capital'. Organisations must 'out think' their competitors:

> In classical economics, the sources of wealth are land, labor, and capital. For most of this century, large-scale, highly efficient manufacturing facilities have brought prosperity to firms and their shareholders. Now, another engine of wealth is at work. It takes many forms: technology, innovation, science, know-how, creativity, information. In a word, it is knowledge. In more and more industries, the most competitive firms succeed by developing, improving, protecting, and renewing knowledge, and then speeding it to market in a stream of rapidly and continually improved products and services. As knowledge-driven competition spreads and intensifies, managers and scholars will find themselves rethinking many familiar, deeply rooted assumptions about what a company is, how it should be organized, what it is managers do, and how it can remain competitive. (Badaracco, 1991, page 1.)

C K Prahalad and Gary Hamel (1990) have introduced the idea of the 'core competencies' to describe the accumulated knowledge of an organisation. It is important to understand how effectively an organisation can deploy this knowledge (but this should not be confused with 'managerial competencies' required by individual managers).

Many of the acquisitions and mergers that were prevalent in the 1970's and 1980's made no attempt to identify or to build on core competencies. While Prahalad and Hamel (1990) note the competence of Philips, the Dutch electronics giant, in its functional leadership in compact data storage and retrieval, the early 1990's have proved a very painful period for Philips as they have been forced to sell-off businesses which were not central to their main activities. It is important to recognise that specific technologies can usually be bought or imitated, although this can be expensive and can involve delays in their incorporation into production, products and services. For many ICT vendors, their core competencies are related not to the manufacture of their products, but to the associated 'added value' services they provide (see Chapter 3).

The identification and use of core competencies are tasks which are very far from simple. Indeed, Prahalad and Hamel (1990, page 87):

> ... find it ironic that top management devotes so much attention to the capital budgeting process yet typically has no comparable mechanism for allocating the human skills that embody core competencies.

In many organisations, a new coordination capacity is required to ensure the effective exploitation of core competencies. The infrastructure of ICTs can assist this process, if there is a learning culture in the organisation (see Chapter 7):

> Looking to the future, the central questions are: what knowledge does a company need to meet its long-term strategic goals? Which capabilities — *not* necessarily which products — will give it an advantage over its competitors three to five years hence? (Badaracco, 1991, page 132.)

Competition is being intensified globally by generic technical and scientific competencies, and new critical skills, many of which are in short supply, are becoming more and more important. Almost by definition, the requirement for management education and development will continue to grow in knowledge-based organisations. Consequently, organisations need to increase their investment in human capital, their key asset.

At the national level, there is a need to consider the scientific and technical component of children's education in schools. A key role for government is to provide the foundations of a knowledge-based society through the schools, colleges and universities, which are essential to create knowledgeable citizens who will be the knowledge-workers providing the basis for the future economy. In Britain, for instance, the Advisory Council on Science and Technology, which advises the UK government on its education and science policy, has agreed that, to achieve economic growth, it is essential to increase and broaden the teaching of science and technology. For the future, it is very worrying that only about half of seventeen year olds in Britain are in full-time or part-time education, while over 80 percent of their counterparts in France, Japan, West Germany and the United States continue their education and development.

Michael Porter (1990) highlights the significance of education in understanding the relative competitive position of nations. For example, in Britain:

The educational system has badly lagged behind that of virtually all the nations we studied. ... The British workforce is well behind in education and skills compared with that of many other advanced nations. Managers in Britain are also much less likely to have college or university degrees than those in other advanced nations. There is a shortage of managers trained in technology entering manufacturing industries, and a technical background has been uncommon in top management. ... Most British companies have done little in-house to offset a weak educational system. (Porter, 1990, pages 497-498.)

In the United States of America:

Perhaps the single most important reason for faltering commercialisation of technology is the eroding quality of human resources relative to other nations. While its overall rate of spending on education as a fraction of GDP is among the highest, America's educational system is faltering badly. ... The top schools and universities are second to none, and many foreign students come to America for training especially at the graduate level. High quality at the top, however, masks grave problems everywhere else. The average American university is not up to the standard of the average German or Swiss university, and the percentage of students majoring in technical fields is lower. ... Even more serious is the educational system for the average worker. American schools set low standards and are weak in discipline. (Porter, 1990, page 520.)

In Japan, there is:

... a long tradition of respect for education that borders on the reverence. ... Japanese are disciplined, hardworking, and willing to cooperate with the group ... While Americans often claim (with some justification) that a lack of creativity results from Japan's rigid system, Japanese education provides most students all over Japan with a sound foundation for later education and training. A Japanese high school graduate knows as much maths as most American college graduates. ... What is unique about Japan's post secondary educational system is the education and training that is provided both for workers and managers in Japanese companies. Japanese knowledge creation has taken place in companies much more than in other institutions. In-company training is rigourous and essential for advancement. (Porter, 1990, pages 395-397.)

The Master of Business Administration (MBA) has clearly been the global brand leader in management education through the 1980's, driven by an enormous popular desire to acquire the title. Gaining an MBA should be an internationally recognised measure of dedication, achievement and understanding of the complex problems of modern business and management. In the future, further differentiation will continue as management education becomes more market-oriented. The business school from which one receives one's MBA will become increasingly important as rankings, such as the American league tables, reflecting the experience of companies spread to

Europe and elsewhere. While the financial pressures facing many higher education institutions have led to their developing MBA programmes, because of the apparently lucrative market, there is an important constraint on the supply-side, given the considerable shortage of experienced high-quality staff necessary to provide the quality of service expected. It is impossible for many schools, with their limited resources, to provide MBA programmes that attempt to do everything. The orientation must be towards areas that they can perform well and can differentiate themselves, including programme type, say:

CONVERSION MBA
Aimed at people in their early twenties, recent graduates with little or no experience of business and management.

MBA
Aimed at people in their late twenties or early thirties, with a minimum of five years' business and management experience, usually in one functional area.

'EXECUTIVE' MBA
Aimed at people in their late thirties, with significant management experience and potential for substantial career advancement (probably to board-level).

Many commentators question the real relevance and usefulness of the 'conversion' MBA programmes (even though the market to fill such places remains buoyant). There is a danger of academic version of Gresham's Law in which the products of bad MBA programmes, not necessarily bad managers, drive out the products of good programmes. What is needed is not merely the MBA label, but the knowledge, skills and experience that make a first-class manager.

Henry Mintzberg (1989, page 79) characterises the teaching of information resources management in some business schools in rather stark terms:

> The field of management information systems, ostensibly concerned with application, continues to try to define itself by what a machine is claimed able to do (but never quite does, although no one dares to find out).

The providers of management education and development, both organisations and business schools, need to ensure that the business potential of ICTs is fully explained to managers so that they can exploit it.

The failure to understand IRM lies with the senior executives that must drive any ICT investments, rather than with the current generation of MBAs and graduates, who have at least some information literacy. All managers cannot, and should not, be expected to possess identical levels and ranges of ICT backgrounds and experiences (see table 1.1).

Table 1.1   *Skills and competencies in ICTs*

	General manager	*Functional manager*	*ICT manager*
Leadership skills	***	*	*
Understanding of general business operations	**	**	**
Understanding of ICTs	**	**	***
Understanding of ICT implementation	*	*	*

Key	***	very high level of capability; individual's primary expertise.
	**	high level of capability.
	*	sufficient capability to permit effective workings with others.
		Can apply 'techniques', but unlikely to generate new initiatives.

The old ideas of computer literacy that required the learning of programming languages and systems theory are outmoded and largely irrelevant. Something is wrong if a manager is writing a computer program. Instead, managers need to be 'information literate', meaning that they should be able to:

- comprehend the strengths and weaknesses of information and communications technologies (including the quality and availability of data);
- understand the ways in which information and communications technologies can help satisfy an organisation's strategic and operational needs;
- use well-documented, generally available ('shrink-wrapped') applications software.

Physicists use the 'half-life' to measure how long a quantity of radioactive isotope takes to decay to half its level of radioactivity. By analogy, the half-life of a BA in Geography is considerably greater than that of a BSc in Computing Science; the outpouring of new material in computing science is much greater than in geography and its effect is much more likely to undermine or bury what is already there. Similarly, the half-life of a geography degree is much shorter than that of a degree in philosophy. The philosopher Socrates (470-399 BC) and the geographer Alexander von Humboldt (1769-1859) could still make contributions to philosophy and to geography, while Charles Babbage (1792-1871) would find it much more difficult to contribute to computing science.

As the rate at which knowledge become obsolete accelerates, the need for continuing education throughout a person's life becomes even more important. However, it need not be more of the same, either in terms of objectives or delivery mechanisms. Sir Douglas Hague (1991, page 14), for example, in a thought-provoking essay entitled "Beyond Universities", argues that:

... pressures for change will receive increasing support from the fact that the knowledge society draws on information and communications technology. It will provide an expanding range of artefacts which will transform what can be done, especially in teaching.

Although the availability of ICTs has obvious implications for the design and content of curricula, there are also implications for the means of delivery, especially given the scale and the distributed nature of the requirement for management training and development. With the need for more (and better) training, information and communications technologies can provide an important new delivery mechanism, especially as an extension of 'open learning' or 'distance learning'. Assuming appropriate course materials can be designed, this delivery mechanism can be both educationally effective and cost efficient. For any organisation, the ability to provide learning at work can have enormous cost savings, especially if the organisation has a geographically extensive network of branches, while for an individual, active, self-paced learning can be very attractive. For example, many retailing organisations with networks of branches are already using technology-based training, such as interactive video, to create active learning environments in their branches.

Case: IRM by distance learning

Scenario: The electronic, or virtually electronic, classroom/campus is an exciting new medium for the delivery of education, especially for managers in full-time employment with several years work experience. Information and communications technologies permit students and academic staff living and working in widely dispersed geographic locations to communicate at the times most convenient for themselves.

The International School of Information Management (ISIM) in Santa Barbara, California is a distance learning institution offering an MSc degree in Information Resources Management through a teleconferencing network; the classroom goes to the students. The courses are offered through a computer teleconferencing network (ISIMnet), which extends the geographic market for their courses by overcoming constraints of conventional, residential-based education institutions. It has also permitted ISIM to bring together a high-quality academic staff from all over the USA (which is a scarce resource in this field) to design and run the courses.

Students receive a variety of study materials, including books, articles and floppy disks at the beginning of each course. Their progress through the curriculum is self-paced and both students and faculty can access ISIMnet at any time of the day or night. ISIMnet ensures private communications by means of the personal 'mail box' which is accessible only to a designated user. The network also allows intensive group interaction without the need to assemble all the participants in one classroom. Group interaction is further enhanced by the availability of additional 'forums'. "Through the Exchange", the electronic equivalent of the campus union, students can 'meet' and 'chat' about anything of interest. They can compare notes; they can make new friends in other parts of the country or the world.

Electronic classrooms, private mail boxes and forums, modern communications tools, promote rather than limit the establishment of close student/faculty and student/student relationships. They are instrumental in restoring intensive, personal interaction to learning as well as to teaching. One student, for example, commenting on their ISIM 'on-line educational experience', stated:

Development of telecommunications distance learning, as provided by ISIM, is excellent. Descriptive words that touch upon my feelings toward this matter of education include, but are not limited by, the most fascinating method for learning, acquiring knowledge and/or pertinent information that I have ever come across.

Source: Boehm and Horton, 1991.

1.2 Society

Notwithstanding the technological changes which we know are difficult to forecast, the effects of social change will be much greater, affecting customers, suppliers, employees and competitors — the way we live and work.

Managers have always had to understand the social context in which they do business. Sound and effective management increasingly recognises the broader significance of social responsibility, which affects every aspect of management. By the end of the 1980's (a decade characterised by the capitalist short-termism of 'junk bonds' and 'golden parachutes'), there was evidence of changing values and actions. More attention was being paid to corporate responsibility and to business ethics; how business is and ought to be undertaken in an ethical manner.

Increased concern about our planet, under the umbrella of global environmental change, could, for instance, provide the impetus for better funding for scientific research and management aimed at enhancing the quality and richness of people's lives. The physical environment being recognised as an important strategic issue for every organisation.

Case: Global environmental change

Scenario: The physical environment is a complex, finely balanced system in which we all live (along with the other animals and plants of the planet Earth). Environmental problems are a major and urgent issue facing the people of the Earth.

Natural resources are being depleted and the environment is being degraded by the activities of both private and public sector organisations. These problems are connected directly with the industrialisation of the last two centuries, associated with increased material consumption and a rapidly growing population.

The effects of the release of carbon dioxide from the burning of fossil fuels leading to the so-called Greenhouse Effect combined with the destruction of the world's forests, which are the major suppliers of oxygen, raise worrying problems. The holes in the ozone layer, apparently caused by propellant gases such as chlorofluorocarbons (CFCs), are leading to increased exposure to ultraviolet light which causes skin cancer and raises the temperature of the planet. The political opening up of Eastern Europe has revealed a nightmare of ecological issues, not least economies such as that of Czechoslovakia which is reliant on the burning of lignite (brown coal) which gives off large amounts of sulphur dioxide and particulates.

While there is uncertainty about the scale and timing of these interlocking crises, the trends are clear. For example, 1990 was the warmest year in Britain since records commenced over 130 years ago and the next five warmest years were all in the 1980's. Many scientists believe that the increase in global mean temperature of 0.45° Centigrade in this century is outside the natural variability of the climate.

National and international programmes are being established to further our understanding and, perhaps, predict natural and man-made global environmental changes, together with their direct consequences and longer-term effects. To make real progress, scientists require high quality measurements from space, the air, the sea, and the ground, together with tests made in laboratories and computer simulations.

The interrelated nature of these environmental issues, which range in scale from the local to the global, means that large-scale data handling is essential (some of which must be completed in real time). Such datasets must be viewed as national and international strategic resources. Various features of global environmental change serve to highlight the requirement for the shared use of data resources: across nations, across organisations, across disciplines and over time. The information requirements are multi-disciplinary, multi-functional and international in nature; collaboration is, and will increasingly be, essential to ensure a focus on the interrelationships between business, socio-economic and

> political activities and the Earth's physical and biochemical environment.
>
> Important issues relating to the 'power' of data, include:
>
> • access and the costs of access to data generated by others;
> • provision and dissemination of information about data.
>
> Remote sensing and other forms of automatic data capture, Geographic Information Systems (GIS), simulation modelling, visualisation and image processing are all important aspects of the necessary data collection, analysis and presentation.

The range of forces that will affect the nature of tomorrow's society, include changing demographic patterns and a new global, political economy. As the service sector of economies develop, it must be accepted that people will be both their own suppliers and their own consumers; despite claims to the contrary, it seems that 'we can take in each other's washing'.

There is a growing shift in the balance of the population which is resulting in an ever greater number of older people in Europe and the USA, especially noticeable in the workforce. It is creating new problems and new opportunities related to consumption patterns and the infrastructure which will be required to support the ageing population, especially in health and social care. Employment structures will be modified, with more part-time, temporary and independent workers and with a greater number of women in the workforce (including a greater proportion in senior positions).

Case: Telecommuting

Scenario: The real transformations that affect people occur where they live and work, and the capabilities of information and communications technologies could now offer much more flexibility and, indeed, enjoyment to people's lifestyles through the provision of a supporting infrastructure.

The future of work does not need to be constrained by today's rigid structure organised around increasingly difficult morning and evening commuting between the home and the workplace. While 'working at home' conjures up images of adult truancy or a late rise from bed followed by some gardening, the majority of managers do take work home with them and believe their outputs are relatively high because they avoid the disturbances of the office. 'Telecommuting' offers existing workers new ways of working and new opportunities for people who may not be able to work in a traditional way; for instance, some mothers with children work at home as computer programmers for ICL and the FI Group. Clearly, the potential for 'telecommuting' depends on the nature of the work.

However, if telecommuting is to be successful it must be well-managed with a clear appreciation of the implications for organisational structures, moving to 'flatter' networks rather than the traditional hierarchy. Managers must be able to specify the tasks explicitly in order to be able to assess performance and project and time management skills will be even more important. The possible benefits to organisations include an improved ability to recruit and retain people and a reduction in the costs of office space. Individuals are likely to have clearer responsibilities.

It is misleading to see 'telecommuting' as necessarily 'high-tech', full-time, or home-based. A telephone may be sufficient to telecommute and local (suburban) business centres may be more suitable than the home from where to telecommute.

In general, homes are not designed to be offices either in their physical construction or in the ways in people use them. It will therefore require considerable adjustments in buildings to provide the necessary space and facilities. Only then can the more difficult tasks of stopping the interruptions from children and the other trials of daily domestic life be tackled.

While there can never be an equality of outcomes, there can and should be equality of opportunity. Little progress seems to have been made on the North-South dialogue which was led by Willy Brandt (1980). The 'Uruguay Round' of the General Agreement of Tariffs and Trade (GATT) seems bogged down in arguments over agriculture. In the majority of 'developed' economies, recent decades have witnessed the rich getting richer and the poor getting poorer. By adding ethnic and racial dimensions, one can see real problems of the poverty of minorities.

The reconfiguration of the geopolitical map of Europe presents a great many opportunities, which many individuals and businesses have already begun to seize. The enormous changes in East-West relations, with the ending of the 'Cold War', the removal of the 'Iron Curtain' and the dissolution of the Union of Soviet Socialist Republics have opened up long forgotten markets and created innumerable new business opportunities. For example, General Electric has acquired a majority holding in Tungsram, a Hungarian light-bulb manufacturer, and Volkswagen has bought a controlling interest in Skoda, the Czech car manufacturer. Less dramatic has been the creation of the European Community's Single Internal Market, datelined for 1992, but in reality a slow evolution. Austria, Norway, Sweden and, perhaps, even Switzerland are interested in joining the European Community in the mid- to late 1990's. Moreover, with all the Eastern European countries and parts of the former USSR enthusiastic to join, the European Community could conceivably extend from the Atlantic to the Urals, with over 600 million people.

The Single Internal Market has attracted enormous strategic attention, not only within Europe but also from American and Japanese organisations. The UK has already seen significant inward investment from Japanese companies to create manufacturing facilities for cars and electronics. The European Community will become a market of such a scale as to provide obvious business opportunities.

1.3 Economy

The future characteristics of the 'economy' are difficult to forecast; the early 1990s have already brought recession to North America, the UK and other western economies. Moreover, it is also difficult to identify the major forces that will affect tomorrow's economies. It is clear that the future is increasingly global or at least 'northern', with barriers between countries and organisations fading away in their economic significance. At the time of writing, it seems reasonable to expect a return to savings and away from debt, given the enormous current scale of both corporate and personal debt.

Organisations increasingly compete and collaborate globally, operating in a number of different 'niche' markets. To be successful, these organisations must be 'world class' in terms of:

- being customer-orientated;
- providing high quality service;
- maximising the use of their competencies;
- bringing new products to market very rapidly.

'Successful' organisations will be those that learn and adapt, that have a simpler, flatter organisation structure characterised by delegation and participation. Management will be less about control and more about leading, motivating and facilitating. Information can and must be at managers' fingers, but they need to be trained to use it effectively.

Notwithstanding the important general changes envisaged for our increasingly knowledge-based economy, it would be incorrect not to highlight the increasingly significant effects of the use of information and communications technologies. For instance, Peter Keen (1991, page 2) in his recent discussion of 'business design through information technology' considers:

... business realities of the 1990's:

- between 25 and 80 percent of companies' cash flow is processed on line;
- Electronic Data Interchange is the norm in operations;
- Point-of-Sale and electronic payments are an element in every electronic transaction processing system;
- image technology is an operational necessity;
- companies are directly linked to major suppliers and customers in electronic partnerships;

- re-organisation is frequent, not exceptional;
- work is increasingly location-independent.

These are conservative, not bold, predictions.

1.4 Information resources management

Information Resources Management (IRM) is a term that has been used for over a decade, although there is still no single, unambiguous definition:

> Information resources management determines how your organisation conducts its business and supports the management of business resources that account for its successes or failures. Information resources management is therefore unique, even for organisations with identical products and services. What your policies will state and how you will implement them will shape how your organisation will operate in the decades ahead. (Strassmann, 1990, pages 493-494.)

While information resources management means different things to different people, the phrase captures the important thrust, which is a concern for the management of an organisational asset rather than for technology. IRM is not a development from the traditional and specialist data processing function. Indeed, it was the failure of DP/IS Departments to focus on the business benefits of large-scale investments that led to an increasing acceptance of the information resources management perspective, at least by general managers, if not DP/IS managers.

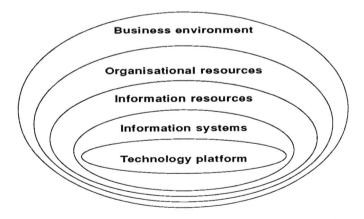

Figure 1.3 *The scope of information resources management*

Information resources management is an umbrella term that covers the full range of management activities necessary to ensure that information is available in order to conduct business and to make decisions. IRM includes all types of data, numbers, text, images and voice, made available using many different information and communications technologies. An infrastructural 'platform' is used to acquire, store, process, distribute and retrieve the data. Figure 1.3 illustrates the scope of information resources management within the overall business resources of an organisation and the traditional ICT emphasis on mere information systems rather than the available technology platform.

INFORMATION

Many authors differentiate between 'data', 'information' and 'knowledge', although the definitions are usually of a very general nature. Data are viewed as raw or only slightly processed, while information is linked directly to a specified decision or process and comprises processed data with an added-value; knowledge is more abstract.

RESOURCES

Traditional economic theory tells us that resources are both scarce and possess value. Although many organisations do not understand the real costs and benefits of data handling, information has become a tradeable commodity, through the rapid growth of information services. Value can be created or added by the integration of different datasets. While the value of datasets generally decreases over time, data are a reusable resource which are not consumed by use.

MANAGEMENT

For the effective and efficient utilisation of any resource, it is essential that it be managed, planning and controlling activities against measurable targets.

In this book, information resources management is interpreted broadly to include:

BUSINESS

How information and communications technologies can be used for competitive advantage.

ECONOMICS

How the information economy is changing markets.

LAW

How information and communications technologies affect the legal frameworks, within which people, businesses and nations operate.

SOCIETY

How information and communications technologies are altering the way in which we live and work.

TECHNOLOGY

The trends in the developments of information and communications technologies, and how organisations use these potential infrastructural platforms.

Figure 1.4 is an idealised representation of the central requirement for organisations to integrate their management of information resources. Information affects all aspects of an organisation, its external links with customers and suppliers and its various internal functions. Unfortunately the wheel cannot show the dynamics of these functions. Information and communications technologies provide the infrastructure which enables information flows, which should be driven by the organisation, specifically the corporate strategy and the management decision-making processes. An external orientation is necessary for the competitive strategy in the marketplace, with an appropriate positioning of products and services. However, unlike many analyses of business strategy which are based solely on outputs, it is also necessary to integrate the inputs from the management of an organisation.

Figure 1.4   *The IRM wheel*

While it is outside the scope of this discussion to consider individual functions, such as marketing or operations management, it is vital that a 'single' corporate perspective be adopted. Although distributed processing means that data can reside anywhere, this feature should not be interpreted as recommending a single large-scale system. The advances in information and communications technologies mean that the various applications can operate in a distributed fashion, accessing data as required.

It is important to appreciate that successful organisations will require new management styles and cultures. Information and communications technologies offer a flexible enabling infrastructure, but are not a sufficient condition. Future organisations must consider sharing information and decision-making to a much greater extent than in the past. Notwithstanding obvious issues of confidentiality, access to data should no longer be a 'power' issue; the source of power should be in the use of the information. This view of information systems is necessary not only to allow flexible, efficient and effective development over time, but also, more importantly, to recognise that different types of decisions have different information requirements as do different decision makers. Thus, simply stated, information is a resource that requires to be managed.

Review questions

1 How should the teaching and learning of management be changed in order to prepare managers for our future knowledge-based society and economy?

2 Highlight three significant features of the information resources management perspective.

3 What forces will affect the nature of management in the future?

4 Why are ICTs regarded as an 'enabling' technology?

Study questions

1 What are the core competencies of your organisation?

2 The gap between the nations of the North (Europe, Japan and the USA) and the South has been discussed for more than ten years. Discuss how it has been, or could be, affected by the adoption of ICTs.

3 The revolutionary changes which have swept through Eastern Europe and the former USSR mean that their economies will have to change. How is this affected by ICTs?

4 Discuss why we work in organisations which are rich in data but poor in information.

Further reading

The only way to keep up-to-date with developments is to read the commercial literature. Readers will therefore find it useful to consult: *Financial Times*, *Datamation*, *Business Week* (especially the Information Processing section), *Economist*, *Fortune*, *Futures*, *Harvard Business Review*, and *Sloan Management Review*.

Books, although quickly out-of-date, are a valuable source of knowledge which is both broad and deep. We list below some books that we found interesting, though it would be sensible to check on more recently published material.

Keen, Peter G W "Shaping the future; business design through information technology" Harvard Business School Press, Boston, 1991.

This is a significant contribution by someone with enormous IT experience and an ability to synthesise future business needs. Business integration and technology platforms are central components of this discussion which is aimed at general managers, rather than IT specialists. Keen argues that effective management will increasingly involve handling IT and he suggests a reorientation of profit from a 'bottom line' perspective to a 'top line' perspective.

Naisbitt, John and Patricia Aburdene "Megatrends 2000" Sidgwick & Jackson, London, 1990.

The sequel to the well-received "Megatrends" by John Naisbitt. This new book, written with his wife, attempts to identify and highlight a range of forces that will affect our lives. They propose:

- *the booming global economy of the 1990s;*
- *a renaissance in the arts;*
- *the emergence of free-market socialism;*
- *the privatisation of the welfare state;*
- *the rise of the Pacific Rim;*
- *the decade of women in leadership;*
- *the age of biology;*
- *the religious revival of the new millenium;*
- *the triumph of the individual.*

Pascale, Richard T and Anthony G Athos "The Art of Japanese Management" Simon and Schuster, New York, 1981.

An early 1980's general management text that highlights seven factors that should be examined by the management of any organisation:

- *strategy;*
- *systems;*
- *structure;*
- *skills;*
- *style;*
- *staff;*
- *shared values.*

Porter, Michael E "The Competitive Advantage of Nations" Free Press, New York, 1991.

A much publicised and somewhat over-rated book which gives a long and rambling case against governmental involvement in industry. It provides country by country analyses of the USA, Sweden, the UK and so on.

Reich, Robert "The World of Work; preparing for 21st century capitalism" Knopf, New York, 1991.

A review with many ideas about how society is changing, the ways in which business is changing, and how individuals work.

Scott Morton, Michael S (editor) "The Corporation of the 1990's; information technology and organisational transformation" Oxford University Press, Oxford, 1991.

This edited volume is an outcome of the "Management in the 1990s" research programme undertaken by the Sloan School of Management at Massachusetts Institute of Technology in conjunction with ten major corporate sponsors. The aim of the project was to understand the management issues to be faced in the 1990s, and to start to develop solutions. The programme did not address technology issues; information and communications technologies were regarded as a key element, but the research did not attempt to predict technological developments. It seemed that ICTs would play a major part in the solution of many of the management problems, and it was also evident that many of the problems were 'caused' by information and communications technologies. It was the applications and implications of ICTs that were to be considered. This edited volume is a difficult, and at times disjointed, discussion of many fundamental management issues that need to be considered explicitly.

Stacey, Ralph D "The Chaos Frontier" Butterworth Heinemann, Oxford, 1991.

The first, inevitable attempt to make the linkage between management's recent interest in change and mathematic's modern development of dynamic systems theory. The concepts of structural stability and self-organisation are introduced, but the reader is left wanting much more than the use of analogies and wondering how dynamic systems can assist managers. No real attempt is made to explore the significant empirical issues of implementation; while the appendices contain a more 'technical' discussion, someone interested in the mathematics should read, say, D K Arrowsmith and C M Place (1990) "An Introduction to Dynamical Systems" published by Cambridge University Press.

2

Where is our organisation going?

Learning objectives:

- to understand the overall logic of strategic management and the importance of implementation and organisational learning;

- to understand the basic techniques of strategic analysis:
    - Strengths, Weaknesses, Opportunities and Threats;
    - portfolio approach;
    - Michael Porter's industry structure analysis model;

- to describe the Strategic Alignment Process.

2.1 Introduction

Every organisation must have some form of strategic management if it is considering 'where is our organisation going?' and, of course, 'where should our organisation be going?' Consideration of these questions is essential, given the changes and uncertainties of the business environment. Conventionally, particularly in 'consultancy speak', the process of strategic management has involved managers answering questions such as:

- where is the organisation now?
- given the external trends, where does the organisation want to be?
- what actions must be implemented to achieve the specified goals?

As part of this process, management formulates an explicit plan of priorities for action with appropriate allocation of resources that will take the organisation forward. Explicit attention must be given to the changing nature and scope of the industry, together with the particular competencies of the organisation. Situation analyses are completed, such as SWOT analysis (Strengths, Weaknesses, Opportunities and Threats), as are portfolio analyses to determine an organisation's best mix of businesses and of products and services. Strategy formulation is undertaken at different levels, usually: corporate; business; and functional.

'Strategy' has become an over-used and much-abused terms, being frequently made unnecessarily complicated. At a simple level, figure 2.1 captures the underlying and interrelated dimensions of any organisation's strategy formulation and implementation: business opportunities, organisational competencies and governance.

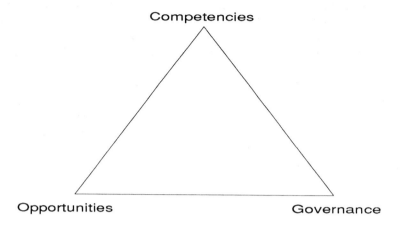

Figure 2.1 *The COG*
(Source: Hugh Macdonald)

Management involves the processes of planning and control, with the associated need for implementation. Strategic management is concerned primarily with the long-term, future direction of the overall organisation. Gordon Greenley (1989) distinguishes fourteen features of strategic management:

- external features
    - market orientation
    - market understanding
    - information inputs
    - empirical research
    - international business
- systems features
    - decision making
    - entrepreneurial thrusts
    - longer time horizons
    - methodological developments
- internal features
    - pro-active strategies
    - multiple strategies
    - interdisciplinary features
    - implementation
    - resource utilisation.

The essence of strategic management should be action rather than the process of developing the strategy or the document itself, with the ability to cope with uncertainty, devolve responsibility and to retain control. Many managers who devise formal mission statements, specify long-term objectives and prioritise implementation plans, not only waste enormous amounts of time and resources, but also delude themselves into believing that they are managing strategically, even though the strategy is never implemented. While some additional flexibility can always be introduced into this process, if only by last minute revisions, the real business issues and competitive assessments are frequently not examined sufficiently thoroughly. All too often, because of unanticipated changes in the business environment managers are obliged to make hasty decisions, without consideration of their strategic consequences and sometimes in contradiction of the strategy. Criticisms of the traditional formal strategic management process could, but should not, be interpreted as abdication of responsibility by management. The essential ingredients are vision, leadership and, increasingly, information which is both useful and actionable. In any event:

> Strategic management is not a separate kind of management at all, it is simply management. You cannot separate day-to-day and 'long-term' control; they are too interconnected. Effective day-to-day management requires tight, short-term control, state of the art Management Information and Control Systems. Without them there will be little management time for the 'strategic' and there will be no tool to implement it. Such systems provide some short-term order in what is fundamentally a disorderly situation. (Stacey, 1990, page 16.)

In this chapter, we introduce some of the ideas of business strategy analysis, both the formulation and the implementation. Formulation and implementation cannot be separated and, indeed, they should be seen as continuous, rather than as a one-off, exercises.

In the next section, attention focuses on strategy formulation, with particular reference being given to some of the techniques that illustrate a portfolio approach and competitive forces. These techniques are discussed with respect to the information-based industries. A descriptive overview of the Strategic Alignment Model from the Management in the Nineties research programme is presented. The concluding comments highlight implementation issues, in the light of Alfred Chandler's (1962) early research on 'strategy and structure'.

The basic rationale of the different approaches is to attempt to explain why some organisations have been successful and why others have failed. A variety of analyses has now been devised to examine the observed relationships between organisational performance and different strategies. It must be understood that, in the same industry, successful organisations could follow different ('niche') or similar ('me-too') strategies.

Almost all industries possess relatively small companies that provide specialist products or services and are able to avoid the major players by focusing on market niches:

Computer companies are among the newest converts to the 'end user' type of niche marketing, but they call it *vertical marketing*. For years, computer companies fought to sell general hardware and software systems horizontally across many markets, and the price battles got rougher. Smaller companies started to specialise by vertical slices — law firms, medical practices, banks, etc. — studying the specific hardware and software needs of their target group and designing high value-added products that had a competitive advantage over more general products. Their sales forces were trained to understand and service the particular vertical market. Computer companies also worked with independent *value added resellers* (VARS), who customised the computer hardware and software for individual clients or customer segments and earned a price premium in the process. (Kotler, 1988, pages 342-343.)

Michael Porter (1980) describes three generic strategies:

COST LEADERSHIP

At an industry-wide level, an organisation can provide an 'identical' product or service at the lowest cost.

DIFFERENTIATION

At an industry-wide level, an organisation can provide a differentiated ('unique') product or service at a premium price.

FOCUS

For an identified market segment, an organisation can form its product or service provision, by either cost leadership or differentiation.

In the market for personal computers, it is possible to identify a number of players who display the characteristics of these strategies. Amstrad remains firmly attached to its 'cheap and cheerful' image, continuing to launch products with chips the rest of the industry consider obsolete; it is a cost leader in the mass market. Compaq has shown itself to be adept at bringing out new and innovative products ahead of most rivals including IBM; it is a differentiated player in the mass market. Part of Compaq's success has been in the market for portable computers, where the technological leader has been Grid. Grid has a focused market strategy, its machines are technologically advanced, but expensive.

Case: Strategic management in retailing

Scenario: Retailing is a rapidly changing and competitive business in which organisations have formulated and implemented a range of corporate strategies.

Corporate business strategy comprises different orientations such as:

- consolidation and productivity: to increase performance from the existing resource to provide increased profit margins, volumes and utilisation of assets;
- repositioning: to meet the changing needs of existing (and/or potential new) customer segments;
- growth: to expand into related merchandise areas, customer service support, trading formats and so on;
- diversification: to expand into new retail opportunities (merchandise, customer service, trading format, and communications). This could include vertical integration or coordination of supply chain activities;
- conglomeration: to develop a group or portfolio of subsidiary companies whose activities may be quite different from each other or may be based on the same market but with different market positioning.

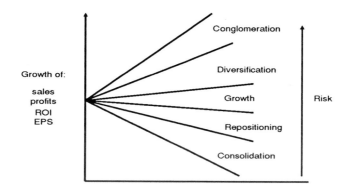

Figure 2.2 *Strategic alternatives for filling the planning gap*

As the strategic direction shifts away from the mainstream, business risk increases (see figure 2.2). It follows that the business can reduce the risk involved by developing effective support strategy expertise. Information resources management is one such element. For instance, some requirements could include:

Consolidation and Productivity:
- merchandise information reporting system (sales and margins)
- merchandise planning system (sales and margins)
    - test market/new product monitoring
    - branch performance monitoring
    - branch order processing
    - stock control/sales/stock systems
    - purchase order management

- supplier performance monitoring
- distribution performance monitoring
- market research competitor performance customer performance

Repositioning:
- competitor performance database
- consumer perceptions)
- customer perceptions) tracking studies
- environmental database: social/consumer change economic data

Growth:
- corporate database:
  - product portfolio performance
  - regional sales performance
  - product portfolio
  - outlet portfolio
- market research:
  - opportunity evaluation
  - product
  - format
  - location
- competitor database:
  - current business performance

Diversification:
- competitor database:
  - current business performance and new business performance
- environmental database:
  - projections
  - social/consumer
  - change
  - economic trends
  - technology trends
  - international trends
- market trends database:
  - emerging market trends
  - market characteristics
  - supply market characteristics
  - consumer expectations

Conglomeration:
- business performance database:
  - sector performance
  - individual business performance

A retailer that develops a range of expertise with information resources management can benefit in two significant ways:

- there should be the advantage of being able to identify and analyse strategic options in considerable depth, possibly sooner than competitors;
- there should be more precise control over the implementation of the selected corporate business strategy.

2.2 Strategy formulation

The process of strategy formulation can vary from an apparently formal and systematic set of procedures for analysis and planning to an *ad hoc* reaction by the senior management of an organisation to perceived problems. In strategy formulation, managers must consider both internal and external forces (see figure 2.3). The opportunities and threats in the industry must be considered within the context of the organisation's strengths and weaknesses, all of which cannot be divorced from the broader social setting and the leadership and vision of the key people responsible for implementation.

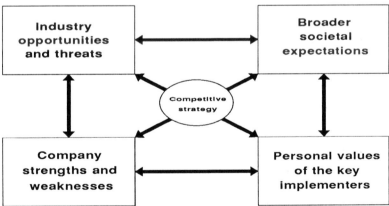

Factors external to the company

Factors internal to the company

Figure 2.3 *The context in which competitive strategy is formulated (Adapted from Porter, 1980, page xviii.)*

Central to the formulation of a business strategy is an examination of the attractiveness of an industry and the appropriate positioning for the organisation (which must be dynamic rather than static). A range of approaches has been devised to undertake these 'environmental scans'. In this section, two approaches are introduced:

- portfolio analysis;
- competitive forces.

The discussion is meant to be illustrative, rather than exhaustive (see Further Reading to follow up the topic of strategic management).

Portfolio approach

As the term suggests, the portfolio approach disaggregates the activities of an organisation into a set of well-defined Strategic Business Units (SBUs), differentiated by industry attractiveness and competitive position — just as one would treat investments on the stock market. Such an approach means that individual strategies can be formulated for each business unit, rather than requiring each strategic business unit to achieve identical objectives. The portfolio approach was developed independently by the Boston Consultancy Group (BCG), McKinsey and Company and the Strategic Planning Institute, though versions, modifications and extensions have been made by many others. One apparent attraction of the approach is that it lends itself to simple visual presentation which makes communication easy. The basic two-by-two matrix can appear to reduce a seemingly infinite number of potential alternatives into an apparently manageable set of discrete and limited options. The analytical techniques of portfolio analysis have been useful not only for strategy formulation, but also resource allocation and performance specification.

To illustrate the types of techniques in portfolio analysis, it is sufficient to outline the Boston Consultancy Group's:

- experience curve;
- growth-share matrix.

Cost advantage has been stressed in strategy as a primary foundation for competitive advantage in a particular industry. Reasons for cost differentials between competing organisations include scale economies, product design, process innovation, organisational learning and so on. The concept of an experience curve is used to explain the relative cost structure over time. Derived from empirical evidence, the experience curve maps the inverse relationships between experience (usually defined as the accumulated volume of production) and the average total cost. However, at this aggregate level, no real causality can be implied, although the Boston Consulting Group summarises in the chain shown in figure 2.4 and defined as a 'Law of Experience':

> The unit cost of value added to a standard product declines by a constant percentage (typically between 20 and 30 per cent), each time cumulative output doubles.

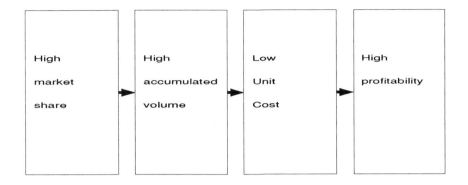

Figure 2.4 *Suggested causality behind the experience curve*

To provide a visual positioning of each business unit, the Boston Consulting Group developed their well-known two-by-two growth-share matrix. For managers, the two axes, relative market share and market growth rate, help to differentiate between 'cash generators' and 'cash users', allowing specific strategic actions to be proposed for units in particular boxes. In some senses, market share can be linked to experience (and its relationship to unit costs) and, therefore, other things being equal, it can be related directly to cash generating potential; on the other hand, growth requires investments, and, therefore, it can be related directly to cash usage. In the two-by-two matrix, the discrete options have been characterised as (see figure 2.5):

- 'star'   - high share and high growth;
- 'cash cow'   - high share and low growth;
- 'question mark'   - low share and high growth;
- 'dog'   - low share and low growth.

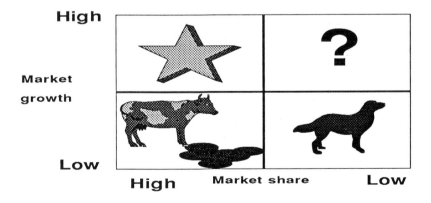

Figure 2.5 *Growth-share matrix*

This BCG matrix can summarise the expected profit and cash flow for each box, and also recommend an outline strategy: milk the cows, divest the dogs, invest in the stars and examine the question marks.

Figure 2.6 provides a set of four idealised diagrams for the consumer electronics industry, providing a descriptive summary of the positioning of competing companies with regard to particular products. Figure 2.7 summarises the profile of 'cash users' versus 'cash generators' in mature and declining markets. Such a profile indicates the type of strategies which could be implemented. For example, the 'cash generators' have higher gross margins, and lower R&D marketing expenses, levels of receivables and inventories and fewer new products than 'cash users'.

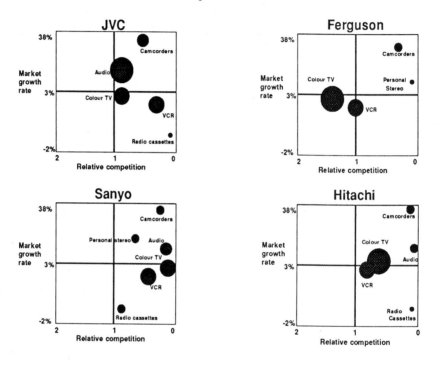

Figure 2.6 *Growth-share matrices for the consumer electronics industry*

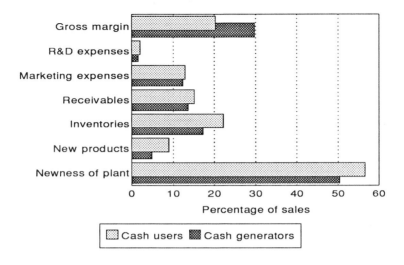

Figure 2.7 *Profile of cash users and cash generators*
(Adapted from Buzzell and Gale, 1987, page 210.)

Case: Profit Impact of Market Strategy

Scenario: In the past, strategies have been both 'successful' and 'unsuccessful', we need to learn from these experiences using empirical data.

The Strategic Planning Institute was founded in 1972 based on work which had been carried out at General Electric since the 1960's. Companies which join agree to provide data for the database and are allowed to use the database and modelling software to test out their potential strategies.

The Profit Impact of Marketing Strategy (PIMS) database has data contributed anonymously from over 450 companies, representing over 3,000 strategic business units for periods ranging from two to twelve years. The data gathered relates to:

• market conditions
• competitive position
• financial and operating performance.

This is analysed statistically and the relationships explored analytically.

To summarise, it is appropriate to quote from the cover of the Buzzell and Gale (1987) book:

Unlike Portfolio Planning methods, PIMS explores many possible dimensions of strategy and market environment, such as investment intensity, product or service quality, labour productivity, and vertical integration, all of which have powerful effects on business performance. For example, PIMS show how the quality edge boosts performance two ways and earns superior profit margins. It verifies how market share and profitability are strongly related but also shows why that does not mean that every business can or should strive to increase its share, as demonstrated by the disastrous 'kamikaze attack' launched in the early 1980's by Yamaha on the market leader Honda. Most important, it analyses why forecasts of cash flow based solely on the growth-share matrix are often misleading and why, in fact, many so-called 'dog' and 'question mark' businesses actually generate cash, while many 'cash cows' are dry.

Source: Buzzell and Gale, 1987.

Competitive forces

Influenced by the early Harvard Business School strategists, Kenneth Andrews and Roland Christensen, Michael Porter's (1980) consideration of competition in strategic management illustrates aspects of organisational positioning and the factors affecting an industry's overall profitability. The industry structure analysis model devised by Porter is used to consider 'competitive strategy' in an industry. It has been enormously influential in recent management thinking, particularly in the development of corporate business strategy. Porter's framework can also be used to illustrate ways in which information and communications technologies affect the nature and strength of competition. Figure 2.8 presents a summary of Porter's five organisation-level competitive forces in an industry.

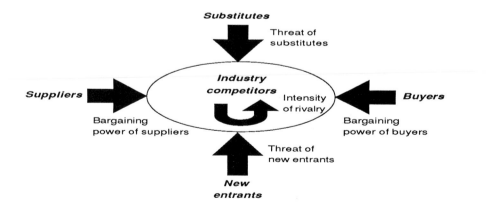

Figure 2.8 *Industry structure analysis model*
(Adapted from Porter, 1980, page 4.)

A brief discussion of possible effects of information and communications technologies on the different competitive forces helps to provide a direct link with potential business benefits for an organisation. The effects can be linked to:

- improved information for decision-making;
- infrastructural support from a technology platform.

The strength of the forces and the interplay between them affects the potential profitability of an industry. While, for convenience of presentation, it is easier to discuss each of the competitive forces in turn, an organisation must consider the interrelationships between the forces and act on a number of different fronts. Moreover, the competitive forces of an industry are constantly changing, affected not only by external socio-economic and political factors but also by the changing business structures made possible by the use of information and communications technologies. For instance, Electronic Data Interchange (EDI) is proving extremely useful in improving the effectiveness of supply chain management, particularly inter-organisational order processing and Just-in-Time manufacturing. However, for the actors in industries using these technologies, it also raises important strategic issues related to the changing power relationships, especially with regard to the management of networks.

Bargaining power of buyers

The bargaining power of both buyers and suppliers affects the possible profit an organisation can make in a specific industry. When buyer power is high, for example, when the buyer is large and/or the available products or services are undifferentiated, there are simultaneously downward pressures on prices and upward pressures on both product quality and service. Buyer power is also high when there is no real cost to change either to an alternative supplier or to another product.

The determinants of buyer power can be divided into:

- price sensitivity:
    - price/total purchases;
    - product differences;
    - brand identity;
    - impact on quality/performance;
    - buyer profits;
    - decision makers' incentives;
- bargaining leverage:
    - buyer concentration versus firm concentration;
    - buyer volume;
    - buyer switching costs relative to firm switching costs;
    - buyer information;
    - ability to backward integrate;
    - substitute products;
    - pull-through.

Information and communications technologies can be used in a number of ways to reduce this buyer power. By introducing or increasing 'switching costs', the technologies can make it more expensive for a buyer to switch suppliers. A buyer, for example, with its people trained in the use of a particular supplier's on-line distribution and inventory management system, has a real disincentive to change suppliers. ICTs can also provide information to help segment buyer groups and to understand the possible variations in profitability between different groups of customers. It may be appropriate to assist buyers through a reduction in their (management) costs of purchasing and thereby remove some of the pressures on price.

Bargaining power of suppliers

The bargaining power of suppliers is great if there are concentrated sources of supply and few substitutes, demonstrated through relatively high prices, susceptible product quality and indifferent service. Some ICT investments have been made to 'automate' manual and relatively expensive processes; in many instances, for example, computer-aided manufacture and robotics have replaced human capital, reduced the bargaining power of labour and improved product specification and quality.

The determinants of supplier power are:

* differentiations of inputs;
* switching costs of suppliers and firms in the industry;
* presence of substitute inputs;
* supplier concentration;
* importance of volume to supplier;
* cost relative to total purchases in the industry;
* impact of forward integration relative to threat of backward integration by firms in the industry.

Threats of new entrants

The problems associated with the threat of new entrants arise because the industry is sufficiently attractive for others to move in. Other things being equal, this causes direct short-term downward pressure on prices from increased availability of products or services.

The barriers to entering a market include:

* economies of scale;
* proprietary product differences;
* brand identity;
* switching costs;
* capital requirements;
* access to distribution channels;

- absolute cost advantages;
  - proprietary learning curve;
  - access to necessary inputs;
  - proprietary low-cost product design;
- government policy;
- expected retaliation.

How can information and communications technologies be used as an entry barrier to defend a market position or offensively to penetrate the barriers created by others? ICTs can be used to improve product and service quality, can provide management with better information for their decision-making, and can represent a capital barrier because of the high costs for a new organisation to enter the industry.

Threats of substitution

Substitutes (new products or services) can reduce or eliminate the market for existing ones. The determinants of substitution threat are:

- relative price performance;
- switching costs;
- inclination of buyers to use substitutes.

For example, the manual and electric typewriter industry has been almost wiped out by word processing systems. ICTs can influence substitution of products and services by:

- affecting the price-performance relationship of an increasing number of products and services;
- enhancing the functional capabilities of products and services.

In terms of better information for management decision-making, for instance, marketing information systems with extensive data on their customers' purchasing patterns can provide new opportunities both to cross-sell additional products and services to existing customers, and to identify changing consumption trends to enable the development of new products and services to satisfy their needs.

Intensity of rivalry

The intensity of the rivalry between competitors in an industry affects the overall profitability; it is usually greater in mature or declining markets. Following de-regulation, the US airline industry has exhibited intense rivalry through price wars, which has resulted in the bankruptcy and take-over of some organisations that were not covering their costs. The rivalry determinants are:

- industry growth;
- fixed costs/value-added;
- intermittent overcapacity;

- product differences;
- brand identity;
- switching costs;
- concentration and balance;
- informational complexity;
- diversity of competitors;
- corporate stakes;
- exit barriers.

The use of ICTs can help overcome the dilemma of a need to lower costs while improving levels of service. Customer Reservation Systems (CRSs) have enabled some airlines to respond to pressure in the industry. Moreover, the integration of associated services, such as hotel and car-hire reservations with airline reservations, has changed the nature of the industry and its competitive rivalry. Banks collaborating in shared networks of Automatic Teller Machines (ATMs) have improved their customer service while keeping overall costs down.

Gregory Parsons (1983, page 184) presents an analysis of information and communications technologies being important to business strategy at three levels:

- industry level:
  - product/service
    . nature of products/services
    . product life cycle
    . speed of distribution
  - markets
    . overall demand
    . degree of segmentation
    . geographic distribution possibilities
  - economics of production
    . relevant range for economies of scale
    . flexibility-standardisation trade-off
    . value-added stream
- firm level:
  - buyers
    . switching costs
    . buyer selection
  - suppliers
    . avoid switching costs
    . backwards integration
  - new entrants
    . entry barriers
    . entry deterrents
  - substitution
    . relative price-performance
    . product features

  - rivalry
    . new basis of competition
    . shared IT
- strategy level:
  - overall low-cost producer
    . reduces overall costs directly
    . enhances the ability to reduce overall cost through other functions
  - overall differentiation
    . adds unique features to products/services directly
    . enhances the ability to differentiate products/services through other functions
  - focusing on niche
    . identify and create market niches directly
    . enhances the ability to create market niches through other functions.

In discussing how information gives you competitive advantage, Michael Porter and Victor Millar (1985) provide another two-by-two matrix to illustrate the effects of ICTs in industry sectors, based on the 'information intensity' of the specific industry. Information intensity is defined as the amalgam of the information content of products and services (ranging, for example, from nothing in a brick to almost everything in a 'quality' newspaper), and of the quantity and cost of information exchange which must occur to complete a transaction (for example, relatively low for most legal documents and relatively high for fashion and perishable goods). Figure 2.9 illustrates the position of different industries by their information content and intensity.

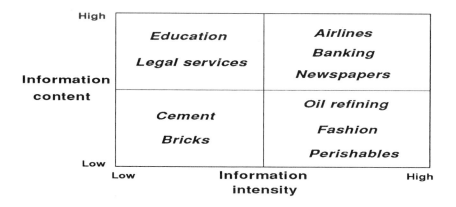

Figure 2.9 *The information intensity matrix*
        (Adapted from Porter and Millar, 1985.)

2.3 Strategic alignment process

The relationship between business strategy and information and communications technologies has been explored for over a decade, though the progress made has been rather disappointing. As part of the 'Management in the Nineties' programme at the Sloan School, a new model was developed which appears to provide more insight into the problem and to offer a practical solution. An important distinction from previous models is that the process is seen as a loop and not as linear; strategy is not handed down on tablets of stone to the DP/IS Department. A second distinction is the inclusion of organisational factors in the loop, usually they are considered separately if at all. To help simplify the problem, it is useful to break it down into internal and external factors and into business and information technology sections, the interactions between these are tuned to achieve alignment. (see figure 2.10)

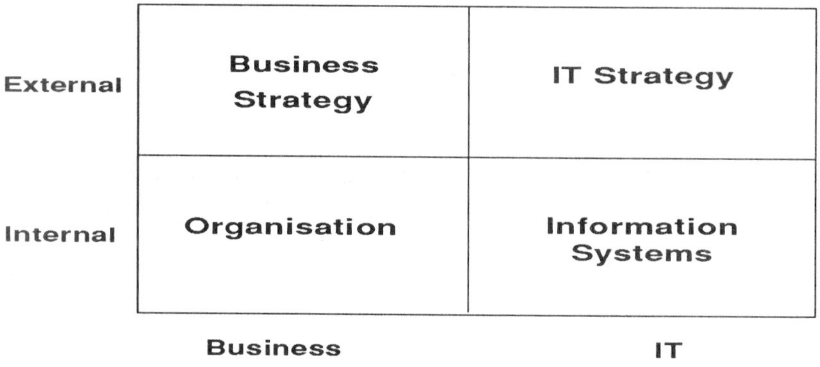

	Business	IT
External	**Business Strategy**	**IT Strategy**
Internal	**Organisation**	**Information Systems**

Figure 2.10 *Framework for the strategic alignment model* (Adapted from Scott Morton, 1991.)

The Strategic Alignment Model (SAM) is used to describe the interactions between internal and external factors, which are not merely linked, but must be aligned. The external factors are the positioning of the organisation in the market and of its DP/IS function as a purchaser of products and services in the ICT marketplace. The internal factors include organisational structure, culture and so on, together with the infrastructure and processes run by the DP/IS function.

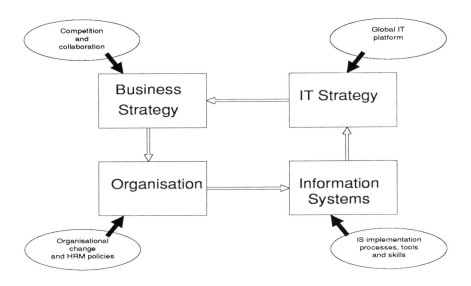

Figure 2.11 *Strategic alignment process*
(Adapted from Scott Morton, 1991.)

The Strategic Alignment Process (SAP) can be seen to have four external forces acting upon it (see figure 2.11). For the Strategic Alignment Process to work, it requires commitment and involvement from top-level managers, rather than merely their blessing. It also requires that all the subsidiary processes be in place to allow consideration of the factors listed below:

- Business strategy:
  - strategic management;
  - redesign of business processes;
  - redesign of business network;
- Organisation:
  - structure, resourcing, work design and processes;
  - education and training;
  - HRM policies;
  - change processes;
- Information systems:
  - applications architecture;
  - skilled human resources;
  - training;
  - implementation processes and standards;
  - accessibility of external resources;
- Information Technology Strategy:
  - awareness of technological capabilities;
  - selection processes for acquisition or delivery of services
  - maintenance and improvement of IT platform.

2.4 Conclusion

Business strategy has only been the subject of systematic analysis for the last three decades. A range of techniques have been developed to assist strategy formulation, but it remains unclear how well these tools will stand the test of time. In a business environment of increasing turbulence, many of the simplistic and rather mechanistic (somewhat deductive) techniques fail to capture the necessarily complex picture of relationships. As complexities are added, the original and attractive clarity of many approaches is undermined. These tools are useful guides, but they do not provide solutions; ultimately, the quality of leadership and management is decisive. In the information age, a greater reliance on detailed empirical analyses, attempting to establish causality, is essential. However, real progress still needs to be made in the linkage of strategy formulation and implementation. Although an apparently 'rationalist' approach may be feasible and desirable, learning and intuition should be incorporated. Henry Mintzberg, for instance, has criticised 'deliberate' strategy, arguing that it should instead be 'crafted'.

Central to this necessary merging of formulation and implementation is clear communication of the strategy with greater involvement and wider ownership across the organisation. Moreover, successful strategy implementation requires the business processes, the organisational structure and the information systems both to be consistent with and to reinforce the strategy.

Review questions

1 Differentiate between strategy formulation and strategy implementation.

2 Illustrate the ways in which information and communications technologies can assist an organisation's competitive strategy.

3 Comment on the strengths and weaknesses of portfolio analysis.

4 What happens in a market where differentiation is a disadvantage?

Study questions

1 Using Michael Porter's framework of five competitive forces, consider the changing nature of the information-based industries (as described in Chapter 3). Is the framework appropriate, and would it help management's strategy formulation?

2 Examine the assertion that the different approaches really only give a framework for managers to communicate and discuss their strategic problems.

3 Explore Peter Drucker's (1954) method for operationalising strategy: Management By Objectives (MBO).

4 For an organisation that you know, consider the recent argument by Donald Harris and David Walters (1992) that

"… unless a strategy is developed for those activities responsible for implementing the strategic direction of the company, it is unlikely that the strategy, nor the corporate objectives it seeks to achieve, will be successful."

Further reading

Ansoff, H Igor "Implementing Strategic Management" Prentice-Hall, Englewood Cliffs, 1984.

An interesting general text that places the development of strategic management into its historical context.

Grant, Robert M "Contemporary Strategy Analysis" Blackwell, Oxford, 1991.

Robert Grant provides a clear and comprehensive MBA-level teaching text which covers the concepts, techniques and applications of business strategy. The integrating theme of the book is 'competitive advantage', including:

- *the resource-based theory of strategy (R Rumelt, J Barney), with particular emphasis on the role of firm, specific, intangible assets (O E Williamson, H Itami) and organizational routines (R Nelson and S Winter);*
- *transaction costs (O E Williamson) and their impact upon the scope of the firm (D Teece);*
- *value chain analysis (M E Porter, McKinsey and Company);*
- *dynamic approaches to the analysis of competition (J Schumpeter, J Williams), including ecological analysis of competitive strategy (B Henderson, M Hannan and J Freeman);*
- *the creation and sustainability of competitive advantage (P Ghemawat), including the role of isolating mechanisms and uncertain imitability (R Rumelt);*
- *agency problems (M James);*
- *reputation effects (D Camerer, D Kreps);*
- *rent appropriation (D Teece);*
- *industry recipes (J C Spender);*

- *cooperative strategies and strategic alliances (J Bower, G Hamel and C K Prahalad);*
- *the contribution of financial theory to strategy analysis including: value maximisation, the role of free cash flow, and option theory (A Rappaport, M Jensen, S Myers);*
- *transnational approaches to global advantage (C Bartlett and S Ghoshal).*

Hax, Arnoldo C and Nicolas S Majluf "Strategic Management" Prentice-Hall, International, New Jersey, 1984.

A clear, comprehensive, albeit unexciting, student textbook. The book is divided into four Parts:

- *the evolution of strategic planning thinking;*
- *concepts and tools for strategic planning;*
- *a methodology for the development of a corporate strategic plan;*
- *the congruence between organisational structure and strategy.*

Hussey, David E (editor) *International Review of Strategic Management* John Wiley and Sons, London, 1990.

This is a critical annual review of developments and best practice in strategic management. Four interrelated concepts, method, process, role and system, are used to structure the contributions by different authors. The main theme of the first volume was building competitive advantage.

Porter, Michael E "Competitive Strategy" Free Press, New York, 1980.

The most influential strategy book of the 1980's. Porter placed competition into a strategic management context through a presentation of frameworks and techniques. A complementary 1983 volume provides detailed case studies.

Stacey, Ralph D "Dynamic Strategic Management" Kogan Page, London, 1990.

A critical appraisal of the traditional strategic management process, arguing for an explicit consideration of dynamics by striking a balance between opportunism and planning.

Successful strategic management does not mean preparing long-term plans — the future is far too uncertain for that. Instead it means improving the total control system of the organisation so that it is fit and flexible enough to play dynamic business games in highly uncertain environments.

3

The information-based industries: their transforming nature

Learning objectives:

- to understand the competitive forces affecting the companies in the information-based industries;

- to understand the strategies and tactics used by these companies;

- to be aware of the technological changes currently affecting the industries;

- to be aware of how individual users and their organisations are affected by the changing dynamics of the marketplace and technologies.

3.1 Introduction

It is essential to understand the industries which develop and supply information system and information-based products and services, in order to understand the uses or potential uses of ICTs. The definition and measurement of these industry sectors are particularly difficult, because they change so rapidly and because their activities are as general as 'a collective electronic means to capture, store, process, distribute and retrieve words, numbers, images and sounds, as well as the electronic means to control different types of machines'. Although these sectors are becoming increasingly significant both economically and politically, measurement of the industries is limited (see, for example, the descriptive account of mapping and measuring the information economy by Miles *et al.* (1990)). In 1986, the National Economic and Development Office (1986, page 6) gave a 'health warning' on their statistics for the UK information technology industry which remains true today:

> Because of the changing nature of the industry, its statistical base is poor, partial and misleading. These figures should be regarded as a general indication of trends and relative magnitude.

The intensely competitive information-based industries are characterised by continuous and revolutionary transformation. The nature of the industries, their established players and their products and services are over-turned every few years. Only IBM has remained throughout, although its strategic focus has changed over the years and its dominance has declined. With each successive wave of computer technology, IBM's global market share has decreased: for the mainframe, its share is about 50%; for the minicomputer, the share is 15%; and for the personal computer, only 10%.

It is essential to view the information-based industries as a mosaic of different, albeit complementary, products and services: people, hardware, software, telecommunications, data, value-added services and so on. Over time, there have been great changes in the profile of the industries; for instance, the trends towards personal workstations and away from mainframe computers. Moreover, differential changes are envisaged for the future (see Table 3.1).

Table 3.1   *Estimated growth of the ICT industries 1993-98*

mainframe computers	1%
medium-sized computers	7%
image processing peripherals	17%
software	15%

Source: Arthur D Little, 1990.

The markets for information and communications technologies are characterised by very short product life-cycles, the need to generate cashflow to fund Research and Development and considerable pressure for sales. A major source of growth has lain in technological innovation, arising in the early years from government-funded research for military and space programmes. Users are under constant pressure to buy more systems which are newer and allegedly better. Therefore, it is not surprising to find that 'the industry' has an image of 'box pushing'; the hard selling of technical products rather than business solutions. However, such technological imperatives are being replaced as the emphasis has moved from manufacturing to customer service. For example,

ICL is an information systems company. It provides IT solutions which allow customers to
- manage their businesses more effectively
- exploit the business opportunities presented by the use of information technology. (ICL, 1990.)

Digital's philosophy is to give individuals, departments, and corporate IS the freedom to select computing solutions that meet their specific needs — while providing the integration that allows the solutions they choose to work with the solutions chosen by others throughout the organisation.

This strategy is based on four principles that underlie Digital's technology decisions. These principles are:

- Distribution
- Integration
- Architecture
- Standards.

... Digital's strategy for the 1990's is to apply the same principles of distribution, integration, architecture and standards to enable systems and applications from many different vendors to work together across a multivendor computing environment. (DEC, 1990.)

Some ICT vendors believe themselves to have achieved the position of 'systems integrator'; being able and willing to recommend a competitor's product or service if it is the appropriate solution for their client's business.

A key development in the growth of services, consultancy and systems integration has been the conversion of computers from sophisticated technical products into commodities. The manufacture of basic memory, processor 'chips' and even computers has become a business for a few volume manufacturers and some specialists in niche markets. For instance, Intel dominates the production of processor chips for personal computers, while Inmos produces very specialised high-powered Transputer chips.

In this chapter, a necessarily selective discussion is presented of these dynamic and exciting industries, covering some of the changing players (both organisations and people), products and services. For convenience of description, the information-based industries have been categorised as:

HARDWARE
Chips, computers, peripherals and related systems which can be touched.

SOFTWARE
Parts of a computer system which cannot be touched; programs which are 'run' on computers.

TELECOMMUNICATIONS
Equipment such as telephone exchanges and local area networks together with the services provided to individuals and firms using these networks.

COMPUTING SERVICES
Services provided to individuals and organisations using computers and networks.

Some general background comments on the evolving structure of the industries need to be made. The industries have been dominated by a few large companies notably IBM and AT&T, with a second group of 'national champions' benefiting from considerable government support. Recently, new pressures have been added because of the increasingly global nature of the industries and the development of supra-national initiatives. As with other industries, the merger and acquisition fever has also been noticeable. For instance, British Telecom (BT) has acquired Tymnet, an international data communications operator, and 22% of McCaw Cellular, a US-based mobile telephone operator. IBM has bought and sold Rolm, the telephone exchange manufacturer, and is now in joint ventures with Apple Computer, British Telecom and Wang Laboratories.

Case: AT&T's bid for NCR

Scenario: At the end of 1990, American Telephone and Telegraph (AT&T) made a successful take-over bid for NCR, one of the oldest firms in the computer business.

In 1956 AT&T bound itself not to enter the computer market, as part of a Consent Decree which allowed it to maintain its near monopoly in telecommunications in the USA. It was allowed only to manufacture a few specialist computer systems for the US Government, mainly for defence contracts. In 1984, at the time of the break up, AT&T was released from the old constraint. It was believed by some observers that AT&T would offer real competition to IBM in the computer market.

In the mid-1980's, AT&T had entered into a joint venture with Olivetti. However, this failed as a result of having been poorly thought through; the companies had different products, different visions and different cultures. In particular, it proved impossible for Olivetti to penetrate the US market. Finally, the project was wound up.

National Cash Register (NCR) was one of the oldest computer manufacturers in the USA, having been in the punched-card business almost since the beginning. In the industry in the 1960's was as one of the BUNCH (Burroughs, Univac, NCR, Control Data and Honeywell), one of the 'smaller' firms found around IBM. At the time of the bid it was the fifth largest computer firm in the USA, operating mainly in niche markets, notably banking, and selling a range of Unix minicomputers.

Table 3.2 *Leading computer companies*

	Employees	*Sales US$ billions*
IBM	383,000	63.4
DEC	126,000	12.9
HP	95,000	11.9
Unisys	82,300	10.1
NCR	56,000	5.9

AT&T's initial offer for NCR was rejected by the NCR Board of Directors as inadequate, although it valued NCR at US$ 6.2 billion. The offer was intended to include the transfer of AT&T's computer division to NCR, with the expanded NCR becoming an independent subsidiary.

John Sculley, CEO of Apple Computer, commented on the bid:

> There is no history of success of computer companies solving their problems through mergers. When you combine two old-line companies, you do not form one new vigorous company.

The general attitude to mergers in the industry is negative. Ben Rosen, the Chairman of Compaq Computers, commented:

> The main beneficiaries of mergers in the computer industry have been competitors, because the companies become focused upon organisational matters and lose sight of their customers.

The creation of Unisys through the merger of Burroughs and Sperry (formerly Sperry-Rand and before that Univac) is seen as an example of this difficulty. Moreover, the idea of 'convergence' of communications and computers has proved difficult to achieve in a single corporation, for example, L M Ericsson and Philips NV have both sold off their information systems business, while STC was broken up, with ICL being sold to Fujitsu.

The AT&T bid for NCR was seen by some in a particularly bad light, since it could be construed as the failure of AT&T in the computer business, especially the joint venture with Olivetti. Charles Exley, Chairman, NCR commented:

It wants to 'buy' expertise, in the form of NCR. The history of failure in such mergers has been devastating.

Table 3.3 *Comparison of AT&T with NCR in 1989*

	AT&T	NCR	
Employees	279,000	56,000	
Net Income	2.7	0.41	US$ billions
Revenues	36.11	5.96	US$ billions

It is difficult to see what AT&T brings to NCR. Perhaps its greatest contribution lies in money and R&D, since AT&T's financial resources could allow NCR to be much more aggressive in its pricing policies. The takeover allows NCR to have access to AT&T's legendary Bell Laboratories. NCR brings its expertise in the computer business and its distribution network.

In winning the takeover battle, AT&T demonstrated its financial muscle. It must now show that it can manage the joint business.

A very important factor behind the changing structures of the industries has been the proliferation of 'start-ups' and 'spin-offs' which have added significantly to the growth of the industries. Ideas apparently blocked or slowed down in a university or an overly bureaucratic corporation have been freed through the formation of a new firm. Areas such as Silicon Valley in California and around Route 128 in Massachusetts have been centres for such spin-offs and start-ups, drawing on people from both universities and commerce. A culture has been established in these areas, which has proved particularly conducive to the creation and support of new information-based firms.

Silicon Valley has seen computer companies come and go, some rise to enormous success, others fail, but in California there is no stigma attached to failure, even to bankruptcy. For example, Apple Computers began like the 'American Dream' in a garage and grew into a great corporation. The inventor, Steve Wozniak, and the entrepreneur, Steve Jobs, developed the Apple Computer for ease-of-use and a broad market; though neither now works in the organisation. Apple Computer became synonymous with the personal computer revolution and within six years the company was in the *Fortune 500*, with over one hundred of its employees listed as dollar millionaires. A less successful story is that of Adam Osborne who was the first person to make computers portable, or at least luggable; his 15 kilogram personal computer was not readily carried. Osborne had his best financial year in 1982-83, with earnings of approximately US$ 100 million. However, his success was brief, from the launch of the Osborne 1 in April 1981 to bankruptcy in September 1983.

In many European countries, the pattern was to establish one or more national champions in the 1960's and 1970's, for example, Siemens in Germany and Olivetti in Italy. These champions were buttressed by government through public sector procurement policies favouring national suppliers (see Table 3.4: note that the ownership and structure of many of these companies has undergone considerable changes since 1986).

Table 3.4 *Top European computer producers in 1986*

		Worldwide DP revenues US$ (millions)	% Turnover achieved in Europe	% Share in home market
Germany	Siemens	4,387	88	65
	Nixdorf	2,075	92	52
	BASF	521	79	n.a.
	Mannesmann	489	91	65
France	Groupe Bull	2,568	94	66
	CGE	1,025	92	48
	CGS	420	70	37
UK	STC	1756	81	63
	Rank Xerox	459	81	n.a.
	Atlantic	431	92	62
Italy				
	Olivetti	3865	70	37
Holland	Philips NV	1763	87	n.a.
Sweden	L M Ericsson	1344	89	n.a.
Norway	Norsk Data	349	91	55

Source: Flamm, 1988, page 169.

The French *Plans Calculs*, for example, were first devised in the 1960's with the intention of developing a French computer industry. In part it was to meet General de Gaulle's requirement to develop an independent French nuclear bomb and its delivery systems, the *Force de frappe*. However, they proved a commercial fiasco, being very expensive and far from successful. The driving force was political rather than commercial and discouraged the formation of companies on a purely commercial basis. IBM France held then and retains a very significant share of the French market. The largest French company was Machines Bull, named after Frederick Bull, a Norwegian, who had patented some punched card machines. In 1991, now called Groupe Bull, it posted enormous losses and began negotiations for a long-term partner. (Salomon, 1986.)

Over the years, the UK government has given considerable support to the native computer industry, mainly to International Computers Limited (ICL). ICL was forged in the 'white hot heat of technology' by Prime Minister Harold Wilson's government in 1968, through the merger of International Computers and Tabulators (ICT) and English Electric Computers. ICL was consistently given preferential treatment, giving it that it obtained almost total dominance of the procurement of computers in the UK public sector, including central and local government, education and the various quasi-autonomous organisations around government. With the election of the Thatcher Administration in 1979, support for industry and preferential purchasing was intended to come to a rapid if not abrupt halt. ICL's financial crisis in 1981 presented the government with a serious dilemma; the failure of ICL would have resulted in major operational difficulties for over twenty government departments which relied on ICL equipment. In the end, the government gave a guarantee of £200 million, despite its ideological opposition to such actions. Eventually, ICL returned to the market, initially through its purchase by STC, the then UK-based telecommunications firm, who later sold control to the Fujitsu group.

Today, the information-based industries are truly global, making it impossible to shelter a national industry. Even the Japanese or USA markets cannot sustain the required R&D or the scale of manufacturing necessary to remain successful; vendors must export to the rest of the world. IBM, for instance, had been intending to move a principal line of business away from the US to demonstrate its international character. Given the development of the European Community's Single Internal Market and the opening up of Eastern Europe, it was not surprising that, in December 1990, they undertook an extensive re-organisation to move the communications division headquarters from New York to London. Kenichi Ohmae (1990, page 199) is a true globalist, arguing:

> ... the only thing that matters is that IBM competes with DEC and Fujitsu.

By comparison with the USA and Japan, the European market is fragmented into a number of distinct national markets, with different characteristics and players, making it difficult for European companies to develop large-scale operations. To overcome this problem, the European Commission and the governments of the European Community have organised a number of programmes to encourage collaborative Research and Development across national boundaries and are moving rapidly to a Single Internal Market in information-based products and services.

The frenetic race for the latest innovation has forced manufacturers into a fight to bring products to market very rapidly. The capacity of rivals to spoil, copy, reverse engineer or 'clone' products has forced companies to go worldwide as soon as practicable, by joint venture or licensing; the alternative is to face the elimination of a potential revenue flow. The need to compete in terms of extreme reliability and low cost has forced firms into a world-wide search for cheap yet reliable components.

While discussing companies which manufacture for telephone exchanges, Christopher Bartlett and Sumantra Ghoshal (1989, page 29) make the following general points on the challenges facing firms in the information-based sector:

> ... the strategic demands in this industry too became increasingly multidimensional during the 1980's. Companies that do not achieve global-scale efficiency, national flexibility and responsiveness, and an ability to develop and diffuse innovations world-wide will not survive the shake-out now restructuring the industry.

To show the differences in attitudes towards globalisation, they identify organisational characteristics that are to be found in companies (see Table 3.5).

Table 3.5 *Organisational characteristics of the transnational*

Organisational characteristics	Multinational	Global	International	Transnational
Configuration of assets and capabilities	Decentralised and nationally self-sufficient	Centralised and globally scaled	Sources of core competencies centralised, others decentralised	Dispersed, interdependent, and specialised
Role of overseas operation	Sensing and exploiting local opportunities	Implementing parent company strategies	Adapting and leveraging parent company competencies	Differentiated contributions by national units to integrated worldwide operations
Development and diffusion of knowledge	Knowledge developed and retained within each unit	Knowledge developed and retained at the centre	Knowledge developed at the centre and transferred to overseas units	Knowledge developed jointly and shared worldwide

Source: Bartlett and Ghoshal, 1989, page 65.

Reprinted by permission of Harvard Business School Press

3.2 Hardware

Computer vendors of the 1950's were manufacturers and aggressive sellers of punched-card machines. Computers were sold mainly as technological products for standalone applications to improve business efficiency. In the 1960's, vendors linked terminals to the previously isolated and inaccessible computers and connected together the computers to provide networks, using 'proprietary' protocols, which locked out the computers of other vendors. During the same period enormous efforts were made to develop the software applications necessary to sell computer systems. In the 1970's, vendors extended their portfolios of specific applications, and in the 1980's, they moved into the provision of solutions to 'business problems'. By the 1990's, some vendors started to see themselves as 'systems integrators'.

Hardware has had an ever increasing power, a trend which is apparently set to continue. The process of miniaturisation has made possible ever smaller systems with at least equivalent, if not greater, power. For example, floppy discs have shrunk from 8 inches diameter first to 5.25 inches then to 3.5 inches, whilst the capacity to hold data has risen from 72 kilobytes to 1.44 Megabytes. Read-only memory compact discs (CD-ROMs), of 500 Megabytes capacity, have proved very useful in the distribution of databases and software. For example, all the telephone directories for the USA can be stored on two CD-ROMs. Magneto-optical discs based on compact discs (CDs) are being developed which can be written to, as well as read.

ICI, the UK chemical giant, has developed 'digital paper', an optical tape system which considerably cuts the price of data storage.

Computers are assembled from a large number of components, some relatively simple, such as the metal cases, and others more complex, such as the integrated circuits. The value-added in this process varies between different types of computer, though the assembly can be as low as 5-10% of the final price; the design of a computer is much more important.

The categories of hardware components that make a finished computer system are:

CHIPS

Integrated circuits, comprising transistors, capacitors and resistors made in miniature on a wafer of semi-conducting material, usually silicon.

PERIPHERALS

Devices connected to a computer, such as printers, and external disc drives.

DISC DRIVES

A device which stores and allows retrieval of data on a magnetic or optical disc.

PRINTED CIRCUIT BOARDS

Patterns of copper conductor strips to link components laminated to a plastic or glass fibre board.

MONITORS

An output device for the temporary display of information, used as part of a terminal of a computer, visual display units (VDU).

The different manufacturers and different industry segments have varying degrees of vertical integration. For example, IBM has traditionally been highly integrated, from chip manufacture to computer leasing and value-added services. In contrast, Intel concentrates on providing most of the personal computer industry with processor chips. Vertical integration allows companies guaranteed access to supplies of technology for new products, though the necessary R&D is expensive.

Chips

In this sub-section, integrated circuits or 'chips' are considered as an example of the manufacture of hardware components. The reason for this choice is that they are, arguably, the most important physical components in computers because of the relationship between the integrated circuits and the operating system, which largely determines the functionality and hence marketability of the computer. The operating system of a computer is closely related to the architecture and 'instruction set' of the chips inside it. Software written for one operating system has to be rewritten or significantly modified before it can be run on another operating system.

A computer manufacturer must convince customers that products have a reasonable life expectancy and that future products will be compatible with existing investments. An important consideration for customers is that their investment in bespoke application software, in staff skills and in hardware is tied to a particular operating system which they would find expensive to replace. In turn, the operating system is tied to one or more chips in the computer. Thus, to stay in business, a manufacturer must have a reliable and continuing source of new and more powerful chips with which to drive new products and sustain the customer base.

The computers of the 1940's were constructed from electronic and magnetic components such as relays and thermionic valves. The invention of the transistor by a team at AT&T's Bell Laboratories in 1947 transformed the design of computers. Transistors were initially individual components, replacing individual valves as amplifiers and switches. They were later grouped together on a single chip of silicon to include transistors, capacitors and resistors which allowed the building of complete circuits. By the 1970's, the complexity of these chips was sufficient to permit the first 'computer on a chip', known as a microprocessor. Microprocessors have since been developed by a number of manufacturers and have been the enabling factor behind many of the developments in the miniaturisation of computers. The technology was known first as Large Scale Integration (LSI) and with subsequent advances as Very Large Scale Integration (VLSI). The growth in power has been enormous, as evidenced by the growth in the number of components on the chip which indicates the number of transistors which can be constructed (see figure 3.1).

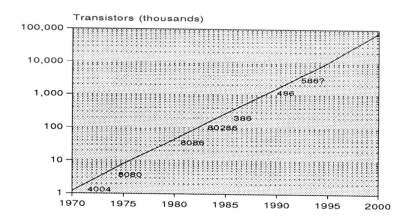

Figure 3.1   *Increase in processor power*

In addition to their use as processors, chips are also used as memory, an important form of which is Dynamic Random Access Memory (DRAM), the working memory of personal computers. These chips can be accessed very rapidly for computations but are 'volatile', in that when the power supply is disconnected their contents are lost. An IBM PC in 1981 would have had 64 kilobytes of RAM, whereas today a personal computer is more likely to have four or more Megabytes. The increased memory allows the user to run larger and more complex programs and to run more than one program at a time.

Globalisation has been a general trend in all industries. In chip manufacture and design it has been especially strong, driven by the high costs of:

- Research and Development;
- building and maintaining production capacity;
- short product life-cycles;
- little variation in customer requirements around the globe.

Case: ICL and Fujitsu

Scenario: In the late 1970's International Computers Limited (ICL) was seeking to maintain its mainframe computer product line. To achieve this objective, it had to make very expensive improvements to the hardware in order to support users' applications and expertise in their operating system.

In most computers, there is a very close link between the integrated circuits and the operating system used. ICL had developed its own proprietary operating system, Virtual Machine Environment (VME), which it used on its mainframe computers. In order to maintain the customer base, it was necessary for ICL to extend and to be seen to be extending the lifetime of VME. Users and software houses needed to have sufficient confidence to develop new applications for this particular environment.

In 1981, ICL sought to reduce the disproportionate costs of Research and Development on its 2900 series of mainframe computers; two-thirds of R&D was being spent on products which generated only one-third of revenues. It wanted to channel more effort into developing products for the more buoyant personal computer and minicomputer markets. ICL thought it was unlikely to have the volume of mainframe computer business to justify in-house semi-conductor production facilities, therefore it required access to chip-making technology.

Fujitsu was identified as the best partner, given the very limited choice in Japan and the USA. The agreement reached was to allow ICL to 'intercept' new technology from Fujitsu, one year ahead of competitors. This would allow the product life of ICL's mainframe computers to be extended from three to, perhaps, five years, always assuming the technology could be used effectively. The breakdown of activities between the two companies is shown in Table 3.6.

Table 3.6 *ICL-Fujitsu agreement on chip technology (Source: Campbell-Kelly, 1990.)*

	Computer		
	3930	3980	1015/1025
Architecture	ICL	ICL	Fujitsu
Design	ICL	ICL	Fujitsu
Software	ICL	ICL	Fujitsu
Manufacture	ICL	Fujitsu	Fujitsu
Technology	Fujitsu	Fujitsu	Fujitsu

The arrangement was successful in that it maintained ICL mainframe computers as an important part of the product line. It is less clear that it was an even partnership since, in 1990, Fujitsu acquired a majority shareholding in ICL. The rationale for the takeover was partly the dependency of ICL on Fujitsu for technology and supply. Moreover, there was also a desire on the part of ICL's parent STC, a telecommunications firm, to dispose of ICL. At the time of the takeover, mainframes constituted around 25% of ICL's business.

Collaboration is an important dimension of competitive strategy, and requires long-term partnerships and understanding. Peter Bonfield, ICL's CEO, offers the following advice on successful collaboration:

1   Treat the collaboration as a personal commitment.
2   Anticipate that it will take up management time.
3   Mutual respect and trust are essential.
4   Remember that both partners must get something out of it (money eventually).
5   Make sure you tie up a tight legal contract.
6   Recognise that during the course of a collaboration, circumstances and markets change.
7   Make sure you and your partner have mutual expectations of the collaboration and its time scale.
8   Get to know your opposite numbers at all levels socially.
9   Appreciate that cultures — both geographic and corporate — are different.
10 Recognise your partner's interests and independence.
11 Even if the arrangement is tactical in your eyes, make sure you have corporate approval.
12 Celebrate achievement together.

US-Japan Semiconductor Agreement;

Scenario: In 1986, the governments of Japan and the USA signed an agreement on pricing and production levels of certain types of semiconductors. The Japanese stood accused of 'dumping' chips in US markets.

While US governments are strongly opposed to supporting industry in any way, the Reagan Administration (1980-1988) was persuaded to make an exception for the manufacture of chips. The Federal Government had for a long time viewed chip technology as of strategic importance, that it played an important role in the technological dominance maintained by the USA in the military field, in the control of missiles and aircraft. The USA has used technology to overcome the problem of being outnumbered in terms of soldiers, missiles, planes and ships by its former long-standing enemy, the USSR. In addition, it was persuaded that the information-based industries depended on the chip-makers and that they were being overtaken by Japanese firms.

The US chip manufacturers argued that Japanese rivals were 'dumping' certain types of chips on the American market, undermining the ability of American companies to compete. The Japanese were accused of selling at prices below the cost to manufacturer and distribute, with the long-term aim of achieving market share and of driving other suppliers out of the business. US manufacturers were also largely excluded from the Japanese market with the notable exceptions of IBM Japan and Fuji-Xerox. The US industry argued for reciprocity of access to markets.

There is a continuing debate in the USA on the need, if any, for an industrial policy (see Porter (1990), Lodge (1990) and Chandler (1990) for a discussion of the broader strategic issues). There has been concern over the decline of industrial manufacturing in the USA from its position of global dominance. In the USA, it is argued by some, that governments are incapable of helping industry, they can only hinder. The US Government is therefore presented with a choice of whether or not to believe that foreign governments are helping their domestic firms and, if so, whether the US Government should attempt to convince those other governments to stop or whether it should emulate their activities.

The US share of the world-wide Dynamic Random Access Memory (DRAM) chip business fell from 100% in 1975 to 8% in 1988, though this is only a small part of the total chip market. The Japanese production capacity was built from nothing in the early 1960's to be the key player in the late 1980's. Japan's Ministry of International Trade and Industry (MITI) provided 50% funding for a cooperative industry VLSI research laboratory from 1976 to 1980. This produced a 256K RAM chip and a thousand patents for chip process technology.

In 1991, trade in semi-conductors, while Japan exported between the USA and Japan was estimated as: US exports $1,116 million, while Japan exported to the USA, $2,442 million for conventional chips plus $2,434 million for computer memory chips.

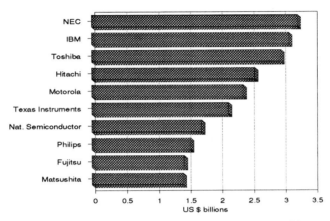

Figure 3.2   *Leading chip producers' revenues in 1987*

The Microelectronics and Computer Technology Corporation (MCC) was established in 1982 in Austin, Texas, as a privately-funded, multilateral research centre with the intention of being profit-making. It was necessary for the US Congress to legislate for the creation of MCC, to exempt MCC from the anti-trust laws. Over twenty chip-makers joined, including AMD, Motorola and National Semiconductor; though IBM and Intel were absent. MCC's research programme includes: artificial intelligence, chip design, software technology, human-computer interaction, and parallel processing. After the Constitution, the Anti-Trust Laws are the most highly regarded in the USA. They prohibit the collaboration of companies to avoid the creation of cartels. Anti-trust laws are based on the view that:

There is a suspicion that when two or more members of a trade meet together, they do so in order to disadvantage customers... (Adam Smith, 1776).

The current and future trends in chip performance appear to lie in ever increasing processing power and storage capacity. This will provide more growth than the software developers seem able fully to utilise. The growing complexity of chips has allowed the construction of systems which are 'fault-tolerant'. These chips continue to work even after a few faults have developed, through the provision of redundant circuits which are used only after the failure of another circuit. There are also battles between Application Specific Integrated Circuits (ASIC) and Reduced Instruction Set Chips (RISC). The net result is more power, for most purposes the technical details do not matter. New semi-conductor materials such as Gallium Arsenide (GaAs) offer yet more processor power, while consuming less electrical power. The switch from electronic to optical computers offers a big jump in processor power, but is still in the early stage of development. New architectures which contain parallelism are also important developments, such as the Transputer.

Computers

The range and diversity of computers is so great that a classification is essential and, although such classifications have proved increasingly difficult to sustain in the face of change, a conventional grouping is:

SUPER-COMPUTERS

The applications of these ultra-powerful computers are in intensive data handling calculations, such as oil exploration, weather forecasting, advanced engineering and defence. They are associated with a few manufacturers, the original leader Cray Research and the Japanese: NEC, Fujitsu and Hitachi Data Systems.

MAINFRAME COMPUTERS

These were the first type of computers ever built, the name is derived from their originally being constructed on a large metal frame. They name is associated with Data Processing (DP) and they carry the bulk of On-Line Transaction Processing (OLTP). IBM is the best known supplier in this market.

MINICOMPUTERS

Originally built in a single cabinet occupying a limited amount of space, they were sold to departments and subsidiaries rather than corporations. Their name is linked with Digital Equipment Corporation (DEC), the first company to design and sell them in the 1960's.

PERSONAL COMPUTERS

Alternatively termed microcomputer. A general-purpose computer designed for a single user with a microprocessor as the Central Processing Unit (CPU).

The value of these categories is being continuously undermined by advances in technology, blurring the distinctions. In the last few years, 'workstations' have emerged that compete against both personal computers and minicomputers, having some of the characteristics of both. Similarly, super-minicomputers are now faster than many mainframe computers.

An important and still growing area of activity is in Original Equipment Manufacturing (OEM). Here one company manufactures components or systems and sells them on to another company which sells them under its own name after 're-badging'. For instance, Digital Equipment Corporation recently entered into an OEM deal with Cipher Data Products to sell tape cartridge drives; DEC already bought tape decks from Cipher. For DEC, Cipher is a new distribution channel reaching a new customer base, which it could not readily reach and helps increase manufacturing volumes, while Cipher avoids the cost of development and manufacturing. Similarly, Hewlett-Packard sells chip-sets to NCR and IBM supplies Japanese language PCs to Hitachi.

The personal computer has become part of a continuum of possible computing platforms from the smallest portable to the largest number-cruncher. It competes with minicomputers and mainframes in the marketplace and in applications on desks. Certain applications which are very demanding in processor power can be run on dedicated processors on the desk-top, for example, display graphics. Other applications require to be accessed by many users or data by many applications; these need a dedicated server or mainframe computer. For the user, it is a matter of convenience which is used.

The personal computer market had been built by vendors other than IBM, notably Apple Computer, founded by Steve Jobs and Steve Wozniak. However, IBM wanted 'in on the act', a share of the money and some influence in the direction of the market. At an early stage IBM had sensed the beginnings of demand for PCs from its corporate customers. It had missed the minicomputer 'revolution', which had been excellent business for companies like Digital Equipment Corporation (DEC).

IBM is an old company, often considered arrogant, with well-established procedures which are not easily overcome. Conventionally, IBM is late into a market, waiting for other companies to establish a base level of demand then it swamps the market. To minimise competition, IBM builds computers to proprietary standards and protects them by patents. The creation of the IBM PC was based at the Boca Raton plant in Florida which was small and almost unheard of, even within IBM. The emphasis was on speed; the project was to take less than one year from conception to having a product in the market. Consequently, the IBM PC had to be built with off-the-shelf components, even the operating system was bought in, from Microsoft. The PC was given an open, non-proprietary, architecture in order to allow other manufacturers to build 'add-ons', such as modems, and to allow software houses to develop applications software for the PC.

The launch of the IBM PC on 12th August 1981 did a number of quite unexpected things. Sales far exceeded IBM's forecasts and it took time for IBM to have the manufacturing capacity available to meet demand. Sales estimates for new products were thereafter IBM grossly exaggerated, such as the PC Junior and PC Convertible. The surge in the market which resulted from IBM's endorsement of the product was quite remarkable. Suddenly organisations and individuals wanted PCs. The IBM logo gave the personal computer a new credibility in large organisations, causing a massive increase in sales. The volume of money being earned created considerable attention within IBM; older established parts of the company wanted a share of the cashflow. Outside IBM, organisations soon realised that the PC could be 'cloned', that is copies could be made which were functionally equivalent if not identical to IBM models, allowing them easy access to the growing market. Everybody in the industry thought they could make money meeting that demand, though few were successful.

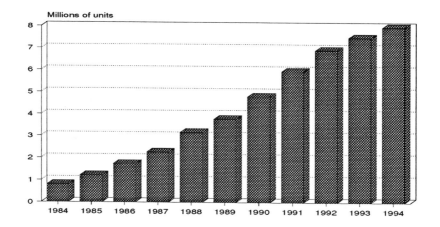

Figure 3.3 *Sales and forecast sales of IBM Personal Computers and clones in Western Europe*

IBM had traditionally sold direct to large corporations. However, the PC had too low a value to support the conventional and expensive IBM marketing and sales operations. Therefore, it had to open up new distribution channels through dealers such as Computerland and retailers such as Sears Roebuck. Marketing and distribution channels have proved difficult to manage, since they effectively control a large part of the market. Access to the distribution channel almost guarantees a minimum level of sales, giving a considerable measure of 'buyer power' to the dealers.

Case: Compaq Computer

Scenario: Compaq Computer rose from nothing to the *Fortune 500* in record time on the basis of innovative personal computers, cloned from IBM.

Compaq Computer, was founded in 1982 in Houston, Texas. It designs, develops, manufactures high-performance personal computers for business and professional users. Compaq has been one of the fastest rising firms in the computer business, based on out-pacing IBM on the development of new models.

Leadership to me is about not being held back by your competition, and also having the credibility and clout with the customers so they'll go with you. Rod Canion, formerly CEO, Compaq.

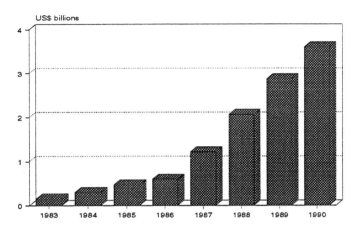

Figure 3.4   *Growth of Compaq Computer sales*

The product lead of Compaq Computer can be shown by comparing product launch dates:

	Compaq	*IBM*
Desktop PC with 386 chip	September 1986	June 1987
Portable PC with 386	September 1987	May 1989
PC with 385 at 25MHz	June 1988	September 1988
PC with 386SX chip	June 1988	May 1989

The 'Clone Wars' had cost IBM market share and leadership. All sorts of existing manufacturers and new entrepreneurs had jumped on the bandwagon so conveniently, if inadvertently, built by IBM. While many had failed to gain a significant market share, some had been successful. Today, over 150 firms worldwide manufacture versions of the IBM PC and PS/2. IBM was finding it difficult to control the market, with firms such as Compaq beating it to produce new models, while others, such as Amstrad undercut its prices.

When IBM launched the PS/2, commentators referred to the move under headlines such as 'The Empire Strikes Back' and illustrated it with Darth Vader. IBM had moved back to proprietary technology, largely abandoning the open appearance of the IBM PC. The PS/2 used technology which was patented, though the processor was either an Intel 80286 or 80386 chip, manufactured under licence by IBM.

The initial PS/2s ran MS-DOS, allowing users to retain their old application software, but with the clear intention of converting to a new operating system, OS/2.

However, there were serious delays in delivering the new operating system. IBM encouraged software houses and value-added resellers to convert programs to OS/2 and to develop new programs for it, by providing them with early supplies of hardware and operating systems.

There was a backlash from the clone-makers who refused to lie down and play dead. A number of manufacturers, including Compaq, Olivetti, Epson, Tandy, AST Research, Hewlett-Packard, Amstrad, Dell, Digital Equipment Corporation, AT&T and Unisys, grouped together to sustain and extend the old IBM PC architecture. A new Extended Industry Standard Architecture (EISA) was devised to allow the IBM PC 'standard' to live on after IBM had tried to kill it. Subsequently, a number of vendors created the Advanced Computing Environment (ACE) with a similar view.

In October 1990, IBM created a design group including Apricot and Olivetti to open up its proprietary Micro-Channel Architecture (MCA) to other manufacturers. Thus, IBM effectively, admitted defeat in its attempt to gain a dominating control of the market. Subsequently, this group collapsed and with it the MCA design. IBM is pursuing OS/2 designs of its own and separately it is attempting to run the Apple System 7 on IBM RISC chips.

The key question is who 'owns' the IBM PC standard, since IBM has clearly lost control. Users had invested massively in machines, software and training for the old PC. However, the users had no means to control the standard, therefore the suppliers were able to step in.

The scale of the PC market makes it useful to subdivide it into smaller and more homogeneous categories:

DESKTOP

The bulk of sales of PCs have traditionally been for desks in offices. Desktop machines are usually connected to a local area network for access to servers, gateways and central computers.

FILESERVER

The more powerful devices which provide additional services for users of networked personal computers. Some local area networks with MS-DOS PCs have fileservers running OS/2 and Unix.

LAPTOP

Truly lightweight PCs are available with the latest chips, available only a few months after desktop models are first announced. Typically these will weigh three kilograms with a battery life of around three hours, important considerations for true portability. At present most laptops have monochrome screens, though this is gradually changing to colour.

PORTABLE

These are slightly heavier models with a weight of, perhaps, five kilograms, powered from mains electricity and not batteries. Usually they have more powerful processors and have better quality screens than laptops.

NOTEPAD

Very small computers, the size of an A4 notepad or slightly larger and, perhaps, 25 mileometers thick, with a scribe or 'pen'. and software which allows limited recognition of handwriting.

RESIDENTIAL

The home market has always been an ambiguous area, which is still dominated by games machines: Atari, Commodore, and so on. There is some overlap in use with portables and laptops.

Case: Wang Laboratories

Scenario: Wang Laboratories were once a highly successful ICT vendor created by An Wang, a scientist and very dynamic entrepreneur. It has since undergone serious problems of strategy direction, product innovation and financial performance.

An Wang was born in Shanghai in 1920. He emigrated from China during World War II to study at Harvard University, from where he gained an MS and a PhD. He founded Wang Laboratories as a one-man operation to market his own invention of magnetic core memory for computers. His initial success was founded on the sale of the patent for the magnetic memory to IBM. He then went on to considerable success in the development of electronic desk-top calculators, dedicated word processing systems and office information systems. In 1982, he handed control of the business over to his son Fred.

The downfall of Wang Laboratories was caused to a large extent by its failure to adapt to the new dynamics of the market. Its highly successful minicomputers and dedicated word processors were being used mainly for office information systems, a market in which Wang Laboratories was the brand leader. Increasingly that market was attacked by vendors of personal computers and networks with 'servers'. Wang Labs found itself in the position of dominance in a declining market, under pressure from IBM in the office systems market and from the whole gang of PC manufacturers. Wang Labs was weak in the PC business, which it had not anticipated would be a real substitute for its existing products.

The first Wang PC had been launched in early 1983. At that time the decision was made to develop a Wang version of MS-DOS, although this incompatibility was intended to allow greater functionality, in time it proved a failing. The low market share held by Wang Laboratories gave it a cost disadvantage in the PC market. After the initial surge in worldwide PC sales, the market stopped growing in 1985, which caused Wang serious problems with both cashflow and stocks of machines which were rapidly becoming obsolete. The Wang PC was over-engineered and insufficiently price competitive.

In one important sense, it appears that the failure of Wang Laboratories can be attributed to loss of control by An Wang. The company had 'leapt' from magnetic memory to desktop calculators and from there to word processing and OIS. It did not make the next jump, rather it allowed itself to be drawn into an unpleasant fight with some of the toughest competitors in the business.

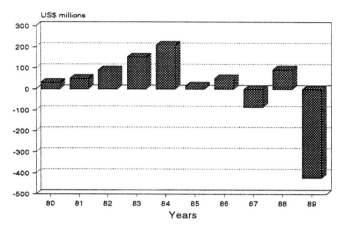

Figure 3.5 *Profit and loss of Wang Laboratories*

Wang Laboratories was not an obvious target for a takeover, since it would be difficult to integrate Wang's proprietary office automation products into another company's product line and its ability to manufacture PCs was of limited value. Therefore, the link created in 1991 with IBM was slightly surprising. The major attraction to IBM seems to have been Wang's customer base with, in the medium term, the intention of running Wang's OIS software on IBM hardware.

The strongest competition for PCs currently comes from Unix workstations. The attractions of such workstations are:

- greater processing power;
- ease of networking;
- independence between the operating system and the hardware architecture allowing portability of software;
- growing dominance of Unix in minicomputer market.

The market for Unix workstations is developing in much the same way as the PC, through standardisation and proliferation. Market growth has attracted software houses which are building an enormous software base. As an indication of the way things may go, Sony and Toshiba have marketed laptop Unix workstations with powers of 15-30 MIPS (million instruction per second).

A 'peripheral' is a device attached to a computer, including:

- disc drives;
- printers;
- plotters;
- tape decks;
- communication cards.

In the late 1960's a number of companies identified a niche market in the production of peripheral equipment for the IBM System/360 series of mainframe computers. With some encouragement from IBM customers, these companies built tape decks, disc drives and magnetic core memory which was intended to be fully compatible with IBM equipment. Thus, a customer needed only to plug it into their existing IBM equipment, hence Plug Compatible Manufacturers (PCMs). The PCMs aimed to beat IBM on price and technical performance which was possible because 'Big Blue' had allowed itself to fall behind in the technology and had adopted pricing strategies which did not reflect underlying costs. IBM responded by moving around the functionality of its hardware, especially switching controllers between boxes and also using its financial muscle to make life difficult for the PCMs.

3.3 Software

Software is a generic term for different categories of program, intangible components, which are 'run' or 'executed' on the hardware. While in the early years of computing, it was the computers that mattered, this has long since been replaced by software which, for both general and specific applications is the key to an investment in the use of computers and the selection of hardware. One buys a computer in order to run software, not vice versa.

The commercial software market dates, in effect, from 1969, when IBM decided to 'unbundle' its software, that is to price separately hardware and software, thus allowing rivals to sell or lease software to IBM customers. The market is characterised by low entry barriers, for example, the capital required is minimal. However, it has proved extremely difficult to build organisations to a large size. Software houses tend to get taken over, either as part of the globalisation strategies of other software companies or as part of the search for added-value by hardware vendors.

The categories of software are:

- packaged;
- customised;
- turnkey.

In the very early days of computing, it was necessary to write software that not only performed the operations required for the business processes but also to control the computer. Two trends then emerged. Firstly, many common operations were transferred into the system software, which in time became the operating system, allowing programmers to concentrate on higher level tasks. Secondly, to obtain the full benefits of existing software some more general software applications were transferred between computers and between organisations. What remains is the area of bespoke software, that is software written to meet particular needs, specific applications for organisations and individuals . Turnkey systems are those where a vendor or Value Added Reseller (VAR) will supply the entire installation, comprising hardware, software and peripherals, install it and set the system running.

While many tasks in business are of a specific nature for particular organisations and therefore require specially written software, some tasks are generic. These tasks, such as word processing, can be addressed by more general software. Most of this generic software comes with standard loose-leaf 'IBM-size' manuals, shrink-wrapped in plastic. The development of such software can best be undertaken by a software house which can spread the development costs over many sales, thus reducing the unit cost. It also allows the supplier to build more functionality into the software. However, it also opens the way for copying of features and cloning; it is unnecessary to do research or development, just copy good ideas from other packages. Figure 3.6 shows the top-selling word processing software.

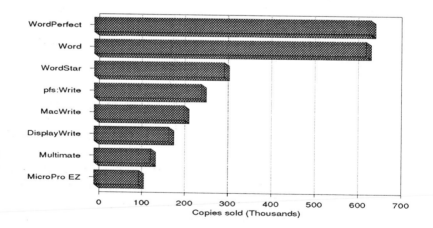

Copies sold (Thousands)

Figure 3.6   *Top-selling word processing software (1987)*
(Adapted from Scott Morton, 1991, page 111.)

Case: Lotus 1-2-3

Scenario: Lotus 1-2-3 has become the world brand leader in the spreadsheet market, a position it is attempting to maintain.

Lotus 1-2-3 has come to dominate the software market for spreadsheets, having displaced SuperCalc which had itself displaced VisiCalc. VisiCalc, the very first spreadsheet, had been invented by Dan Bricklin in 1979 to help solve financial and management accounting problems while studying for a Harvard MBA. VisiCalc was a major factor in the success of the Apple II computer, providing a real reason for buying it.

Lotus 1-2-3 has been able to dominate the market by its ease-of-use and its flexibility. The success of Lotus 1-2-3 was linked to the spectacular success of the IBM PC.

The Lotus Development Corporation was initially very reluctant to issue site licences which would have allowed their customers to economise on purchase costs. Initially, Lotus 1-2-3 was protected by a method requiring each user to have a special system disc which had to be read each time the software was loaded into memory. The relative dominance of Lotus in the marketplace allowed it to charge full prices and to ignore demands from users for more liberal licensing. A site licence allows a user organisation a discount for bulk purchases and generally provides server versions, allowing several simultaneous users on a LAN. Eventually, Lotus succumbed to the demands of its customers to granted site licences.

One of the strategic issues in selling software is the availability of distribution channels.

A major problem for the Lotus Development Corporation was to avoid being seen as a one product company, which inevitably focuses attention on short-term assessments of sales. In an attempt to diversify, Lotus launched integrated packages incorporating word processing and database management systems in addition to a spreadsheet. Jazz (Apple Macintosh) and Symphony (MS-DOS) both failed; they were unable to compete with combinations of more conventional products.

Recently, Lotus has improved 1-2-3 with the release of versions 2.2, 2.3, 3.0 and 1-2-3 for Windows. These products attacked the markets of packages built around Lotus 1-2-3. For example, Harvard Graphics, a sophisticated business graphics package, has the capability to import data and basic graphs directly from a Lotus 1-2-3 spreadsheet for further processing. Many other packages are 'add-ons' for Lotus 1-2-3, such as Allways.

Lotus faces direct competition from Borland Corporation with its Quattro spreadsheet. It must also endeavour to judge how the technology will change. Having diverted considerable efforts into developing a version of 1-2-3 for OS/2, Lotus was unable to recover the costs from sales. It then had to develop another product, 1-2-3 for Windows. However, it faces stiff competition in the Windows market from Microsoft's Excel (based on its Apple Macintosh product).

Lotus Development Corporation has also 'ported' Lotus 1-2-3 onto Unix workstations, such as those made by Sun Microsystems. In doing so it has recognised the growth of the Unix market and its importance in the office sector. Lotus 1-2-3 faces competition from minicomputer and mainframe spreadsheets, such as System W.

Lotus also faces competition from other suppliers who have built spreadsheet interfaces to their software. For example, the relational database Oracle contains a module allowing interrogation of a database using a spreadsheet which is very similar to Lotus 1-2-3. Lotus has responded by buying other software houses, including the suppliers of a word processing package and an electronic mail system.

Finally, Lotus has resorted to the courts to protect its product, successfully suing Brown Bag Software and others for producing clones of Lotus 1-2-3. The basis for these actions in the US courts has been that products have the 'look and feel' of Lotus 1-2-3, a type of action which appears to be restricted to courts in the USA at present.

The spreadsheet has been one of the driving forces in the uptake of the personal computer. However, it has now become a standardised product, almost a commodity. It is not clear that it can go much further. Programs with the functionality and an interface very much like a spreadsheet are found in many other packages, so that the end of the line may be in sight for the spreadsheet.

A major market segment has been for business graphics which allow the user easily to create charts, illustrations and slides. Packages such as Harvard Graphics have been able to transform the ability with which a manager can produce professional business graphics. Evidence of this can be found in the proliferation of such packages: Lotus Freelance and Cricket Graph.

Case: Oracle

Scenario: The market for relational database management systems is very competitive, with products being made available on a multiplicity of computer platforms.

Oracle was founded in 1979 by Lawrence J Ellison in Redwood City, California, to make and sell relational database management systems. Three principles govern Oracle's approach to products:

- compatibility;
- portability;
- connectability.

The aim is to provide software which works identically on a number of hardware platforms including IBM, DEC VAX/VMS and ICL VME. An important consideration has been the implementation of the international standard, Structured Query Language (SQL).

The various component parts of Oracle include:

• menu system;
• forms interface;
• report generator;
• database for free text;
• spreadsheet;
• links to other databases, including dBASE IV.

The growing power of personal computers and servers has allowed Oracle to 'port' its software down into the PC market. Corresponding moves by rival software suppliers to move from PCs to servers and minicomputers have proved extremely difficult, the complexity of this requires a new structure, effectively require the supplier to rewrite the software.

To help its customers develop their own applications, Oracle supports Computer Aided Software Engineering (CASE) with:

• business analysis techniques;
• data dictionary;
• graphical workstation for designers;
• form and report generator.

Oracle has developed sets of its own generic applications for areas such as: finance, general ledgers, accounts payable and receivable, personnel and purchasing. Value Added Resellers have also been encouraged to develop other applications. In addition to its after-sales services, Oracle offers a wide range of consultancy and training.

Oracle is number one in the world market for relational database management systems, ahead of rivals such as software houses like Informix, Sybase and Ingres and of hardware vendors IBM and Digital Equipment Corporation. Over one hundred employees have become US dollar millionaires. Oracle achieved its remarkable growth by pushing very hard for sales. Often, the push was too hard, resulting in booking orders which did not materialise or for products which could not be shipped for months and so could not be invoiced; sales staff received commission immediately. 1991 saw a major restructuring of the firm, with many staff being forced to leave.

One of the clearer failures in the software market has been that of integrated packages. The basic idea was sound, in that most users required access to a number of the pieces of application software discussed above. Therefore, why not bundle the software into a single package, with consistent interfaces and with easy mechanisms for transferring between the various parts? The failure came because the products, such as Jazz and Works, were 'stuck in the middle', they had not the same level of functionality as single products, thus secretaries rejected them as word processors and managers rejected them as spreadsheets.

A separate market for operating systems emerged only with machine independent operating systems, such as Unix and MS-DOS. An operating system is a set of programs that jointly control the system resources (processors, disc drives and so on) and the processes using those resources. From the user's perspective, it is an environment within which a number of programs are run. Computer programs are written in programming languages (such as C++ or COBOL), which are 'compiled' into 'code', which then can be executed on a particular computer with a particular operating system. To move a program to another operating system requires it to be recompiled and/or rewritten.

MS-DOS is currently the leading operating system for personal computers. A variety of versions of MS-DOS exist for different manufacturers, in particular IBM's PC-DOS. As explained above, IBM has moved to a proprietary operating system for its PS/2, called OS/2, originally provided by Microsoft but IBM have since taken over full responsibility. This has allowed Microsoft to concentrate on improving MS-DOS and further developing Windows. IBM has also opened links to Apple to develop the Apple System 7 operating system to run on IBM RISC chips.

Case: Unix

Scenario: The market for Unix systems has grown enormously, particularly in the last two years.

The Unix operating system was invented by Dennis Ritchie and Kenneth Thompson at Bell Laboratories, part of AT&T. It was announced in 1973 at a conference held in IBM Yorktown Heights. Unix is a multi-tasking and multi-user operating system with built-in telecommunications and database facilities, which is advantageous to users because it improves the performance of the system. It is easy to customise and has accumulated a very long list of applications software. Much of its initial popularity was achieved through use in universities and colleges from which it spread by means of students to technical applications in industry (see figure 3.7).

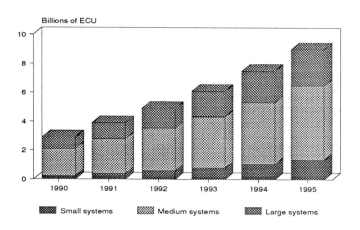

Figure 3.7 *Forecast growth in sales of Unix 'boxes' in Europe (Adapted from Ovum, 1990.)*

Unix is 'portable' in that it can be made to run on most computers. It is not tied to a particular chip or set of chips unlike, say, MS-DOS or IBM's VM. Most of Unix is written in the C programming language with a small amount of machine specific code, only the latter has to be modified to run on a particular computer.

Following the Consent Decree in 1956, mainly related to its activities in telecommunications, AT&T was excluded from the computer market. It was therefore unable to exploit Unix commercially, though ironically, this helped in its adoption, since AT&T licensed Unix to a large number of computer companies. This position changed with the Modified Final Judgement in 1984, when AT&T was freed to enter the computer market and could take a real interest in exploiting Unix.

Given that AT&T had never controlled Unix very closely, a number of versions had appeared, notably System V and Berkeley. Attempts have been made to turn Unix into a standard called 'Posix'. However, much faster moves are taking place in the market, with two entrenched camps arguing over which is the better version of Unix. At risk for the two groups are stakes in the rapidly growing Unix market.

Open Software Foundation: Altos, Intel, IBM, Data General, Digital, Philips, Groupe Bull, Toshiba, Hewlett-Packard, Wang, Nixdorf, Hitachi, MIPS, Texas Instruments and Oracle.

Unix International: AT&T, Sun, Fujitsu, ICL, Gould, Intel, Unisys, Motorola, Olivetti, Xerox, NCR, Prime, Amdahl, Control Data and Oracle.

The suppliers of mass-produced 'shrink-wrapped' software identified Unix as a suitable platform for expansion. The large and growing number of Unix 'boxes', especially workstations has created a sufficiently large market to spread the cost of converting MS-DOS software and of writing new software. In turn this is driving up sales of Unix boxes. Unix versions of the spreadsheet Lotus 1-2-3 and the word processing package WordPerfect are already available.

Unix accounts for at least 10% of global IT revenue. It attracts more hardware revenue than any computer vendor except IBM. Unix will grow to take 20% of IT revenue shortly after 1992. Tony Cleaver, IBM (UK) Chief Executive Officer.

In terms of everyday use, its makes little difference to a manager whether a workstation runs Unix, MS-DOS or some other operating system. The screen appearances are converging on similar graphical user interfaces and the more popular software packages are increasingly available for both Unix and MS-DOS operating systems. Consequently, operating systems are becoming commodities, like hardware.

Much of the current attention being given to operating systems is on the development of Graphical User Interfaces (GUIs), such as MOTIF (Unix), X-Windows (Unix), Microsoft Windows (MS-DOS) and Presentation Manager (OS/2). These allow the user to issue simple instructions rather than the often arcane and character-based commands of many operating systems. Since its launch in the mid-1980's, for instance, Microsoft Windows has attracted the interest of a considerable number of software houses and is now a common requirement for more recent releases of 'user-friendly' software.

A WIMPs (Windows, Icons, Menus and Pointers) environment is much more 'user-friendly' than traditional operating systems. WIMPs are based on approaches developed at Xerox Corporation's Palo Alto Research Centre which were made first into a commercial success by Apple Corporation (see figure 3.8):

WINDOWS
allow a number of areas of the screen to contain different processes, not necessarily on the same machine.

ICONS
allow the representation of documents, software and processes by relevant pictures.

MENUS
usually pop-up or drop down, allow users a selection of options.

POINTERS
such as a mouse or tablet, allow the user to select items from menus and to activate windows and icons.

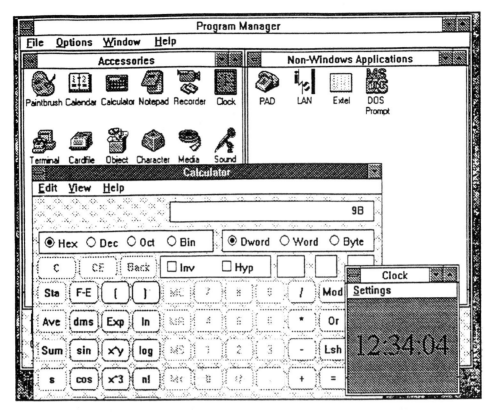

Figure 3.8 *A typical WIMPs screen*

3.4 Telecommunications

The technological convergence of computing and communications has had important strategic implications for many industries and companies. Communications can be viewed as the network 'nervous system', whether of an organisation or of an economy, just as the canals and railways did in earlier centuries, permitting effective and secure flows of data.

It is possible to categorise the telecommunications marketplace as follows:

EQUIPMENT
Hardware and software systems provided to telecommunications operators and their customers.

BASIC SERVICES
Telephone services between users and, in most countries, leased lines and data services.

VALUE ADDED SERVICES
Services provided using a basic service, 'adding value', for example, by providing access to a database or managing a telecommunications network.

Technological advances have radically altered telecommunications in the last forty years. There have been considerable reductions in costs through the automation of telephone exchanges and in the use of sophisticated electronics. The well-known phenomenon of convergence of computers and communications has not only linked two technologies which were once quite distinct but also forced together two very different application areas and two previously unrelated markets while creating opportunities for new services and, indeed, new organisations.

The new technologies have been used to develop new services, such as voice mail. The boundaries between many old services have all but been eliminated, notably between voice and data which are carried together and it is difficult to see any new market barriers which would last any length of time. The established trading patterns and traditional economies of scale and of scope in the telecommunications industry have been overturned in both business and residential markets. The use of telecommunications has made services tradeable in ways that could not previously have been imagined. For example, Reuters has been transformed from a rather staid, if extremely respectable, provider of newspaper stories into a very dynamic provider of financial information and a rival to stock exchanges.

General economic pressures have led to a re-examination of subsidies to, and cross-subsidies within, telecommunications authorities and monopolies. Political forces in Western Europe, Japan and the United States of America drove the re-regulation of telecommunications. The 1980's saw a major movement in favour of free markets, though with the retirements of Ronald Reagan and Margaret Thatcher this may not be true of the 1990's. The political ideas driving re-regulation fit naturally with the political changes in Eastern Europe and the former Soviet Union. For example, Hungary is well advanced in the privatisation of its national Post Telephone and Telegraph authority (PTT) and its telecommunications manufacturing companies, together with the introduction of competition. However, some countries can be accused of putting too much faith in the free market, overlooking the potentially positive roles of state regulation and intervention, while in others the pace of change is slow, notably in Austria and Switzerland where the telecommunications regimes remain rigidly controlled.

Deregulation, in the sense of abolishing all controls, is generally undesirable since governments need to retain some residual controls in addition to general legislation: health and safety, submission of company accounts, taxation and so on. Countries need to retain control over:

- monopoly and oligopoly in industries;
- provision of basic telephony service to rural areas (universal service);
- formation of joint ventures;
- maintenance of international competitiveness.

There have been massive structural changes in the global telecommunications industry. The traditional view of telecommunications in Europe was of a state monopoly with a number of domestic and often nationalised manufacturing industries providing the necessary telephones, exchanges and other equipment. State control or state sponsorship have been extensive and represent a form of vertical integration. Five scenarios for regulation can be distinguished:

- state monopoly: retention by the state of total control, both in provision of services. *Status quo ante* would require massive state financing and detailed direction.
- regulated private monopoly: licensing a single provider of telecommunications on a non-competitive basis, but with restrictions on activities and profitability, for example, AT&T in the USA prior to 1984. More than one operator could be licensed, restricting each to a separate area, such as mobile telephony;
- heavily regulated competition: more than one operator, operating under control of activities and profitability.
- lightly regulated competition: more than one operator with considerable degrees of freedom for firms to compete in some or all sectors market if they wish, subject to some constraints, such as, profit and interconnections. The UK, following the 1991 White Paper, is in this category.
- unregulated competition: removal of all constraints on operation in telecommunications, allowing any company to offer any service.

The traditional trade-off has been that an organisation, for example, the Post Office in the UK or AT&T in the USA, would be allowed a monopoly in exchange for a guarantee of 'universal service' and acceptance of control over its prices and/or profits and/or return on investment. The historical view of universal service was the agreement to provide a telephone to any location, even the most isolated. However, in the 1990's, a basic telephone is of limited value, when the urban resident in a major Western city can expect two fully digital lines suitable for voice or data at a speed of 64 kilobits per second and the business user can have anything from two to one hundred and forty Megabits per second.

The provision of telecommunications services has, for all practical purposes, ceased to be a natural monopoly, though it often lingers on as an unnatural one. It is no longer the grudging provision of black bakelite telephones to shops, offices and homes. The market has become highly fragmented instead of monolithic. The main historic argument for the monopoly related to the wasteful duplication of transmission systems. Telecommunications has ceased to be a labour intensive process characterised by gangs of unskilled and semi-skilled workers laying cables under streets or stringing wires between telegraph poles. Although telephone 'lines' can still be traditional copper cables, they can also be provided using microwave, satellite or optical fibre. The multiplicity of potential access 'lines' removes the natural element from the monopoly, since there can now be competition without wasteful duplication of infrastructure. The keys to success lie in the quality of service, innovation and the rapid deployment of new technologies.

In the past, economies of scale in transmission were of vital importance, today they are less obvious. For example, Mercury Communications Limited was able to build its figure-of-eight optical fibre cable backbone around the most populous part of England in a very short period of time, by running optical fibre cables alongside the railway tracks of British Rail. Ironically, the recent changes in regulations now allow British Rail Telecom (BRT) to compete in the telecommunications market.

When it is decided to introduce competition then the different networks need to interconnect. Where such interconnection occurs and where one supplier makes use of services from other suppliers it is necessary that the sharing of revenues be regulated through agreed access charges. Ideally, the user should have easy access to the maximum number of networks and services. Where non-competitive services are retained, then there must be regular reviews of tariffs and the quality of service by a regulatory body.

It has proved inadvisable to mix monopoly services and competitive services other than in the very short term. If it is decided that there should be a monopoly service in addition to any competitive services, then the boundary fixed between the two must be sustainable. Companies cannot be permitted to provide both regulated and unregulated services since it is virtually impossible to regulate them because of the difficulties of untangling the allocation of overheads, transfer pricing and so on. In the United States of America, the Federal Communications Commission (FCC) has had considerable difficulty with this problem trying to keep up with these shifting boundaries in its Computer I, II and III judgments.

Case: United Kingdom telecommunications

Scenario: The UK Government had made significant moves in re-regulating its telecommunications services. It required to take stock of the position and lay out a framework for developments for the 1990's.

In 1984, the Government broke the telecommunications monopoly of the newly privatised British Telecom by the award of a licence to Mercury Communications. In order to encourage Mercury, the Minister for Information Technology (Kenneth Baker) promised no further competition for seven years. That period expired in 1991 and the Government announced its intention to open the market to further competitors.

In November 1990, the government published a consultative document outlining its proposals for the future. The overall aim was to maintain the UK's position as one of the most dynamic and open telecommunications markets in the world. Monopolies had already been broken in telephone equipment, in subscriber wiring and public call-boxes. A government White Paper was published in March 1991 after consideration of over 200 comments on the consultative document.

The main proposal was that the 'duopoly' (BT and Mercury) be ended, with new licences to provide telecommunications services being open to other organisations unless there was a specific reason not to grant the licence. This would apply to the local loop, that is the connection between the exchange and the subscriber, as well as long distance and international lines.

The new regime allows a number of new entrants to the telecommunications market, which could include:

International telecommunications:
- US Regional Bell Operating Companies (such as, Nynex and US West)
- satellite operators (such as, British Aerospace, Racal and EDS)

Trunk network (long distance):
- British Rail Telecom (BRT);
- British Gas;
- British Waterways;
- Post Office;
- London Underground;
- electricity utilities;
- satellite operators.

Local services:
- cable television;
- Personal Communication Network (PCN) mobile telecommunications operators;
- water companies;
- Telepoint operators.

Source: Department of Trade and Industry, 1990 and 1991.

Equipment

Production of exchange equipment is controlled by a few global firms which have the volume of sales necessary to recover the massive Research and Development costs. In contrast, telephones have become a commodity market. The relatively low labour costs of telephone manufacture mean that they remain open to many European manufacturers, probably organisations making 'white' or 'brown' goods or computers.

The conventional categorisation of telecommunications equipment is:

CENTRAL OFFICE SWITCHES
Public telephone exchanges (but not private branch exchanges).

TRANSMISSION EQUIPMENT
Inter-exchange and local loops, multiplexers, copper and fibre optic cables.

CUSTOMER PREMISES EQUIPMENT
Private branch exchanges (PBXs) and key systems, telephone sets, mobile equipment, facsimile machines and so on.

The costs of Research and Development have been rising steeply in recent years, caused by the growing complexity and sophistication of equipment. There has been a major change from mechanical to digital systems in which the switching is performed by software; exchanges have become computers running complex switching software. Manufacturers have had to establish or gain access to new expertise in this area which, once achieved, has allowed them to add a wide range of new facilities to their equipment. In order to re-coup the rising costs of Research and Development, telephone manufacturers have been forced towards globalisation, by establishing a broader base of customers, they have been better able to write off R&D costs.

Case: Alcatel

Scenario: Regulatory, political, financial and technical forces came together to force telecommunications equipment manufacturers to look for new business structures.

Alcatel NV was created in 1986 from the French firm CGE (Compagnie Générale d'Electricité) and the telecommunications divisions of the American multinational ITT (originally International Telephone and Telegraph). The main actors were Rand Araskog (ITT) and George Pebereau (CGE). The intention was to form an organisation sufficiently large to compete with the world's largest telecommunications equipment manufacturers: AT&T, Ericsson, and Siemens.

ITT had been built by over 250 acquisitions by Harold Geneen. The corporation was a true conglomerate displaying great diversity. However, in the 1980's fashions changed and ITT was held to be too diverse and lacking in strategic logic. Therefore, ITT found itself obliged to fend off corporate raiders who wanted to carve up the corporation and to sell off parts of the corporation.

The telecommunications divisions had been under pressure from governments in the various countries in which ITT operated; they were expected to sell their subsidiaries at knock-down prices to the local government or its proxy. The problem for ITT was that the markets were controlled by the same governments, leaving ITT very exposed to pressure.

Telecommunications technology had moved from electro-mechanical to digital, increasing the costs of Research and Development and opening up possibilities of collaboration with other electronics firms. AT&T and Philips had already created such a joint venture, known as APT.

ITT had developed a fully digital central office switch, the System 12, at considerable cost. At this time the Bell System in the USA was being reconstructed following the settlement of the anti-trust case against AT&T, leading to a series of major purchases of exchanges. However, ITT had been too slow in developing its product offering and was unable to bid for this business.

Linking ITT with CGE was both imaginative and was well-received. It involved decisions by the French government, which had nationalised CGE in 1982. The important point for the French was to create an organisation which was more than a national champion, a firm which was a global competitor. A major factor in this process was the French government, which held a controlling interest in CGE. What was unusual was that they recognised that CGE could no longer operate on a national level and required to expand overseas if it was to continue to be competitive.

Source: Araskog, 1990.

Basic services

In the 1940's and 1950's, it became clear that the transmission of voice over telephone networks could be achieved more efficiently by digital means, through the conversion of analogue or continuously varying signals into a digital signal. Once digital, the voice signal could be transmitted with other types of data, for example, Integrated Services Digital Network (ISDN). The use of computers and software as telephone exchanges has allowed extremely sophisticated switching. Centrex services have been offered, in which the facilities of a private branch exchange are provided on the public exchange. Wide Area Telephone Services (WATS) have been offered in the USA, providing a national freephone or 0800 service. Virtual Private Networks (VPNs) have been developed in which the functionality of a private network is achieved on the public network, using the sophistication of the switching software.

The categories of basic services are:

TELEPHONY

Originally analogue, telephony is increasingly digital transmission. Digital technology has allowed the introduction of more sophisticated services, such as Centrex, itemised billing, freephone, WATS and others.

LEASED LINES
A telecommunications link between two fixed points, such as between a branch office and headquarters.

DATA SERVICES
Originally developed to allow access to shared resources, data services have become an important form of national and international communications between people and computers and between computers.

A leased line between two fixed points, say, between a branch and head office is connected by the telecommunications operator and can be freely used by the client organisation, charged on a fixed cost basis, independent of the level of use. 'Break-out' from a private network of leased lines allows, for example, a company with a network linking branches throughout the UK to route calls to the London area across its network from the Edinburgh branch to the London office before they enter the public network. Using this facility, an organisation can make substantial savings on call charges. A major technical advantage is that allows the user freedom to optimise the use of the line, subject to licensing concerning the attachment of equipment.

One of the important recent changes in UK regulations and increasingly in other European countries is that companies are allowed to re-sell excess capacity on their leased lines. It can often be economic to operate a leased line at only 10-20% of capacity leaving a considerable margin for resale. By releasing some of the 'extra' capacity the user can recover a proportion of its embedded costs and, perhaps, make a profit.

Mobile telephony has grown in leaps and bounds, where it has been unfettered by government regulation. Traditional analogue mobile communications was replaced in the mid-1980's with digital telecommunications allowing many more users and a higher standard of service. A second generation known as Groupe Special Mobile (GSM) is already beginning to replace the diversity of mobile standards, equipment conforming to GSM can be operated in all Western European countries and soon in Eastern Europe. In private applications cordless technology is being used as the basis for 'wireless' office switches (PABXs and key systems), with cellular systems replacing wiring and allowing users to roam within an office or factory.

The scale of activity in mobile telephony is shown by the *Fortune*'s 1990 review 'deals of the year', which listed the following:

- McCaw Cellular acquisition of 42% of Lin Broadcasting (US$ 3.8 M);
- Lin Broadcasting acquisition of 46% of Metromedia (US$ 1.9 M);
- Contel acquisition of franchises from McCaw (US$ 1.3 M);
- CTE acquired 95% of publishing and cellular telephony group Providence Journal (US$ 0.67 M).

For the residential and business user, the latest technical developments lie in Integrated Services Digital Network (ISDN), though its practical applications remain unclear. ISDN allows a traditional single copper telephone line to carry two simultaneous channels which can be used for voice or can carry data at 64,000 bits per second. Thus a user can conduct a telephone conversation on one channel while using the second channel to access a database or to provide a common electronic blackboard for discussion. Business users can have two Megabits per second, allowing 30 channels. Among the applications is Group 4 facsimile which is a major technical advance on Group 3, the current standard, in that it allows transmission at full photocopier standard and in colour. However, Group 4 machines are still very expensive. Facsimile is a difficult market to forecast, since there is competition from electronic mail, voice mail and from more sophisticated document transfer techniques which allow incoming documents to be edited. The French service, known as *Numéris*, is the most advanced in Europe in its implementation. Its development has been very clearly orientated towards business needs with considerable experimentation involving users in Brittany and Paris.

The next stage is to be Integrated Broadband Communication (IBC) which will operate at speeds of 140 Megabits per second in the late 1990's. It is not clear what will be done with it!

Value-added services

The definition of 'value-added' is a legal rather than an economic one. It is used to define services where competition is permitted, as distinct from monopoly services. The categories of value-added services are:

ON-LINE DATABASES
Databases with information on particular themes. For example, FT Profile, which contains articles from a number of major newspapers and magazines.

ELECTRONIC DATA INTERCHANGE
The electronic exchange of purchase orders, delivery notes, invoices and so on between trading partners.

ELECTRONIC MAIL
A system of exchanging electronic messages between individuals. It operates in a similar way to the post office, though with mailboxes held at one of a number of central locations.

Value Added Services embrace a wide range of time and cost-saving facilities for transferring information electronically rather than on paper. Their introduction can transform the efficiency of virtually any sector of business by the elimination of paper work and whole tiers of administration, substituting electronic links between trading partners. (see also Inter-organisational systems in Chapter 6). On-line database access is concerned with information retrieval and information dissemination; person-to-computer communication, with the information from the computer often stored and accessible in a highly structured form. Electronic Data Interchange (EDI) is primarily concerned with transactions; a computer-to-computer, highly structured and well formatted document. Electronic mail is about communication; a person-to-person unformatted type of communication.

The diversity of types of benefit of value added services include cost savings, quality improvements and, through their imaginative use, changes in the nature of the very product. For example, the National Bingo Game comprises the simultaneous playing of the same game of Bingo in some eight hundred clubs in the UK, allowing larger prizes and more excitement as well as giving the traditional game a more 'modern' image. The electronic linking of the clubs for the game helped transform a falling market. The benefit of product enhancement lies in managers examining what the organisation does and asking whether it can be improved through value-added services; or, even develop a product around it.

Databases and on-line information services provide valuable information in a convenient form, or by broadcasting news or information which may be of value to expected users and can save many hours of searching through directories and libraries. Speed of communication and ready access to information can make major contributions to the effectiveness of management.

Case: Reuters

Scenario: Reuters has undergone considerable changes in the way it does business and in the services it delivers to its clients.

Reuters was founded in 1850 by Paul Julius Reuter (1st Baron Reuter). He established an information service by using pigeons to bridge a gap, in the telegraph services, between Aachen and Brussels. Ever since, Reuters has been in the business of providing information at high speed. To do so it has used several generations of technology, from telegraphy to fibre optics.

Reuters was owned by the 'press barons' and various UK local newspapers as the result of a deal struck with the UK government during the Second World War to preserve its supposed independence. The shares were to be held according the original documents "in the nature of a trust rather than ... an investment. Later, shares were sold to newspapers in some Commonwealth countries. Reuters traditionally competed with Associated Press and Agence France Press.

In the early 1960's, a 'Stockmaster' system was introduced to replace tickertape delivery of stock market information. Reuters was one of the first organisations to realise the potential of linking clients to computers. This allowed the subscriber to receive the information in real-time and to do so in a selective manner. The service was based in the USA, with Reuters acquiring the rights to distribution elsewhere. To do so they built a network of computers and leased lines across Europe, Africa and the Far East.

In 1970 the service was improved by moving from a 'hardwired' system to software. This allowed:

- greater flexibility in use;
- subscribers to contribute information;
- subscribers to trade on the system.

Use of the system was given a major boost in 1971 by the collapse of the Bretton Woods fixed exchange rates. The Reuters Monitor Service became a prerequisite for foreign exchange (FOREX) trading in the very volatile conditions which resulted. In 1981 it was updated with the launch of the Reuters Monitor Dealing service. These systems were video-based, supplying screens of data in preset formats.

In 1981 Reuters declared its first dividend in forty years. This caused the owners, the newspaper proprietors, to take a new interest in the firm. Eventually a public floatation was arranged, providing funds for the further development of Reuters network services. The money accruing to the press barons was channelled into the modernisation of their production facilities.

Reuters has three sources of information:

- journalists;
- direct feed from exchanges;
- subscribers.

Information from the service is provided to users on teleprinters, VDUs, digital feed into clients' computer systems and workstations. Increasingly, the emphasis is on the processing of information at clients' sites; therefore, workstations and computer systems are important. Reuters Monitor System is capable of providing enormous amounts of information to subscribers; arguably too much information.

The growing sophistication of users' activities downstream of Reuters is a cause for major concern. The digital feed of information to clients presents problems in pricing. As the client then processes the data it is difficult to know what to charge for the service.

Reuters has maintained its reputation for sobriety and neutrality. It is necessary to maintain the integrity of the network through adequate security measures both on the entry of data and its transmission.

The ethos at Reuters is one of individuals working for a clear common goal, derived from the journalistic background and is consequently highly literate.

Source: DTI (1990).

Prodigy is an electronic information service provided jointly by IBM and Sears Roebuck, a leading retailer in the USA. It is designed to allow home computer users access to a range of information services, such as catalogues, recipes, stock prices and travel timetables. This is reflected in Prodigy's revenue streams; a low flat fee to the subscriber, a relatively large commission on purchases made over the system and an on-screen advertising charge. However, it has been found that a large number of subscribers like to interact with each other on the system, rather than simply receive information and purchase goods. Electronic bulletin boards were established and an extensive 'free' electronic mail system developed, the consequence of which was that Prodigy's systems costs exceeded revenues. Prodigy reacted by charging for electronic mail, but has now lost many subscribers to other networks, such as H&R Black's CompuServe and McGraw-Hill's BIX.

Case: Minitel

Scenario: The French government has been very successful in establishing domestic and business use of Minitel, the French version of videotex. Today, it faces considerable marketing and technological challenges.

The French government introduced Minitel in 1984. It was a version of the British invention, Prestel or videotex. The aim was to conduct a limited experiment, then to follow it up with a major national launch. It was recognised that France had been slow to adopt earlier telecommunications technologies and that it had a poor infrastructure. Accordingly, the scale was grand, over five million Minitels have been installed to date. The key to this was the argument that the Minitel would replace the printed telephone directory with an on-line database.

One of the most important features of Minitel was the kiosk tariff structure. This offered a predetermined tariff with a number of bands which the customer could easily understand. France Télécom could easily collect this money since each band had its own telephone number. Having dialled the four digit number, the subscriber then keyed in the name of the service, for example, Coke or Orangina. Thus, the consumer saw a 'branded' product. The service operator was paid in respect to the number of minutes of connect time recorded by France Télécom.

Perhaps the most difficult part of assessing Minitel is the significance of *messagerie rose*. One of the important early innovations was to allow subscribers access to an electronic version of the personal announcement column of a newspaper. These services rapidly developed into a national scandal, with all too obvious names like CUM, GoGay and SM being offered. The publicity generated through the adverts, for example, on Parisian bus shelters, and the controversy in the newspapers, made Minitel famous or infamous. On one or two occasions the national digital network, Transpac, crashed under the strain. Whilst it is not easy to interpret the figures from France Télécom, it appears that today these services represent no more than 10% of the traffic and possibly less than 4%. In January 1992 the French government ruled that a number of these services were pornographic and subjected them to a tax of 50% of revenue, effectively driving them out of business.

Today the position is very complicated. France Télécom has been very quick in 'rolling out' ISDN, which offers the potential for photovideotex. However, it has not addressed the question of how to convert Minitel to this more sophisticated standard. The rules of the commercial game have been altered with the creation of a single internal market for telecommunications services on 1st January 1991. The French national auditors, the *Cour des Comptes*, issued a very critical report in 1989, arguing that the money spent on Minitel would have been better used by reducing tariffs for business.

EDI is concerned with the automatic transfer of structured messages representing transactions (such as invoices, orders and acknowledgements) directly between the computers of trading partners. For example, instead of a supplier having its computer generate the relevant paper work, sending all of this paper to its trading partners by mail, who then have to re-key the information into their own computers, for local processing, the computers can directly exchange the information. The result is a quicker, cheaper and more accurate transmission of information. Major users of EDI services include the motor and shipping industries, the financial services industry and the distributive and retail trade, where many millions of pounds are saved each year through its use.

Electronic mail services increase the speed and effectiveness of business by providing a virtually instantaneous means of communicating messages person-to-person or to potentially interested groups by means of 'bulletin boards'. A number of public services have been launched, including BT's Telecom Gold. Commercial electronic mail services have proved problematic, having failed to attract significant volumes of business.

3.5 Computing services

There are quite different national approaches to the purchase of software. Where a British company would have a large DP/IS Department to create and maintain the software necessary to run the business, a French company would put the business out to a software house.

Case: Hoskyns

Scenario: Hoskyns, a very large UK software house, has recently changed hands.

Hoskyns is a software house, consultancy practice and facilities management operation based in London. It sells products such as its Project Manager Workbench and CASE tool, Prism.

Following the purchase in 1990 of Plessey by GEC and Siemens, Hoskyns was an obvious candidate to be sold off. There had been considerable interest in Hoskyns. Firms mentioned were US West, AT&T and Japanese software houses. One of the major problems was that the company's assets were volatile, since the staff could easily have been scared off in any takeover bid which was seen to be hostile.

Eventually it was sold to the French firm Cap Gemini Sogeti (CGS), a French-based computer services firm with over 14,000 staff. It is one of the largest such firms in Europe. Its activities include:

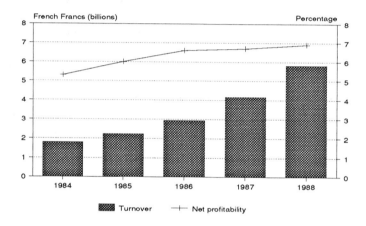

Figure 3.9 *Growth in CGS turnover*

Consultancy:
    strategy, planning and IS architecture.
Systems Integration:
    prime contractor, turnkey solutions, dedicated hardware design,
    applications and systems products.
Development:
    defining applications, developing basic software, developing
    applications software, implementing products, conversions,
    maintaining DP applications, security, running DP Centres, recruiting
    DP staff, training and seminars.

Hoskyns appears to have found reasonable owners and settled down to a relatively steady state of growth.

A Value Added Reseller (VAR) is an organisation which buys hardware or sometimes software and uses it to provide a service. For example, turnkey systems for computer aided design.

Consulting

Consulting can be a useful professional, advisory service that assists managers to analyse and solve problems in their organisations. With the appropriate selection of consultancy practice and particularly the consultants who will work on a specific assignment, it is possible to capture and learn directly or indirectly from the experiences of other managers and organisations. It must be stressed that selection and management of your consultants is not straightforward, but, ultimately, these tasks, along with problem identification, determine the success of any project. The basic objective of consulting is to enhance management practices, and the service can be provided by an internal group or an external organisation. A major application arises from the need for an outside view either independent or quasi-independent. Consultants can be used as a catalyst for change, although some seem to shy away from the tasks of implementation.

A range of consulting organisations exist from the large general practices usually associated with large accountancy firms to small firms comprising one or two people with specialist interests and experiences. A number of categories of consulting activities can be identified:

STRATEGIC STUDIES
Developing a business strategy or an information systems strategy for an organisation.

SPECIALIST STUDIES
Studies where the consultant is providing a level of expertise not found in the company, such as networking, assessment of CASE tools, etc.

PROJECT MANAGEMENT
To superintend the work of internal and external organisations in the completion of a particular project.

BODY-SHOPPING
The provision of the necessary consultants, project managers, systems analysts and programmers for a particular project.

RECRUITMENT
Supplying permanent or temporary staff.

There is a considerable movement by manufacturers to add value to their own products by moving into consultancy. For example, Microsoft has recently established a broad-based IT consultancy in the UK, and many manufacturers have internal consultants (such as IBM, ICL and DEC) within their specialised vertical marketing departments.

Case: European Security Forum

Scenario: At the instigation of Coopers and Lybrand a collaborative body was established to help companies work on the security of their information and communications systems.

Organisations no longer merely use ICTs, but they depend on them and any disruption can be damaging (see Chapter 6). For example, because of a software bug, the London branch of a US bank paid out a total of £1 billion twice. Although the money was recovered, the company suffered both public embarrassment and the loss of interest on the money.

Coopers and Lybrand recognised that organisations are dependent on their ICTs and that they need to take measures to ensure the security of their ICT resources. They invited over sixty organisations to participate in the European Security Forum; each is a leader in its particular area of activity. The security of each organisation is surveyed and put into a database, in order to:

- to compare with other members;
- to develop a longitudinal model;
- to help identify 'best practice'.

Each year a number of studies are conducted into areas chosen by the members of the Forum. The aim is to help the members become 'wide awake' to security issues.

Source: Kapp, 1990.

3.6 Conclusion

The information-based industries are best characterised by chaos, a state of permanent revolution, dominated by large-scale transformation. The different elements of the sector and the individual companies show little continuity over the years, other than the preeminence of change. It is difficult to believe that this position will alter in the next few years or indeed longer, the forces at work today seem set to remain dominant.

The 1990's have already seen a flurry of joint ventures, mergers and acquisitions, the value of which will take some time to assess:

- IBM and Apple Computer;
- IBM and Wang Laboratories;
- Borland and Ashton-Tate;
- AT&T and NCR;
- ICL and Nokia.

It is clear that many technological components of sophisticated business systems are being reduced to mere commodities. Consequently, costs fall for customers and profit margins for suppliers. This trend is forcing suppliers to re-examine their manufacturing and to build up long-term relationships with reliable suppliers, to license technology and to enter into joint ventures. Users are increasingly able to benefit from lower costs and, through open systems, reduced switching costs. Equally, it is driving vendors to find new areas of added-value.

Product life-cycles have become absurdly short, often achieving obsolescence before the product reach the market, making time-to-market of great strategic importance.

> High-tech products tend to have two things in common; they fall in price rapidly as production builds up (they possess steep learning curves) and they get replaced fairly frequently (they have short life cycles). The trend in high-tech is towards things becoming steeper and shorter. So the competitive advantage is going increasingly to outweigh almost everything else. (Valery, Survey "High Technology" *The Economist* 23 August 1986.)

This situation creates a vicious circle for suppliers driving them to ever faster introduction of new products to keep ahead of rivals. The problem it poses for customers is how to exploit the technology sufficiently rapidly to allow them to move on to the latest generation.

> If we overspend 50% on our engineering budget, but deliver on time, it impacts 10% on revenues. But if we are late it can impact [sic] up to 30% on revenues. Reduced product cycles will be the key competitive differentiation in the future. (John Young, President and CEO, Hewlett Packard.)

Rivalry is at best fierce and often cut-throat, ICT vendors cannot expect to receive any quarter from rivals. This is forcing vendors into new forms of collaborative ventures, which allow companies to insure their R&D against rapid change in the market. Suppliers have to rely on one another, for their choice is to hang together or hang separately.

Review questions

1 The declining cost/performance of computer systems seems endless; to what extent is it driving changes in the industry?

2 Review ten years of the personal computer from the perspective of (a) the manager and (b) the manufacturer.

3 Unix seems likely to become the dominant operating system for computers of all sizes, what were/are the driving forces behind this?

4 Discuss the trade in information and comment on its characteristics as a 'commodity'.

5 In what circumstances do you consider it appropriate for an organisation to employ consultants? How can you maximise their value to your organisation?

6 Discuss how companies in the information-based industries cope with the management of continuous and tumultuous change.

Study questions

1 Assess the progress to date of the acquisition of NCR by AT&T. In retrospect, does it make strategic sense?

2 Explain how the changing structure of the information-based industries affects relationships between suppliers and users.

3 Describe how the 'collision' of the markets for personal computers and workstations is affecting suppliers.

4 Compare and contrast the telecommunications equipment and service industries.

5 Discuss the critical success factors of value-added resellers.

6 Mobile telephony is expanding at very rapid rates. Can this be justified in terms of business benefits for users?

7 Integrated Broadband Communication (IBC) is the next development in telecommunication. What would you do with it?

8 Evaluate IBM's joint venture with either Wang Laboratories or Apple Computer.

Further reading

Information concerning the industry appears in the Financial Times, Datamation, Infomatics, Telecommunications, Business Week and Fortune.

Araskog, Rand "The ITT Wars: a CEO speaks out on takeovers" Henry Holt, New York, 1989.

The slightly bitter story of the creation of Alcatel through the transfer of the telecommunications sections of ITT. It is seen as part of the effort to save ITT from attacks by speculators intent on carving the firm up.

Bartlett, Christopher and Sumantra Ghoshal "Managing across Borders: the transnational solution" Hutchison, London, 1989.

A highly practical book for organisational success in global competition. Stress is placed on both the need for a coherent business strategy and the capability to organise and manage its implementation.

Campbell-Kelly, Martin "ICL: a business and technical history" Oxford University Press, Oxford, 1989.

A solid business history of ICL up to the early 1980's, though often going into considerable technical detail.

Chandler, Alfred "Scale and Scope" Harvard University Press, Cambridge, 1990.

Chandler's latest alliterative history of capitalism, following the 1962 "Strategy and Structure". It emphasises the challenges facing both organisations and societies. It is disappointing that history stops in the 1950s.

Delamarter, Richard "Big Blue: IBM's use and abuse of power" Pan, London 1988.

This is a somewhat splenetic attack on IBM based on what should, in the view of the author, have been the basis for an anti-trust action against IBM. It should, for balance, be read with a pro-IBM view, say, Buck Rodgers "The IBM Way" Harper & Row, 1986.

Flamm, Kenneth "Creating the Computer: government, industry and high technology" Brookings Institution, Washington, 1988.

A thorough and professional history of the development from a North American perspective. Heavy going and rather technical at times.

Hendry, John "Innovating for Failure: government policy and the early British Computer industry" MIT Press, London, 1989.

History indicates that innovation, without exploitation, which Hendry blames on a lack of strategic alignment.

Gilder, George "Microcosm: the quantum revolution in economics and technology" Simon and Schuster, New York, 1989.

From an origin in quantum physics and its embodiment in the integrated circuit, George Gilder explores the meaning and future of modern technology. While arguing that the computer is the most important product of his so-called 'quantum era', Gilder does not argue for the centrality of this machine, but for the primacy of human thought and creativity.

Jacobsen, Gary and John Hillkirk "Xerox: an American Samurai" Macmillan, New York, 1986.

A fascinating business case study of a firm in the dynamic and competitive global market.

Lawrensen, John and Lionel Barber "The Price of Truth: the story of Reuters millions" Mainstream, Edinburgh, 1985.

A racy account of the history of Reuters and of the politics of its floatation.

Lodge, George "Perestroika in America: restructuring business-government relations for world competitiveness" Harvard Business School Press, Cambridge, 1990.

A general account of the need for industrial policy. In particular, it covers the chip business and Spot-Image, the French satellite imaging business.

Mackintosh, Ian "Sunrise Europe: the dynamics of information technology" Basil Blackwell, 1986.

An early warning of Europe's potential techno-economic catastrophe, with an important policy emphasis.

Methé, David T "Technological Competition in Global Industries: marketing and planning strategies for American industry" Quorum Books, London, 1991.

A book that focuses on the DRAM industry, which rapidly grew from its early origins at Intel, through other American chip-makers to be dominated both in terms of technology and market share by the Japanese. The analysis by David Methé looks at the dynamics and places more of the blame for the demise of the American semiconductor companies on a lack of innovation, rather that financial constraints on R&D.

Miles, Ian *et al.* "Mapping the Information Economy" British Library Research Report 77, London, 1990.

The first serious attempt to look at an important and difficult problem. While much of the specific material will date rapidly, the general themes and arguments underlying the discussion should stand the test of time very well.

Ohmae, Kenichi "The Borderless World" Collins, Glasgow, 1990

The most recent of a series of provocative books from this Japanese management consultant. It is an excellent illustration of the 'inter-linked economy', albeit with a bit of futurology.

Sculley, John "Odyssey: Pepsi to Apple" Fontana, London, 1987.

This book tends to suggest that John Sculley could walk on water, but otherwise is an excellent account of the differences between life at Pepsi-Cola and Apple. Frank Rose in "West of Eden" (Arrow Press, 1989) gives a more balanced and slightly more technical view.

Wang, An "Lessons: an autobiography" Addison-Wesley, Wokingham, 1986.

An account of one of the most successful entrepreneurs in the IT business. It is a rather too rosy view, stopping well before the recent problems overwhelmed the firm.

4

Doing business in the information era

Learning objectives:

- to appreciate how business scope and business processes can be redefined using the potential of information and communications technologies;

- to be able to consider changes in terms of a framework comprising:
  - automate;
  - informate;
  - empowerate;
  - transformate;

- to understand the importance of the analysis of information gathered from data processing for business strategy and customer service.

4.1 Introduction

Notwithstanding the rapid technological developments of the 1970's and 1980's, it is a sobering thought that the majority of developments in the information and communications technologies lie in the future. Moreover, the vast majority of organisations have been unable to exploit the business potential of the existing technologies.

In Chapter 5, there is a detailed discussion of computer-based information systems. At this stage, it is sufficient to note that the usefulness and relevance of ICTs should be demonstrated through their applications in terms of:

- providing information as an input into management decision-making;
- offering a technology platform as an infrastructure that creates opportunities for new ways of doing business.

The design, specification and implementation of any information system must be driven by an understanding of the information needs of the management (see Chapter 6). In order to achieve that understanding, managers and organisations must know:

- what information they need;
- what information they have access to;
- what information they can use effectively.

Max Hopper (1990, page 121), the champion behind SABRE, American Airlines' customer reservation system, recently argued:

> Astute managers will shift their attention from *systems* to *information*. Think of the challenge this way: In a competitive world where companies have access to the same data, who will excel at turning data into information and then analysing the information quickly and intelligently enough to generate superior knowledge?

In terms of what information is required, interestingly, Peter Drucker (1990, page 83) comments on his work at the Pentagon nearly fifty years ago:

> I made my first appearance before a Congressional committee, which was headed by an obscure politician of whom nobody had ever heard, whose name was Harry Truman. He cut me into tiny little pieces and fed me to the fish. And then he became a kindly old gentleman and invited me to his chambers. I am not a drinker, but he poured a bottle of bourbon into me without any noticeable effect. And when I thought I would survive — though I didn't yet enjoy the prospect — he said, 'Sonny, don't ever do again what you did today.' And I said, 'Sir, what did I do?' He said, 'You quoted fractions to Senators. If we understood fractions, what would we be doing in the Senate?' And then he said, 'Go back to that so-and-so General of yours and tell him never to do again what he did.' I said, 'What did General Jones do, sir?'. He said, 'He did something that needs to be explained, there is nothing you can explain to a U.S. Senator.' From that moment on I was the first Truman booster. He was absolutely right. This is wisdom.

In fact, for information presentation, some managers, like numbers, some managers like graphics and some managers like things to explained informally.

While it is always helpful to focus on 'best practice', looking at it the other way can also provide useful insights.

> Inefficient use of information wastes money. Many examples of inefficiency can be found including:
>
> - information which is collected but not needed;
> - information stored long after it is needed;
> - useful information which is inaccessible to potential users;
> - information disseminated more widely than is necessary;
> - inefficient methods used to collect, analyse, store and retrieve information;
> - collection of the same basic information by more than one group of people in the same department;
> - duplication storage of the same basic information.
>
> (Central Computer and Telecommunications Agency, 1990, page 4.)

The recent technological convergence of computing and communications is important; its realisation in 'open systems' permits the linkage of hardware and software from different vendors. While different organisations are at different stages in their investment in and use of ICTs, the historical perspective can be summarised as:

- improved operational efficiency (since the 1960's);
- increased management effectiveness (since the 1970's);
- enhanced organisational competitiveness (since the 1980's);
- development of total customer service (from the 1990's onwards).

In this chapter, information is considered as an input to management decision-making; this allows the identification of various types of application and indicates the need for careful 'up-front' planning in the design of computer-based information systems. A general discussion of 'doing business in the information era' is presented, particularly distinguishing between the characteristics of the 'computer era' and the 'information era', indicating the evolution of applications that some organisations have followed. These reviews provide the foundation for an information systems strategy linked to a corporate business strategy. Particular attention is given to the need for a dynamic, rather than the traditional static, perspective.

Computer-based information systems and management decision-making

In the 'classic' work of Robert Anthony (1965), managerial activities were classified into one of three categories, these have been influential in the development of thinking on management of information systems:

- strategic planning (goals, strategies and policies);
- management control (implementation of strategies);
- operational control (efficient and effective performance of individual tasks).

Examples of activities under these categories are given in Table 4.1.

In terms of the development of applications of ICTs, the general historical trend is upwards from operational activities towards more strategic applications. Moreover, within an organisation, the stage of growth can vary by function (with the accounting/finance function often at the forefront).

Using Anthony's classification, a useful framework was developed by Anthony Gorry and Michael Scott Morton (1989) who differentiated between the information requirements of management planning and control activities. Figure 4.1 summarises the relationships between different types of decisions and their information characteristics. Planning and strategy decisions, for example, are relatively unstructured and require qualitative, as well as quantitative, information. By contrast, many control activities, such as monitoring raw materials, inventories and sales, require simple structured decisions based on quantitative data. Further differences relate to time; a future, rather than a current or historical perspective. Table 4.2 illustrates some of the information requirements for some marketing tasks.

Table 4.1   *Typical planning, control and operational systems*

Planning systems	sales forecasting
	operating plans
	capacity planning
	profits/earnings forecasts
Control systems	sales analysis
	budgetary control
	management accounting
	inventory management
Operational systems	order-entry processing
	tracking shipping documents
	shop floor scheduling
	purchase orders

Source: Ward *et al*. 1990, page 3.

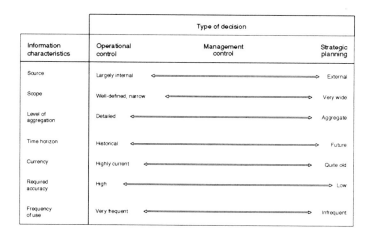

Figure 4.1   *Information requirements by decision category
(Source: Gorry and Scott Morton, 1971.)*

Table 4.2 *Information and marketing tasks*

Task	Information requirements
Analysing the market	Sales/profit: • total • by products, area client • market rates of growth • cash flows by each segment Client attitudes: • brand awareness • brand loyalty Number of customers: • by product • by area • by purchasing patterns Units sold per unit input: • advertising to sales ratio • personal selling effort to sales • shelf space to sales
Defining marketing objectives	Sales/profit performance Market share Cash flows Competitive strengths/weaknesses Technical, legal, political and social influences on the market Resources and skills in the organisation Buyer loyalty Channel loyalty Customer needs and buying power Financial position Manufacturing competencies, capacity and flexibility Research and development strengths
Developing appropriate marketing strategies	Data on current strategies: • cost • effectiveness Identification of strategic options: • cost • potential effectiveness Targets Budgets
Controlling performance	Units sold per unit input: • advertising to sales ratios • personal selling effort to sales ratios • shelf space to sales ratios

Source: L K Parkinson and S T Parkinson, 1987.

The nature of a decision affects the type of information required and, therefore, the design and specification of computer-based information systems. It is far from clear that computer-based information systems have been useful and relevant for management decision-making. While it is easy to argue that particular information should be helpful for management decision-making, it is much more complicated to know how and why a manager makes use of the information provided by a computer-based information system. More generally, Henry Mintzberg (1989, page 9) characterises much of his management writing as 'celebrating intuition':

> If you ask managers what they do, they will most likely tell you that they plan, organise, coordinate and control. Then watch what they do. Don't be surprised if you can't relate what you see to those four words.

The effectiveness of individual managers to receive, process, store, retrieve and apply data varies enormously. Moreover, with the advances in both information and communications technologies and in automatic data capture, it is becoming more important to recognise the severe limitations of the brain in handling complicated decision-making tasks and dynamic business environments. Cognitive psychologists have demonstrated that more information is not necessarily helpful; in fact, in times of information 'overload', managers use less information in their decision-making than when having an 'optimal' amount of information. Current research into human-computer interaction is helpful in the development of systems which are more user-friendly, a necessary, but not a sufficient, condition for better information resources management. For instance, the failure to exploit fully information systems has long been recognised as a non-technical issue; the 'information literacy' of managers and the 'information culture' of their organisations are key determinants. Nigel Piercy (1990, page 254), in his consideration of marketing information systems, suggests that:

- managers seek information to justify what has already been decided;
- marketing information may be used to make sales people 'properly optimistic';
- managers may seek information as a way of delaying decisions;
- marketing information may serve an 'organisational' function, for example, providing common ground or a shared frame of reference, acting as a collective memory, or functioning as a stabilising factor, or even providing reassurance.

The beliefs of managers concerning the potential of information systems are important constraints. The idea of an 'information culture' tries to go beyond the interaction of the organisational culture and the use of information and communications technologies (see chapter 7). It is intended to describe attitudes towards the use of information. A key consideration here is numeracy. In a highly numerate group, it should be possible to use sophisticated statistical analyses and operational research (optimisation) techniques in a sensible and balanced way. In other groups, such analyses may be viewed as culturally unacceptable or may be treated with spurious seriousness. There remain two opposing problems:

- the development of user expectations which are extravagant and unrealistic (at least at a reasonable cost);
- the lack of user awareness about the effective and efficient use of information in different application areas.

In considering the nature of managerial work, Mintzberg (1989, page 12) highlights four myths, of which one is:

Folklore: The senior manager needs aggregated information, which a formal management information system best provides.

In keeping with the classical view of the manager as that individual perched on the apex of a regulated, hierarchical system, the literature's manager is to receive all important information from a giant, comprehensive MIS. But a look at how managers actually process information reveals a very different picture. Managers have five media at their command — documents, telephone calls, scheduled and unscheduled meetings and observational tours.

Fact: Managers strongly favour the oral media — namely, telephone calls and meetings.

While some researchers have started to explore decision-making in relation to the use of information, the real relevance of this work to practising managers remains unclear. Efforts to research decision-making are overly academic, attempting to programme it. It seems that academic interest in analysis is not aligned with tasks actually performed by managers: synthesis, understanding and reducing uncertainty. 'Successful' information systems, for instance, often make the specification of alternative decision options and their implications much clearer and evidence is beginning to demonstrate that the resulting information can be threatening (and sometimes unacceptable) to some managers. In considering future developments of computer-based information systems, it is important not to neglect the necessary investments in intellectual capital and the capacity to explore new ways of working (see also Chapter 7).

Moving from the 'computer era' to the 'information era'

It would be naive to believe that 'best practice' in information resources management is equally attainable in all organisations, large and small and across all sectors. The information culture of organisations varies because of different customs and values. The history of the use of information is different in different industries and organisations and this must be recognised explicitly; indeed, there can be enormous variations within a single organisation. The information culture of organisations, especially information literacy among the senior managers who must drive the strategy, can be an important practical constraint. In planning the future, it would be wrong to neglect the current technology platform and the history of its development. Whether 'successful' or 'unsuccessful', past experiences can be significant constraints on future strategic plans.

The evolution of computer-based information systems — their past, present and future roles — has been idealised in various models of 'stages of growth'; these categorise the various phases through which organisations consider, design, implement and operate information systems strategies. The various models identify and describe distinct stages in the growth of computer-based information systems, important differences are in the areas in which applications are developed and the types of business benefits achieved.

Richard Nolan (1979, page 125), for instance, proposed:

> There is now a ... descriptive theory of the evolution of a DP activity — the stage theory. One can use this theory to understand where the company has come from, which problems were a result of weak management, and which problems arose from natural growth. More important, one can gain some insight into what the future may hold and then can try to develop appropriate management strategies that will accomplish corporate purposes.

In what has had a considerable effect on the management thinking on computer-based information systems, Nolan proposed six stages of growth as figure 4.2 portrays:

INITIATION

The stage when the organisation gets its first (mainframe) computer. There is a purely operational systems focus with batch processing to automate clerical operations to achieve cost reductions. There is a lack of strategic interest by senior management.

CONTAGION

The initial excess capacity is reduced through rapid growth as users demand more applications based on high expectations of benefits. There may be a move to on-line systems. The high level of expenditure as the DP Department tries to satisfy all user demands begins to be noticed by senior management. In fact there is probably little control, although there may be a tendency to centralise the activity in order to improve control.

CONTROL

In response to growing management concerns about cost, system delays and difficulties, and a feeling that investments are expected to show a return, formal plans are produced and methodologies and standards are enforced. This action often produces a backlog of applications and a growing set of dissatisfied users.

INTEGRATION

An increased proportion of the expenditure is on the integration of existing systems through databases to remove unnecessary redundancy. The DP/IS Department begins to provide a service to users, rather than merely solutions to problems.

DATA ADMINISTRATION

The focus is now on information requirements, rather than data processing *per se*. Information begins to be shared within the organisation as a corporate resource. Database capabilities begin to be exploited as users value information.

MATURITY

By this stage, the planning and development of information systems is closely integrated with business development.

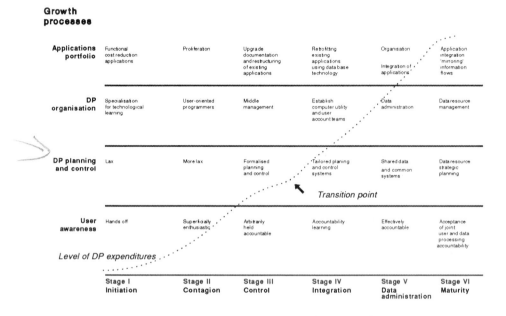

Figure 4.2 *Nolan's six stages of growth (Source: Nolan, 1979)*

For empirical analyses, Nolan suggested six indicators by which to measure an organisation's information systems and their management:

- the rate of DP/IS expenditure;
- the technological configuration (such as batch and on-line);
- the portfolio of applications;
- the DP/IS organisation;
- the approaches to planning and control in DP/IS (internal or external);
- the characteristics of user awareness (such as reactive, proactive or involved).

Element	Stage 1	Stage 2	Stage 3	Stage 4	Stage 5	Stage 6
Strategy	Acquisition of hardware, software, etc	IT audit Find out and meet user needs (reactive)	Top-down IS planning	Integration, coordination and control	Environmental scanning and opportunity seeking	Maintain comparative strategic advantage Monitor futures Interactive planning
Structure	None	Label of IS Often subordinate to accounting or finance	Data processing department Centralised DP shop End-users running free at Stage 1	Information centres Library records, OA, etc in same unit Information services	SBU coalitions (many but separate) Decentralised systems	Centrally coordinated coalitions (corporate and SBU views concurrently)
Systems	Ad hoc unconnected Operational Multiple manual and IS Uncoordinated Concentration on financial systems Little maintenance	Many applications Many gaps Overlapping systems Centralised Operational Mainly financial systems Many areas unsatisfied Large backload Heavy maintenance	Still mostly centralised Database systems Uncontrolled end-user computing Most major business activities covered	Decentralised approach with some controls, but mostly lack of coordination Some DSS, but ad hoc Integrated office technology systems	Decentralised systems but central control and coordination Added value systems (more marketing oriented) More DSS internal, less ad hoc Some strategic systems (using external data) Lack of external and internal data integration	Inter-organisational systmes (suppliers, customers, government links) New IS-based products External/internal data integration
Staff	Programmers/ contractors	Systems analysts DP manager	IS planners IS managers DB administrator Data administrator Data analysts	Business analysts Information resource manager Chief Information Officer	Corporate/ business/IS planners (one role)	IS Director/ member of board of directors
Style	Unaware	Don't bother me (I'm too busy)	Abrogation/ delegation	Democratic dialectic	Individualistic (product champion)	Business team
Skills	Technical (very low level) individual expertise	Systems development methodology	IS believes it knows what the business needs Project management	Organisational integration IS knows how the business works Users know how IS works (for their area Business management (for IS staff)	IS manager - member of senior executive team Knowledgeable users in some IS areas Entrepreneurial marketing skills	All senior management understand IS and its potentialities
Superordinate goals	Obfuscation	Confusion	Senior management concern DP defence	Cooperation Entrepreneurial Intrapreneurial	Opportunistic	Interactive planning

Figure 4.3   *A revised 'stages of growth' model*
(Source: Galliers and Sutherland, 1991)

The current stage of maturity of information resources management varies considerably across industrial sectors, organisations and functions within individual organisations. While empirical evidence to support or refute proposed hypotheses is scant, some indications of the information culture of an organisation can be derived from an examination of its applications portfolio and the attitude of the DP/IS Department towards users. Comparisons of expenditure on ICTs are difficult to complete and are generally misleading (noting, for example, the 'illegal' expenditure on personal computers in many organisations); price-performance ratios have fallen enormously over time through technological advances. In any event, the basic philosophy of information resources management suggests that it is not the quantity of investment that is important, but how well it is managed and used. Moreover, organisations introducing and developing information systems strategies today will be different from only a few years ago; the technology and the professional knowledge of information resources management have advanced enormously in recent years. A major criticism of the evolutionary models results from their origin in a period dominated by mainframe computers; today, it is less relevant as an aid to help identify key areas for development (although there has never been a rigid methodology that could be brought out to provide answers).

While a significant reason for the attractiveness of Nolan's stage model is its simplicity, it is now a major weakness. Charles Wiseman (1985), for instance, argues that there is no opportunity to consider or explore strategic opportunities for information systems (see also John Ward *et al.* (1990)). Robert Galliers and Tony Sutherland (1991) recently revisited the stages of growth model, not only the original Nolan model, but also subsequent modifications. They proposed a revised six-stage model (see figure 4.3) founded on the Seven S's of Richard Pascale and Anthony Athos (1981, page 81):

STRATEGY
Plan or course of action leading to the allocation of an organisation's scarce resources, over time, to reach identified goals.

STRUCTURE
Characterisation of the organisation chart (that is, functional, decentralised, and so on).

SYSTEMS
Procedural reports and routine processes, such as meeting formats.

STAFF
'Demographic' description of important personnel categories within the organisation, such as engineers, entrepreneurs, MBAs, and so on. (n.b. 'Staff' is not meant in line-staff terms.)

STYLE
Characterisation of how key managers behave in achieving the organisation's goals; also the cultural style of the organisation.

SKILLS
Distinctive capabilities of key personnel or the organisation as a whole.

SUPERORDINATE GOALS
The significant meanings or guiding concepts that an organisation imbues in its members. Superordinate goals can also be described as the shared values or culture of the organisation.

Important differences exist between the computer and information eras with regard to resources, staffing and business orientation. Passing from the 'computer era' into the 'information era' means the increasing strategic significance of communications and data rather than computing *per se*. For people, there is a need to go beyond the technical Data Processing skills to broader business and management skills in two ways:

- developing the general management background of technical ICT specialists;
- developing the ICT awareness and competencies of managers.

There is an evolution from internal and administrative functions, such as payroll and accounts, to external and strategic aspects, such as the direct linkage with suppliers and customers. Peter Keen (1991, pages 15-16) views information and communications technologies as 'a means to a business end' and discusses seven dimensions of business design in which these technologies can be exploited:

- competitive positioning;
- geographic positioning;
- redesigning and organisation;
- redeploying human capital;
- managing the economics of information capital;
- positioning the IT platform;
- aligning business and technology.

Towards a strategic framework for information resources management

Once specified, a corporate business strategy must drive the information systems strategy and the specification of the technology platform or enabling infrastructure of computer-based information systems. The main reason for the early (and still relevant) investments in information and communications technologies was to improve efficiency, especially in operational areas. More recently, an increasing number of strategic investments have been made, often as 'acts of faith', in the hope that 'IT can be a source of competitive advantage'. There is no evidence to demonstrate that information and communications technologies can be a source of sustainable competitive advantage, although they are increasingly competitive necessities in many industries.

Investments to improve productivity have been characterised by the term 'automate'. In a significant contribution to management thinking, Shoshana Zuboff (1988) extends the traditional automation perspective by proposing the term 'informate', with an explicit emphasis on the information content of administrative and productive processes in an organisation. Charles Wiseman (1985) refers to the 'hybrid' nature of many investments in large information systems; for example, the Electronic Point of Sales (EPoS) systems used by retailers contain a large component of 'automation' (data capture, verification, collation, storage, analysis and distribution), as well as potential information about purchase patterns and the need to replenish stock. Similarly, Customer Reservation Systems (CRSs) operated by airlines provide detailed data allowing analysis of local markets and route patterns, which have become vital in their deregulated market. Computer Aided Design (CAD) systems for architecture and construction can also provide the 'informating' base for a future asset management system.

Case: University applications

Scenario: As a by-product of processing applications to universities, large volumes of data are available for competitor analysis and the identification of trends in applications.

As part of the process of applying to enter a British university, potential students must complete a form for the Universities Central Council on Admissions (UCCA). Details from these forms are entered onto the UCCA computer system and are made available to the universities to which the applicants have applied.

The principal purpose of this data is to help in the administration of applications. Photocopies of the whole form are sent to each university where they are considered by admission tutors, who look for bright candidates with an aptitude for the subject and who are likely to achieve the entry standards in their school examinations.

By careful analysis of the data it is possible to identify a number of patterns. Postcodes of individuals and schools can be used to identify the areas from which students apply, do not apply, decline offers and those who are admitted. Parental occupation codes and postcodes give insights into the socio-economic groups applying. It is also possible to identify the type of schools from which applications are made. On a crude level it would be cost-effective to eliminate applications from those people who will be rejected, simply because they do not come near the academic admission standard. A more interesting exercise is to target schools which have wrongly understood the admission standard and persuade them to encourage their brighter students to apply.

> Given that the data includes the set of five courses and universities to which the applicant has applied, it is possible to carry out a competitor analysis, between courses and institutions.

Following John Beaumont and David Walters (1991), the automate/informate categorisation can be extended to provide a strategic orientation, by incorporating two additional capabilities:

- 'empowerate';
- 'transformate'.

The traditional structural perspectives of organisations (hierarchies and bureaucracy) are becoming obsolete through the use of networks. Given the advances in the speed, capacity and accuracy of information and communications technologies, many multi-site and multinational organisations, such as banks, are using infrastructural 'empowerate' capabilities to permit local action while maintaining head office control. Technology in the form of teleconferencing already permits this development. The benefits of this enabling infrastructure are only realisable if the organisational culture permits a sharing of information and decision-making and a focus on core competencies. Important issues that cause concerns are organisational structures and cultures. Typically, in British organisations, information and communications technologies have been used to reinforce centralised decision-making. This in turn has developed a culture within which 'head office' is seen as the focal point of decision-making to the extent that for some organisations any move towards decentralising decision-making would prove to be an uncomfortable organisational innovation.

'Empowerate' should not be confined to an internal organisational perspective; inter-organisational networking, such as Electronic Data Interchange, is of growing significance in supply chain management. The potential competitive benefits of such inter-organisational linkages should not be underestimated, especially for organisations which achieve control of the trading network, such as American Airlines and United Airlines with their SABRE and APOLLO CRSs. Moreover, collaboration can be a successful part of a competitive strategy to enhance customer service, as illustrated by shared Automatic Teller Machine (ATM) networks (such as the Bank of Scotland network which accepts cash dispenser cards from Lloyds Bank, Royal Bank of Scotland and the Matrix group of building societies together with credit cards from American Express and Visa).

'Transformate' is used to indicate that information and communications technologies can support new ways of doing business and even new businesses. The original airline CRSs are now linked with other travel and leisure organisations, such as car rentals, hotels, and entertainment. Peter Drucker (1989) has described the likely nature of some future organisations as 'information-based'. Benetton, for example, has reduced its exposure to risk by using information-based organisational methods of linking production to retailing, all controlled by itself. By subcontracting production and by franchising retailing, Benetton is able concentrate on their technical skills in the transmission and processing of information and on their flair for design.

It is important to view the four components ('automate', 'informate', 'empowerate' and 'transformate') as complementary, rather than as some kind of natural progression to enhanced success through ICT investment. The balance of the components should be developed from the corporate business strategy. Figure 4.4 illustrates an idealised representation of this integration. The information systems strategy is the outcome of this integration and provides the basis to determine the required technology platform.

AUTOMATE

To improve condition and productivity decisions. For example, the use of EPoS to rationalise the merchandise range and to reduce stockholding to optimal levels.

INFORMATE

To emphasise the information content of administrative and productive processes within an organisation. For example, the use of EPoS data provide an input into labour scheduling at the level of an individual store, within staffing budget set by head office.

EMPOWERATE

To permit action at individual local branches while maintaining head office control. For example, to develop specific local market offers by permitting the use of local management input to introduce a specific local differentiation.

TRANSFORMATE

To use information and communications technologies to support new methods of doing business and to plan and control new business ventures. They may be applied within the business or externally to make links with customers and suppliers more cost-effective, such as supply chain management. The management of information and Decision Support Systems become distinctive competencies which can be used to operate within other business sectors.

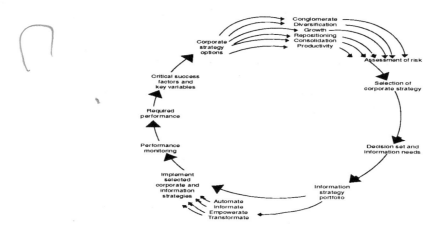

Figure 4.4 *Matching corporate strategy and information strategy*

To date, this representation is unrealistically static. Senior management must ensure that the development of an information systems strategy is integrated with the overall corporate business strategy and its changing requirements. The information needs of organisations and their managers differs as a result of:

- the strategic direction of the organisation;
- the perception of risk;
- the stage in the strategic life-cycle;
- the information culture and information literacy of the managers.

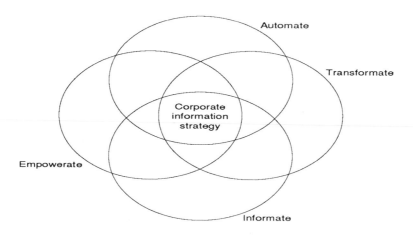

Figure 4.5 *The elements of a corporate information strategy*

The four components introduced earlier form the basis of the framework. The corporate information systems strategy is likely to be some combination of each of the four components. They should initially be supportive of each other, overlapping where there is a requirement for interactive support (see figure 4.5). The four components are 'balanced' to produce a corporate information strategy. Such a balanced approach would seem unlikely for a particular organisation, more likely is the situation where one (or more) of the elements is more prominent.

Case: Information resources management in retailing

Scenario: Retailers make large investments in information and communications technologies. Following some of their strategic options outlined in Chapter 2, the information resources management framework is used to analyse them (see figure 4.6).

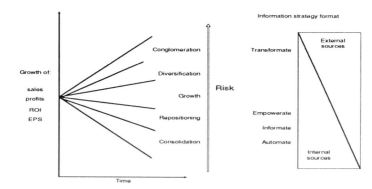

Figure 4.6   *Developing an information strategy to meet the needs of the corporate strategy*

An organisation focusing on a strategy of consolidation and productivity would require an information systems strategy that aims at 'automation'. It would use its information outputs to evaluate product range and branch performance, together with an evaluation of the optimal stockholding at branches and in distribution centres. Such a strategy would take the form shown in figure 4.7a. Here the information systems strategy is directed at the requirement to use information to evaluate performance of the existing business with a view to improving the return on assets.

As the consolidation and productivity strategy is seen to become effective a shift of emphasis will be to expand the use of the data so far generated; to 'informate'. The managerial emphasis is focused upon planning and control, for example, using EPoS data to provide an input into labour scheduling at branch level; in addition, there may be space management and store design planning. The shift from 'automate' to 'informate' is one in which the business moves from the use of

---

information to evaluate and rationalise its activities towards using information to manage the business. Thus, labour scheduling and space allocation are management activities that automate from centrally controlled facilities; at branch levels, they are implemented with little or no modification. This emphasis is shown in figure 4.7b.

Consumer behaviour is continuously changing. The implications for the business are that it may require a more local view of its activities to be taken or, possibly, for an overall review of the positioning of the business in the market place. Both implications require the business to consider differentiation issues. The former require some devolution of decision-making to branch management if local opportunities are to be maximised. At this stage, the emphasis in information resources management shifts towards 'empowerate' (although 'automate' and 'informate' capabilities remain important). Repositioning strategies also require a similar approach, however, the devolution that occurs is within a central level of head office activity. Examples of 'empowerate' can be seen in the moves by food multiples towards 'local ranging', in which local consumer demand is reflected in the goods and services offered, and local management is 'empowered' with sufficient authority to decide upon the composition of the ranges. The creation of niche retailing activities within mass merchandiser companies is similar. Here, autonomy is given to a group of managers. Figure 4.7c shows this 'empowerate' emphasis.

Continued success and growth are usually achieved by replication and development of the existing business by the addition of related product and service offers. There is a point at which these no longer provide the rate of growth required and consequently diversification and then conglomeration are considered. It is at this point that the emphasis in information resources management moves once more. The shift towards 'transformate' requires the ability to use information and communications systems to support new methods of conducting business. It is likely that the organisation will first examine the existing business in an attempt at improving its cost-effectiveness. For example, supply chain management systems may be developed to improve merchandise availability at distribution centres and at the point-of-sale, while at the same time optimising stockholding throughout the chain. Customer contact and handling may be improved by developing customer databases, while market penetration may be increased by using expertise in information analysis. These issues are also important for mergers and acquisitions. For example, Tesco's acquisition of Hillards was completed successfully and separate information systems integrated in a very short space of time. An earlier illustration was when Sir Terrence Conran combined Habitat and Mothercare, founded on the creativity of the former and the strong systems of the latter.

Information and communications systems enable service organisations to communicate with and provide a service to customer groups who may live in areas of low population density (where the existing retail format could not be operated economically or for those customers whose lifestyles do not permit ready and early access to existing format offers). The developments in home shopping are of interest here. Other examples, perhaps not so obvious but nevertheless important, are developments in-store whereby a retailer can expand the merchandise on offer (and add service) across items that are difficult to handle for both the retailer and the customer. Perishable products such as expensive food, exotic fruit and vegetables have been dealt with this way by US department stores. Price catalogues are yet another example of the in-store use of available technology, allowing customers to compare competitive price offers by interrogating a database. (see figure 4.7d)

The 'transformate' emphasis also considers the managerial decisions and information required for diversification and conglomeration strategies. Typically these are the issues identified through critical success factors and key variables. An evaluation of revenues and margins, productivity profiles, and added-value costs and benefits link together with information on market structures and market shares, provide a basis for deciding upon whether market entry should be attempted and if so how. Following a decision to make an entry the information system should be used for detailed planning and control of the strategy implementation. Figure 4.8 suggests how the information systems strategy might develop, providing an idealised representation of how the changes over time could be both dynamic and incremental.

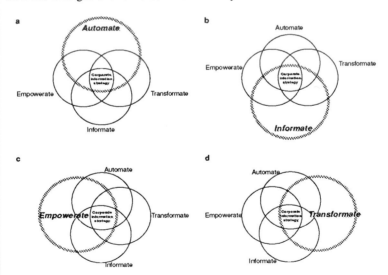

Figure 4.7 *The focus within an information strategy*

As alternative strategies are expanded the associated risk can be expected to increase. The purpose of the information strategy is to reduce risk by providing information to relevant management decisions. Within the context of the model proposed, the information strategy is structured to meet both the decision type and information needs of the decision-maker.

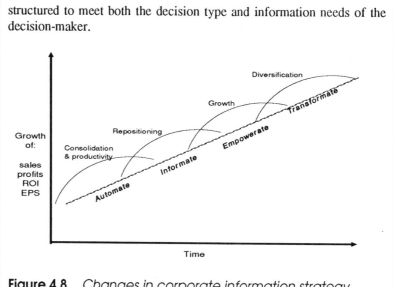

Figure 4.8 *Changes in corporate information strategy*

Levels of transformation

It is essential for us to be able to look beyond the many clichés in the strategic applications of information and communications technologies. A few heroic managers may get by with well-known examples and a lively imagination, however, relying on heroic managers is dangerous since they are in short supply. Instead we need tools for everyday managers.

As part of the 'Management in the Nineties' programme, Venkatraman devised a five level categorisation of the organisational changes and the benefits related to the application of information and communications technologies (see figure 4.9) (Scott Morton, 1991):

LOCAL EXPLOITATION
Use of ICTs in departments and other small-scale organisational units, independent of the organisation as a whole.

INTERNAL INTEGRATION
The integration of the various computer-based information systems operated in the organisation to provide a technology platform.

BUSINESS PROCESS REDESIGN
Using the introduction of ICTs as a lever for changes in the ways in which the business processes are conducted.

BUSINESS NETWORK REDESIGN
Alteration of the links to suppliers and clients. This goes well beyond efficiency benefits, often significantly affecting the strategic balance.

BUSINESS SCOPE REDESIGN
The definition of the boundaries of the business through the use of ICTs.

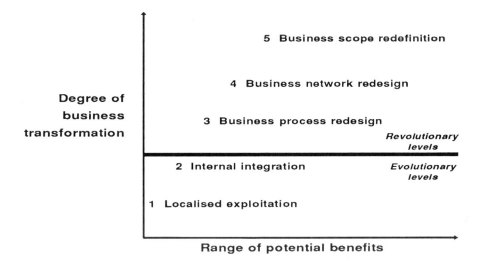

Figure 4.9 *Five levels of IT-induced reconfiguration*
(Source: Venkatraman in Scott Morton, 1991, page 127.)

'Localised exploitation' is found when ICTs are used as efficiency measures in departments, for example, payroll. It has similar problems to the idea of 'islands of automation', in that the exchange of information is difficult, if not impossible. Integration achieves the linking together of different local pockets of ICTs, overcoming the problems of the 'islands of automation'. However, it remains a largely technological integration and leaves almost untouched the ways in the which the business operates.

Beyond integration lies the redesign of the processes, network and the business itself. To achieve these changes implies revolutionary change in the organisation and not the evolutionary change of the first two levels. Only at levels of organisational revolution is it possible to exploit the full benefits of the technology platform.

A business process is a sequence of interdependent tasks and functions that produce outcomes that contribute to the success of an organisation; processes describe tasks and not the detail of the work to be done. The idea of process is now well established in business from the work in Total Quality Management (TQM) (see, for example, Harrington, 1991). The quality management work on improving business processes can also be applied to an information-based perspective, since it is related to the operation of the business as a whole.

The idea of redesigning the 'network' refers to the group of suppliers and customers, rather than to an electronic network. By using electronic links, it is possible to change the relationships with suppliers. While most companies have thought of electronic trading in terms of transactions, it is possible to go much further:

TRANSACTION
Reduced costs and errors, with very limited strategic potential.

STOCK-AVAILABILITY
Confirmation of orders before placing, with possible channel expansion.

PROCESS LINKAGE
Simplification of procedures, with possible development of product derivatives and special products.

EXPERTISE
Direct savings through close working and sharing, leading to enhanced capabilities.

The uppermost of the five level, redesigning the scope of a business, requires vision and it cannot to be taught by methodology.

Case: 7-Eleven

Scenario: Using a sophisticated electronic network, 7-Eleven both improved their performance in its existing business and added new activities.

The 7-Eleven convenience stores were established in the USA in 1946 by the Thompson family as part of their family business, the Southland Corporation. It was called 7-Eleven because it opened at 7am and closed at 11pm. These were operated as a franchised chain.

In 1974 a licensee, Ito-Yokado Co Ltd, started business in Japan, where it operated its own stores and franchised the 7-Eleven name to other retailers. By 1990, it had grown to over 4,000 stores, making it the largest chain of convenience stores in Japan. This growth has been achieved in selected areas by creating clusters of about sixty small stores around a regional office, allowing it to dominate the market. The target of Ito-Yokado has been to open more than 350 stores each year. According to the Annual Report, Ito-Yokado:

... did extensive research this year to determine the effects of store location on actual sales levels. This data was used in selecting optimal site locations for each of 313 additional stores opened this year, making our total number of stores 2,964.

Ito-Yokado has not only opened new stores, it has closed some, though typically only 10 or 20.

One of the major achievements of Ito-Yokado has been to reduce the stock held in each shop. This fell by about 50% in the ten years from 1980 to 1990. Direct Product Profitability (DPP) has been achieved, in which it is possible fully to identify the costs and profits attributable to individual products. The turnover of stock has been optimised by the elimination of goods which turnover slowly and the expansion of goods which turnover quickly. In extreme cases the goods on a shelf are turned over three times in one day. That is, the first set of goods on the shelf are sold out, perhaps newspapers in the morning, to be replaced by sandwiches for lunch, to be replaced in turn by beer which is likely to be bought on the way home from work. A 7-Eleven store might place an order at 10.00 for delivery that afternoon at 15.00 with an error on the delivery time of fifteen minutes either way, but no more. The order is passed to a central computer system through the regional office. Orders are then sent to the suppliers, typically, by 11.00. At 13.00 a van will leave the factory or processing plant to deliver the goods. The EDI network links together:

- stores;
- head office;
- distribution centres;
- dedicated manufacturers & wholesalers;
- independent manufacturers and wholesalers.

The strategy for information systems evolved in the following way:

1974	No on-line computer system;
1975	Introduction of computer processing;
1979	Establishment of an on-line network;
1982	Introduction of Electronic Point of Sales (EPoS) system;
1985	Unification of EPOS data and merchandising;
1987	Using a 'total system' to move ahead of the competition.

At first, ICTs were used to reduce inventories in stores and so to increase profits, allowing 7-Eleven to reduce the inventory by 50% in the period from 1980 to 1990. Over the same period, the gross profit margins rose from 25% to just over 28%.

Since 1987, 7-Eleven has collected payments for electricity and gas bills on behalf of the utility companies. This business has risen in quantity to 500,000 transactions each year. The service is provided on the pre-existing network at minimal incremental cost to 7-Eleven. It offers an additional service to existing customers and provides a service which might attract new customers into the stores. The utility company had to issue a new style of invoice with a bar code and four parts. The customer retains the first copy, the second copy is kept by the store, the third by the 7-Eleven regional office, while the fourth part goes to the utility company. 7-Eleven does not charge the utility companies for this service, instead it retains the money for five days, taking advantage of this one-off effect on cashflow and long-term improvement in bank balance. The payments are immediately notified to the utility companies, in order that customers are not penalised. The service to collect payments was extended in 1990 to life assurance.

Such has been the success of 7-Eleven in Japan, that Ito-Yokado bought out the Southland Corp in March 1990.

Source: John Dawson, the Institute for Retail Studies (University of Stirling) and International Computers Limited.

4.2 An emancipatory perspective

It is appropriate to explore the wider scope of information, information systems and information technology in terms of decision-making processes, organisational structures, and competitive positions — business strategy formulation and implementation. Why should ICT investments be made and what returns can be envisaged? It must be recognised that new decision-making processes become feasible with computer-based information systems; it is incorrect to view it merely as a speeding up or automating of existing, time-honoured processes.

In a 1989 survey of one hundred chief executives and over two hundred information executives, conducted by Louis Harris and Associates, identified four main constraints on the effective use of computer-based information systems:

- a fundamental need to change basic business process prior to implementation of new information systems;
- a failure properly to train people in the use of information systems;
- a need to identify ways to improve communications between information systems and internal customers;
- cultures that resist change.

In the 1990s, much greater attention is being given to customer service, an orientation which has direct implications on both the information required for management decision-making and the necessary ICT infrastructure. In addition to detailed internal, operational information, managers must have information on the products and services of suppliers, competitors and customers. ICTs can allow an organisation to provide a quicker, flexible and personalised service to customers, and also change the nature of the service they provide. Indeed, William Davidow and Bro Uttal (1989, page 181) argue:

> ... the more an infrastructure (the backbone of service) depends on information systems, the faster it must change, and the more investment it will absorb.

The attractions of information analysis are gradually being recognised, with some organisations reaching out to form 'information partnerships'; collaborations between non-competing organisations become more feasible:

> They can make small companies look, feel and act big, reaching for customers once beyond their grasp. Partnerships can make big companies look small and close, targeting and servicing custom markets. (Konsynski and McFarlan, 1990, page 115.)

Review questions

1   For your current work, define your information requirements.

2   Discuss the relevance of the 'stages of growth' framework for today's information and communications technologies

3   For an organisation that you know, consider the usefulness of the proposed management framework of 'automate', 'informate', 'empowerate', and 'transformate'.

4   Through observations in your organisation, examine how decisions are taken by specific individual managers.

Study questions

1   Consider the assertion that managers have too much data but insufficient information.

2   Explore the notion that collaboration will become an increasingly significant dimension of competitive strategy.

3   Will it be sufficient in the future for your organisation simply to do things more efficiently and more rapidly?

4   For an organisation you know, identify potential information partners and show how both sides could benefit from the sharing of information.

Further reading

Journals: Harvard Business Review, International Journal of Information Resource Management, Sloan Management Review and Strategic Management Journal.

Mintzberg, Henry "Mintzberg on Management" Free Press, New York, 1989.

An excellent, clear discussion of 'inside our strange world of organisations'. Many challenges are made about the conventional wisdom of management, based on Henry Mintzberg's experiences of 'bottom-up management'. The usefulness and relevance of information is placed in its organisational context of strategy, structure and power. (All MBA students should read Chapter 5, "Training Managers, not MBAs".)

Simon, Herbert A "The New Science of Management Decision Making" Prentice Hall, Englewood Cliffs, 1977.

An early, important and influential attempt to explore the effects that the computer has had, and by extrapolation will have, on organisations, the people who work in them, and the society in which they operate.

Synnott, William R "The Information Weapon" John Wiley and Sons, New York, 1987.

A clear book for business managers, with a wide range of different case studies, which places IT/IS at the strategic level. In total, 63 information weapon strategies are proposed!

5

Computer-based information systems

Learning objectives:

- to know about the range and scope of computer-based information systems;

- to understand applications of:
  - database management systems;
  - decision support systems;
  - interorganisational systems.

5.1 Introduction

For the majority of managers, information technology and information systems are daunting, tinged with uncertainty and tainted with obfuscating jargon: CPU, MIPS, RAM, DSS, VDU, 4GL and DBMS. A manager needs to have an understanding of the basic concepts and principles of computer-based information systems, but not an understanding of the technicalities of hardware or computer programming. As managers, we are not interested in technology or systems *per se*. We need useful and relevant information for our decision-making and therefore our concern is how to gather 'data' and how to transform it into 'information'. The categories of data include:

- numbers;
- text;
- image;
- voice.

Although computer data are usually thought of as numbers, decision-making by managers is based primarily on textual data from reports, memoranda, letters and so on. Even though organisations have been using computers for decades, large amounts of (textual) data are not held in a digital, 'computer readable' form. Another important source of information which is not easily made machine readable is through meetings, both formal and informal, and from conversations, both face-to-face and by telephone.

Rationality in the use of data cannot be assumed; moreover, data are neither value-nor context-free. The criteria for determining the relevance and quality of data, whether provided by a computer-based information system or by other means, are in terms of its being, or being perceived to be:

- on time;
- appropriate;
- detailed;
- frequent;
- objective;
- comprehensible.

In this chapter we describe, categorise and analyse the various types of computer-based information systems and some of their uses in organisations. This classification is not particularly easy since there have been considerable and continuing technical advances, perhaps greater changes in organisational requirements and a marked shift from a technical to a business perspective. The categories of computer-based information systems which are discussed in this chapter are:

MANAGEMENT INFORMATION SYSTEMS

Using computers for their processing and analytical power, these are systems for detailed and repetitious operations, for example, to process cheques and income tax returns, from which it is possible to analyse the information to provide regular and exception reports.

OFFICE INFORMATION SYSTEMS

A toolbox of facilities (word processing, electronic mail and so on) for a community of users with some semi-formal transaction processing and 'reach through' access to a variety of databases and other information systems.

DECISION SUPPORT SYSTEMS

Modelling and simulation software to help answer 'what if...?' questions, with facilities to allow tailoring for individual decision-making styles. A special category of DSS is the Executive Information System (EIS) installed in boardrooms.

KNOWLEDGE-BASED SYSTEMS

A category which covers a wide range of systems which process 'knowledge' or 'intelligence', including: expert systems and machine translation.

INTER-ORGANISATIONAL SYSTEMS

Systems which cross organisational boundaries, for example, Electronic Data Interchange between suppliers and assemblers in the automobile industry and customer reservations systems for airlines.

5.2 Management information systems

Computers have been used in organisations for their processing and for their analytical power in a wide range of applications. Most applications are repetitious processing of very similar transactions. Given that the processing systems are in place and operational, it is possible to summarise the information to provide regular and exception reports.

The categories considered in this section are:

ON-LINE TRANSACTION PROCESSING
Systems for detailed and repetitious operations, for example, to process cheques and income tax returns.

DATABASE MANAGEMENT SYSTEMS
A computer-based information system for the storage and retrieval of data, allowing users to ask questions with the result displayed on a screen or printed on paper.

On-line transaction processing

There have been marked changes in the nature of information systems over the last fifty years. At the end of World War II, data processing, insofar as it was identifiable, was by means of electro-mechanical adding machines using punched cards. War-time work in the USA and the UK significantly altered this picture, through the accelerated development of new technologies. In the UK, Colossus was developed to decipher German codes and in the USA, ENIAC was developed to calculate the trajectories of shells fired from new guns.

In the late 1940's and 1950's, International Business Machines (IBM), under the leadership of Tom Watson, Senior, remained firmly in its traditional business of manufacturing, selling and leasing electro-mechanical calculating machines using punched cards. However, the delivery of Eckert and Mauchly's Universal Automatic Calculator (UNIVAC) to the US Census Bureau in 1951 prompted IBM to respond; IBM had been founded to build systems to satisfy the large-scale data handling requirements of the US Census in the 1890's. In developing electronic computers, both IBM and UNIVAC drew heavily on their work for the US Government and in particular for the military. For example, SABRE, the first real-time tr⎯⎯⎯tion processing system for airline bookings, owed considerable debts to SAGI Strategic Air Command's early warning system, which had allowed IBM t expertise in both time-sharing systems and networking.

Case: Lyons' Electronic Office

Scenario: The introduction of the first commercial data processing system in the UK occurred in the somewhat unlikely setting of a leading chain of tea-shops.

Lyons operated a chain of tea-shops known as Lyons' Corner Houses throughout the United Kingdom. In 1896, Lyons had introduced their first adding machine into one of their tea-rooms, which had been followed by a series of efficiency improving devices and systems. Lyons employed mathematicians to help them improve the efficiency of their operations. Raymond Thompson and O W Standingford encouraged the Lyons Board to build a computer; at that time it was impossible to buy one. Thompson and Standingford visited the USA in 1947 and saw the work on early electronic computers of John von Neumann and his colleagues. Returning to the UK, they sought out Maurice Wilkes at the University of Cambridge who was working on EDSAC (Electronic Delay Storage Automatic Computer), an early scientific computer.

We believe that they have been able to get a glimpse of a development which will, in a few years' time, have a profound effect on the way in which clerical work (at least) is performed. Here, for the first time, there is a possibility of a machine which will be able to cope, at almost incredible speed, with any variation of clerical procedure, provided the conditions which govern the variations can be pre-determined. (quoted in Simmons, 1962, pages 26-27.)

The Board backed the project, giving initial support for the further development of EDSAC at the University of Cambridge. In 1949, the project was brought inside Lyons under the control of J M M Pinkerton. EDSAC had been devised for scientific computing which was relatively intensive in its use of processing but involved relatively little input and output, whereas business applications had much less processing but much more input and output, reading in details of orders and printing out invoices.

By 1951 a computer, Lyons Electronic Office (LEO), was undertaking small-scale non-essential work for Lyons and some outside work, such as calculating shell trajectories for the Army Ordnance Board. The payroll at Cadby Hall, Lyons' headquarters, was computerised in 1954, as was the processing of the daily orders from the 150 Corner Shops and the analysis of the tea stocks. In the spirit of the time a documentary film was made in 1957.

Lyons sold eleven LEO II computers and 150 LEO IIIs. However, in 1960 Lyons sold its computing interest to English Electric which was subsequently absorbed into International Computers Limited (ICL). In

> the process of the mergers, the LEO architecture was lost. Lyons turned to IBM to supply it with data processing equipment.

Throughout the 1950's and 1960's, there developed a growing diversity of uses of computers for data processing and information systems. From the original pay-roll systems these grew to include almost the entire accounting function, with the consequence that in many organisations the responsibility for DP/IS lay with the finance department. In the 1970's the idea was even suggested that it would be possible to map the entire information flows of the organisation as a single integrated management information system.

A major shift in transaction processing has been from batched and centralised to on-line and decentralised processing. Work was originally assembled into 'batches' then processed later, usually overnight. The next stage was centralised on-line processing, involving work being processed individually as items arose by a single central system. This was followed by distributed on-line processing which is again an on-line system, with the items being processed as they occur, with the important distinction being that it is on a variety of machines. Where there is intensive input and output this can be handled by a local processor, giving better response times, with more powerful and more specialist processors available when required. This distribution is organisational, functional and geographic, giving rise to more complex problems of managing the 'system', insofar as it can still be called a system. The reliance on telecommunications has grown and is now almost complete.

In most organisations there are barriers to distributed computing, including:

- networks from a number of vendors with different protocols;
- duplication and incompatibility of data;
- outdated and inefficient application software;
- inadequate skills base.

The challenge to organisations is to build an 'open systems' infrastructure which can overcome these problems through all the parts being designed to work together. The characteristics of this would include:

- vendor independence;
- supports organisation-wide functions;
- permits authorised users to access applications and information anywhere from any workstation or system;
- allows interoperability of networks and systems;
- portability of applications, allowing transfer to other systems;
- unified network management.

A distributed computing environment enables applications and processes to be located anywhere on a network of geographically dispersed systems and still be managed from a single central location. To users, it appears to be a single, local system. The benefits to the organisation are that it:

- allows the business to respond to change;
- permits resources to used where and when they are needed.

The final goal, for the present, is a single logical system, comprising many different physical components and many different locations.

Performance of a system can be measured in many ways, for example, the time taken to process a transaction or the number of transactions per seconds. Availability can be measured as the percentage of time for which the system is available or as minutes of unscheduled time when it is not. Reliability is measured in terms of mean time between failures. Recoverability is the facility of bringing the system back to the same state as it was before it failed. If a transaction processing system fails, for whatever reason, it is essential that transactions are not lost. In some cases the mechanism is to execute to completion or to roll-back if it fails, that is all the operations take effect or none at all. On recovering from failure, the system recovers all transactions already processed, they must never be 'lost'.

The client-server model has been developed to provide a continuation of existing systems, by improving their functionality. The aim is to facilitate the movement of processing onto lower cost computers, taking the load off central mainframes.

Database management systems

The term database is used to describe a computer-based information system for the storage and retrieval of data. Most of these systems look very similar to the user, in that they take the form of typing a question or 'query' with the result displayed on a screen or printed on paper. However, there are significant differences in terms of:

- technology used;
- types of data stored;
- basic units of retrieval;
- methods of defining queries.

The idea of the Data Base Management System (DBMS) was developed in the late 1960's as one result of growing problems with traditional computer applications based on individual programs and data files. Each application, for example, a payroll, would have its own set of programs and data files, which were so closely intertwined that to change a file usually involved changing the corresponding program and vice versa. Thus, to add new categories to a file would involve changes to existing programs, which would usually be working perfectly well. Such processes became known as 'unproductive maintenance'.

The proliferation of programs for different applications meant that items of data were often duplicated on several files, increasing the demand made for relatively expensive storage capacity and, more importantly, causing problems with consistency and updating. The data values quickly became inconsistent, for example, different stock levels for the same item in the programs used by the production and sales departments. The only way to access files was using a program, so that even the simplest query involved writing a program or having one written. This was a time-consuming task in itself and often subject to long delays because programmers were tied up in unproductive maintenance or in the development of new systems.

It was realised that these problems were the result of a piecemeal, application-centred approach. A new data-oriented approach was needed, avoiding the haphazard creation of separate files for each new application. The data likely to be used in all the computer-based information system required to be brought under some form of central control. A major advance in technology facilitated this development, when high-speed, high-capacity magnetic discs replaced magnetic tapes. Previously, magnetic tapes had to be loaded manually from racks onto tape decks connected to the computer and the records in the files processed sequentially. Magnetic discs allowed files to be processed to be available continuously and interactively and so to be processed in any order. Even a high-speed tape deck is much slower than a magnetic disc for transaction processing. Tapes are still used today, mainly for back-up and to transfer data between systems.

The principles developed for the data-oriented approach are:

DATA INDEPENDENCE

Data files are not tied to programs and, therefore, it should be possible to change or add to a file or program without affecting the other. In particular, creating new applications should not require the modification of existing files.

MINIMISATION OF DATA REDUNDANCY

Wherever possible, there should be only one copy of each data item in order to ensure consistency.

FLEXIBILITY OF DATA ACCESS

It should be possible to interrogate the database without having to write a program. There should be a 'query language' which should be easily learned by non-technical users.

DATA INTEGRATION

All data should be available from a single system, therefore it should be possible to combine and extract data in an almost limitless number of ways.

UNIFORM SECURITY, PRIVACY AND INTEGRITY CONSTRAINTS

The limits necessary for security, privacy and integrity should be defined once for each user or class of users across the whole system thereby minimising the risks of inaccurate data entering the system, incorrect processing of data or inappropriate access to data.

A database management system (DBMS) is a sophisticated piece of software which organises data according to these principles and provides access for two principal groups of users:

- technical programmers working in programming languages;
- casual users of the database.

At the lowest level of the DBMS is the internal operation of the machine, where data are stored on discs. Users do not need to know anything about the physical locations of data or the mechanisms of storage and retrieval. Indeed, they are usually prevented from doing so. All that the user requires is the set of definitions used to describe the data items he or she wishes to access and manipulate.

A conceptual model is used to define the whole information resource at an abstract level; all entities, all relationships between entities, security restrictions, audit controls, validation procedures and so on. (It does not contain any of the implementation details.) This model is at the heart of the database, containing all the data and the connections between them, with a structure which minimises redundancy. There are three different types of model which have been used in databases:

- hierarchical;
- network;
- relational.

These models have been the subject of much debate as relational databases have emerged from the laboratories into organisations. There have been long technical arguments over the merits and technical performance of relational databases which have very desirable functionality, but been very slow. It was not until the mid-1980's that sufficiently powerful computers became available to run relational databases at the speeds necessary for transaction processing. Today, they can perform sufficiently quickly to satisfy the requirements of most and possibly all applications. This is the result of faster hardware and improvements in the software. Although all three models are still in use, the relational model is taking over from the other two models.

The breakthrough in conceptual simplicity for relational databases came with the realisation that both connections and values could be represented in the same way and in a form familiar to everyone, through the use of tables. A relational database is seen by the user as a collection of tables (known in mathematical jargon as relations), a table being an unordered collection of rows. In computing terms, a table can be thought of as a file, with the rows representing records and the columns representing fields. In the example given below, the tables show people in the School of Management at the University of Bath with room numbers and telephone numbers. This model is not only easy to understand, it is also easy to manipulate, change and update. The user now works with complete tables, instead of individual rows as in the other models.

Table 5.1 *Specimen database tables*

Surname	Forename	Title	Staff number
Beaumont	John R	Prof	90016
Baden-Fuller	Charles FW	Prof	82056
Targett	David W	Prof	90018
Doyle	John	Dr	86035

Staff number	Telephone	Room	Subject
90016	6742	WH3.26	Business Strategy and Information Management
90018	6856	WH3.14	Business Strategy
82056	6684	WH3.15	Information Systems
86035	5626	LIB3.9	Decision Sciences

With the older hierarchical and network models, expressing queries is similar to and could be almost as difficult as writing programs. With the relational model queries are easier for the user to express, though at the expense of creating more work for the system. To make retrieval of data possible, the tables must have the correct links set up between them. Database design is the process of selecting a set of tables to represent an organisation's data with all the necessary connections but with the minimum of redundancy. For a large number of data items with many interconnections this task can be a complex process. (See also the discussion of entity-relationships in Chapter 6.)

The concepts and procedures are the same for all relational databases, though the languages in which they are expressed vary from one package to another. A query language is a means of obtaining information from a database. It is usually a subset of English with a very restricted grammar, dictionary and syntax. For example, if you want details of all professors, without a computer would involve referring to a table of all staff and going down the title column picking out all the rows where the title is professor. To express this as a query involves giving the table name and a condition, such as Title = "Prof". However, it is necessary to be careful since many databases are 'case sensitive' in that "prof", "Prof" and "PROF" are all seen as being different. Conditions in queries can use the mathematical operators:

=	equal to
>	greater than
>=	greater than or equal to
<	less than
<=	less than or equal to

This language allows the construction of queries such as "Age <= 40". The logical operators can also be used:

AND   both
OR   either
NOT   not

These are better represented pictorially in figure 5.1. The logical operators allow queries such as "Age <= 40 AND Title = 'Prof'" or more complex still with three combinations, such as "Title = 'Prof' OR Title = 'Reader' AND Age <= 40".

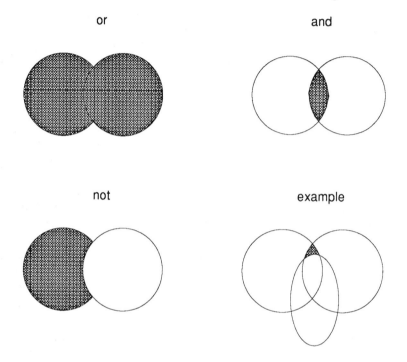

Figure 5.1 *Venn diagrams*

An alternative and more user-friendly way of expressing conditions is to let the user fill in the search criteria in the relevant headings and columns of an empty version of the table, for example,

Title	Age
Prof	<= 40

If all the rows are not required, then the query can specify the names of the necessary columns. Retrieving data from one table requires the specification of the table name, a condition for selecting some of the rows and the names of the columns to be displayed.

Case: Structured query language

Scenario: In order to improve the interconnection of databases and to make easier their wider adoption, a standardised 'query language' has been developed.

The Structured Query Language (SQL) is a language for interrogating databases. It was originally developed by IBM to allow access to data held on several database systems in different IBM computing environments and was adopted later as an American standard and subsequently approved by the International Standards Organisation (ISO). SQL, pronounced 'sequel' or sometimes 'ess-cue-ell', is a set of facilities for defining, manipulating and controlling data in a relational database. It is used in preference to a natural language because it is unambiguous, even if it is less powerful and less familiar to managers.

A strong case can be made for a standard such as SQL. Training costs are reduced because movements of staff between organisations, departments and computing systems does not require re-training. Applications which have been written on, say, a PC can be moved to a mainframe computer. There is easier inter-communication between different systems, especially as we move towards distributed database systems. However, there are disadvantages to standards, notably it can stifle creativity — a standard can only ever be a sub-optimal system because innovation would not comply with the standard. SQL is not the ideal relational language — there are several deficiencies and idiosyncrasies.

Today, SQL is being used worldwide in a range of database products, including:

- Oracle;
- Ingres;
- Borland/Ashton-Tate's dBase IV;
- IBM's DB2 (mainframe).

SQL is intended to support the definition, manipulation and control of data in relational databases. Data manipulation, retrieval or updating of data, can be either interactive or can be run from inside an application program written in a conventional programming language, such as, COBOL. Interactive SQL generally involves a user working at an interactive terminal and receiving the output to a screen. SQL within a program will provide the data for further processing, for use in on-line transaction processing, leading to a report.

SQL allows users to create 'tables' and 'views'. A view is a 'virtual' table in which the DBMS allows one or more users to treat as a table data from two or more 'real' tables. SQL permits the modification of data in tables with three commands 'insert', 'update' and 'delete'. The most important of the SQL commands is select which allows you to extract data from the database. For example,

Select   name, subject, age
From   staff
Where   title = 'Prof'
Group by   subject
Order by   age

This command selects the columns containing the names, subject and ages of all professors, groups them by subject and within each subject, orders them by age.

SQL has built-in functions for mathematical operations: count, sum, average, maximum, minimum and so on.

The data dictionary is a key element in the DBMS; it stores and manages all the 'metadata', that is the data about the data. It is the main tool used by the database administrator to manage an organisation's information, to maintain the integrity, consistency and reliability of the database. The data dictionary is itself a database which contains definitions of the records, data items, relations and other data objects held in tables. It also holds information about where the data itself is physically stored.

DBMS have a report generator which is used to improve the appearance of the output generated from queries by providing:

- overall headings;
- individual column headings;
- column formatting;
- automatic page numbering;
- computation of totals and sub-totals;
- creation of new columns, for example, by multiplying two existing columns.

Thus, a query can be stated in SQL or a similar language and formatted to make the output easier to read.

Case: Metadata — Global environmental change

Scenario: The availability of high-quality data is an essential requirement for research into global environmental change. Moreover, researchers must also know what datasets are available.

To facilitate data exploitation, there is a significant need for information about data, 'metadata'. The majority of the uses of datasets are secondary in the sense that they go beyond the primary use for which they were collected originally.

In the UK, the Inter-Agency Committee on Global Environmental Change has recently established a Global Environmental Change (GEC) data facility with a prime objective to construct and maintain a Master Directory providing a GEC data inventory. It is intended that the metadata, through this GEC Master Directory, should be available both on-line and as floppy disks or CD-ROMs.

This development raises a number of issues regarding details contained in a directory. As a minimum, the level of detail should be by discipline and the natural groupings of data within that discipline. Queries should return all the enquiries containing the combination of keywords specified in the query. Possible fields could contain:

Identification and availability:

TI   proper title (description of content and time/place coverage)
CT   common title (short informal name by which data may also be known)
AU   statement of responsibility for creation (author: person or corporation)
DC   date of creation
ED   edition statement, which may include a date or revision number
PU   publisher (statement of responsibility for maintenance/distribution)
PL   place of publication
FR   frequency of update (yearly/monthly/regularly/ad hoc)
AV   terms of availability (eligibility for each class of user; price, if any)

Subject and Content:

AB   brief abstract or description of content and origin, a statement (150 words maximum) and, where appropriate, sub-fields:

A01   purpose for which data were generated/collected or currently serve
A02   population of interest (for example, describe persons or objects)
A03   period or time coverage
A04   geographic coverage
A05   extent of aggregation
A06   method/instrumentation used to collect or generate the data
A07   source of (hard copy) information used in digitising

A08	spatial referencing system (for example, Ordnance Survey national grid, unit postcode)
A09	scale
A10	resolution
A11	projection scheme
A12	spatial data structure (statement such as: raster/grid; vector/polygons, lines or points; full topological, raster image or NTF release and structure level)
A13	data quality or processing statement
SU	suggested keywords or subject terms

Computing characteristics:

SO	software requirements
SI	a brief indication of size (such as, 3MB or 2GB)
FO	exchange format (optional)

Access and management:

CO	contact name: statement of responsibility for maintenance
CA	contact address (postal address, telephone number, electronic mail address)
AK	brief acknowledgement/copyright statement
DO	citation (title) or reference to relevant documentation

The Data Base Administrator (DBA) is the person responsible for ensuring that the DBMS is set up and used in a systematic and disciplined way. The specific tasks assigned to the DBA usually include:

*   creating and maintaining the database;
*   providing access to users;
*   setting up adequate security checks on sensitive data;
*   carrying out routine back-up procedures so that the database can be recreated in the event of a failure.

The idea of free text retrieval is to store large, often enormous, amounts of text in a database where it can be searched by keyword, indexed terms or any word in the text. This is essential in the storage of correspondence, invoices and so on, if they are to be retrieved. ICL has developed Content Addressable File Store (CAFS) for this purpose. Sitting on ICL mainframe computers, CAFS allows the user to search very rapidly through large databases.

To go one step further, Document Image Processing (DIP) allows the scanning, storage and retrieval of images of documents. The aim of DIP is to reduce the physical storage space required for documents while making them available more readily and more rapidly. The enormous storage capacity of Write Once Read Many times (WORM) optical discs (for example, two Gigabytes on one disc) makes it feasible to store documents as scanned images, each page taking up to one megabyte. WORMs have an expected life of ten years, so that they can be used for archiving documents, if this proves to be a legally acceptable storage medium. For some years DIP was a solution in search of a problem, for example, Wang experimented with DIP systems in the early and mid-1980's, though were unable to create or discover a market. As with so many ICT applications, DIP is showing steeply declining costs and is already available on PCs. The companies involved in producing DIP systems include both conventional ICT vendors and photographic firms: Wang, DEC, IBM, Kodak, Agfa, NCR, Unisys and Philips.

Data protection

Concerns over the protection of data arose from fears concerning control over access to data and the purposes for which it might be used, specifically data about individuals. Moreover, the transfer of data across national borders might mean that data passed out of the jurisdiction of one government into another where the laws are different, changing the restrictions on the uses which can be made of data.

In the United Kingdom, the data protection debate was begun in February 1970 with a motion on a Private Member's Bill by Brian Walden, MP. This was followed by the investigation of the Younger Committee, appointed by the government, which reported in 1972 leading to a Government White Paper in 1975. A second committee was appointed in 1976 under Sir Norman Lindop which reported in 1978, to be followed by a second White Paper in 1982. Finally, the first legislation, the Data Protection Act (1984) was passed with a timetable for implementation over three years. restricting the use of data about private individuals. All individuals and organisations processing and storing data in the UK must register the fact with the Data Protection Registrar. Individuals about whom data are held may, on payment of a fee, obtain access to that data to verify it. If the data are incorrect or have been incorrectly transferred to another party, the individual is entitled to compensation.

The principles behind the UK Data Protection Act are that personal data:

- shall only be obtained and processed lawfully and fairly;
- shall only be held for specified, lawful and registered purposes;
- shall only be used for registered purposes and only disclosed to registered recipients;
- shall be adequate, relevant and not excessive for registered purpose(s);
- shall be accurate and where necessary kept up to date;
- shall not be kept for longer than is necessary for their stated purpose;
- individuals shall have right of access to any data held about them which is capable of being processed automatically;
- appropriate security measures shall be taken against unauthorised access to, or alteration, disclosure or destruction of, or accidental loss of, personal data.

Exemption from the Act is granted to the police and to military and security services on the statement of the government minister concerned.

Registration Number CO297153

Purposes for which data are to be held or used:

PO33   Pensions administration
PO08   Purchase/supplier administration
PO01   Personnel/employee administration
PO15   Reservation, bookings and ticket issue
PO04   Marketing and selling
PO06   Public Relations and external affairs
PO22   Education or training administration

Types of individuals about whom data are to be kept:

SO01   Current, past employees, trainees, voluntary workers
SO06   Current, past, potential claimants
SO39   Current, past potential relatives, dependents, friends, neighbours, referees, associates, contacts of any of those described above

Classes of data to be held:

C001   Personal identifiers
C002   Financial identifiers
C003   Identifiers issued by public bodies
C011   Personal details
C021   Current marriage or partnership
C022   Marital history
C023   Details of other family, household members
C062   Recruitment details
C063   Termination details
C068   Payments, deductions
C087   Pension details
C131   References to manual files, records

Figure 5.2 *Extract from the registration under the Data Protection Act for the University of Stirling*

Equivalent or more restrictive legislation has been implemented in most European countries in compliance with the Council of Europe's "Convention for Protection of Individuals with regard to Automatic Processing of Personal Data". The convention arose from concerns about the ability personal data at ever diminishing cost with easy retrieval of the data and in the absence of established legal protection. The power of the individual state is significantly diminished by the ability to access information from anywhere in the world. For enforcement and for convenience of individuals and organisations, the legislative frameworks need to be similar!

- personal data should be collected, stored and communicated only for specified and legitimate purposes with the permission of the data subject or under the legal authority;
- personal data and the uses to which it is put should be accurate, up-to-date, relevant and not excessive;

- on request, the data subjects should be entitled to know that data are held about them and to have access to that data, where appropriate, they should be able to correct it.

The European Community is currently considering a proposal for a directive on data protection under its Open Network Provision (ONP) which is much more restrictive than current legislation in the UK. At the time of writing, this document remains in draft form and it is unclear how the final political negotiations will turn out. However, to take a simple example, they could make illegal the identification or logging of the number of an incoming telephone call, which is technically quite simple.

Commercial on-line databases

For many years, there have been abstracting journals which printed brief details of all monographs, articles in journals, contributions to edited volumes and so on, together with indexes. Such journals allow researchers to identify all works on a particular topic by searching, albeit painstakingly, through the abstracts and indexes. The advent of computers meant that the work of generating and sorting the indexes could be automated. Later it was possible to produce camera-ready copy directly from the computer. However, the major breakthrough came with the development of direct access to the databases containing the abstracts and indexes. Initially, this capability was used to supplement manual searching, but gradually on-line searching drew equal in importance and then overtook manual searching. In some cases the full text of the journals has been made available on-line, for example, the Harvard Business Review. This is a major improvement, since it avoids many of the problems with trying to comprehend the indexing of another person who might have a different understanding of the subject matter and its importance. Full text searching allows the user to obtain part of the text or the complete text at the time of searching, however, there is a risk of overdoing the search.

Specimen abstract for this book:

Authors: Beaumont, John R; Sutherland, Ewan
Title: Information Resources Management
Publisher: Butterworth-Heinemann
Date: 1992
Keywords: Business Strategy, Management, Information and Communications Technologies, Social
    Sciences

Abstract: A general management text that focuses explicitly on the increasing need to manage information as a resource. The use of cases complements the discussion. One chapter is devoted to the changing nature of the information-based industries.

At first, access to these databases was by use of a conventional terminal connected to a telephone line and a modem working at the comparatively slow speed of 300 bits per second. As time went by speeds were increased with the developments in technology. Data networks such as Telenet and Tymnet, have been used for the international links, either directly or from a packet switch exchange near the user.

The late 1980's saw developments in disc storage technology both in cheaper hard discs and in Compact Disc Read Only Memory (CD-ROM). CD-ROM allows large quantities of data (up to 500 Megabytes per disc) to be distributed worldwide comparatively cheaply; a disc costs £1 and weighs only 10 grams. CD-ROMs are well suited as a distribution medium, being relatively cheap, small in size, light in weight and relatively robust. Although 'hard' discs provide faster access times and faster data transfer rates, they have to be updated from CD-ROM, conventional floppy discs or by telecommunications link. The attraction of having the database locally on a CD-ROM is that instead of paying usage fees a single fee is paid, therefore beyond a certain level of use, the marginal cost is zero. An early example of a CD-ROM database in the UK was produced by the Post Office and Hitachi, to provide a complete database of UK post codes and addresses. More recently, British Telecom have provided a CD-ROM version of the UK telephone directory, partly in response to business attitudes to the 43.5 pence charge for telephone number enquiries.

5.3 Office information systems

The choice of the term 'office information systems' (OIS) is intended to avoid phrases which suggest goal orientation or unambiguous prescriptions for success. Office automation can conjure up images of robots sitting at typewriters and otherwise dehumanised offices, with the terms 'electronic office' and the 'office-of-the-future' sounding little better. The prescriptive approach of office automation singularly failed, with the 'paperless' expectations of the late 1970's and early 1980's simply not having been delivered. Over a period from the mid-1970's to the mid-1980's word processing software and hardware was developed which had quite remarkable effects on the employment of clerical and secretarial staff. The electric typewriter and the associated pools of typists were driven out, first by standalone word processors, then office information systems and personal computers.

The creation of OIS has been at best idiosyncratic and at times quite anarchic. A number of technologies have been thrown at this ill-defined problem. At one time the solutions lay in microelectronics and then in telecommunications, at another time facsimile and then voice mail, support for tasks then document processing; higgledy-piggledy these coalesced into OIS. The confusion is demonstrated by IBM, which at one time offered five separate office systems running on dedicated machines, personal computers, minicomputers and two incompatible types of mainframe computers. The driving force behind this has been the continuing belief in the 'office market'. This was based on some rather dubious figures which alleged productivity in offices was not rising and that capital investment in offices was much less than in factories, from which it followed that offices could be made much more efficient by increased investment. This has been reinforced by bursts of massive growth in sales for PCs, facsimile machines and so on.

A fundamental problem in discussing office information systems is the vague and ambiguous nature of the term 'office'. To a child it is place where daddy goes all day, to the parent it is somewhere to escape from the children, to the accountant it is an overhead, to the factory worker it is somewhere that people drink coffee all day, and so on. Clearly, at one level, the office is a social setting, while at another level it is a place of business. We do not really need to know what an office is, though it does help to understand the processes which occur there.

While much of the work in the field of computer-based information systems replaces people, the recent aim in OIS has been to support managers in their work by providing them with facilities which make them more productive, both more effective and more efficient. Office information systems are designed to assist the activities of the office through the use of information and communications technologies. They are used by both individuals and by groups and should require individuals to use only the knowledge that they would normally use in their everyday work.

Where tasks are highly repetitive they can and will be automated using conventional information systems. Between the highly repetitive and utterly unpredictable tasks lie a number of procedures which are carried out infrequently and where an information system created with the full force of a structured methodology (see Chapter 6) would be inappropriate; the potential rewards would not justify the costs. Generic office tasks are best tackled using software written for a wide market which is rich in facilities, such as word processing, spreadsheets and business graphics; this is clearly work for software houses or hardware vendors. OIS also have facilities which allow users to build their own small scale applications, if necessary, they can be assisted in this by more experienced support staff.

The design of OIS is aimed at producing a set of software to run on a workstation providing a mixture of services for users, a form of 'one-stop shopping'. This requires consistent interfaces across the different pieces of software in order to make the OIS easy-to-use for non-technical users. It is necessary to provide access to a range of applications, including:

- word processing;
- spreadsheets;
- decision support systems;
- electronic mail;
- business graphics;
- electronic publishing;
- databases (personal, work group, organisational and external).

Different individuals have different profiles of use of the facilities available; indeed the same user will vary his or her use from day to day. Manufacturers have built systems by combining different workstations, servers, minicomputers and mainframes on a variety of networks. It is then up to the user organisation, in collaboration with the advisers, to construct the best system from the prepared units and to select the best system from a number of suppliers.

Word processing software slowly evolved from rather crude screen representations to powerful 'WYSIWYG' (What You See Is What You Get), showing many styles of lettering and complex page layouts. Software packages have gradually expanded to include sophisticated facilities equivalent to those originally found in Desk Top Publishing (DTP) packages. This has come about partly as a result of competitive pressure within the word processing market and also from the convergence of the word processing and DTP markets. An important enabling factor was the availability of high quality laser printers with technically advanced functions and more powerful PCs which could accommodate the necessary software, main memory, disc space and speed of processor.

Word processing software incorporate a range of useful facilities:

- spelling checker;
- thesaurus;
- dictionary;
- style checker.

A computer program cannot easily grasp the complexities of natural language semantics and most spell checkers are doing little more than proving that the text is a sequence of individually correct English words. Style checking is a much more complex task, although basic software is now being marketed for this application.

Case: Preparation of this book

Scenario: The authors, Beaumont and Sutherland, working respectively in Bath and Stirling, wanted to produce a manuscript for this book which would look like the final book using straightforward word processing software.

The software chosen was Microsoft Word version 5.0, allowing the authors to produce high quality output on a variety of printers at different stages in the drafting process. MS-Word is relatively easy to use, with a menu system at the bottom of the screen which can be made to disappear if an experienced user prefers. The menu, whether continuously visible or not, allows easy access to functions which are seldom used.

Stylesheets were used to manage consistency throughout the book. For instance, a style 'IT' was created for the text in this paragraph, which defines the font of the characters, the lines at the sides of this box and the grey shading, while a second code, 'IB', was created for the case heading. A single change to the stylesheet changes the appearance of all chapters of the book. It was possible to match the style of the manuscript to the style used by the publisher.

MS-Word allowed us to incorporate graphics from Cricket Graph, Harvard Graphics and Extel Microview.

There is a need to be able to incorporate documents and objects from other sources, for example, database reports, electronic mail messages and graphics. A more complex consideration is how to transfer text from one package to another, without having to re-key it. The crude method of converting it from the internal file format used by one package into ASCII characters, requires that all formatting information be stripped out. The more sophisticated approach used in Office Document Interchange Format (ODIF) is intended to allow the retention of all formatting information either as a printable image or as in processable form which would allow further editing. Even with the ODIF approach it will still be necessary to make approximations, for example, in the choice of a particular font, which is dependent on the printer. Going one step further, Office Document Architecture (ODA) is a structure for documents which comprises both a logical and layout structure. However, few editors or word-processors yet support ODA.

A major area of growth in shrink-wrapped software has been for business graphics, such as Harvard Graphics. The attractions of do-it-yourself graphics are considerable, allowing the user to produce high-quality:

- illustrations for reports;
- overhead projector slides;
- 35mm slides.

Electronic mail

Electronic mail is well-established in the academic communities of Europe and the USA. It is of growing importance in trans-national corporations and in other large organisations, having spread there from the universities and ICT vendors. Electronic mail is a recent adaptation of previous forms of communication with which it now competes in the market place.

Facsimile (fax) has been around in various forms since the middle of the nineteenth century. It is a systems of transmitting scanned images, rather than a character-based transmission. Facsimile is generally referred to by the different 'group' standards. Group 1 fax is long abandoned, while Group 2 is out of production and declining in use. Group 3 is the dominant standard today, transmitting a single page of A4 text in approximately two minutes over a conventional telephone line. Group 4 provides a very high quality of output, similar to a good photocopy machine, though at a significant cost in equipment and telecommunications charges. The higher resolution of Group 4 requires the transmission of much more data which will be feasible only when the higher speeds lines of Integrated Service Digital Network (ISDN) are more widely available. It is possible to buy or lease portable Group 3 facsimile machines to connect to mobile telephones. Thus you can receive a facsimile message while driving down the motorway in your Jaguar. However, sending facsimile messages should not be attempted while driving!

An electronic mail message consists of an electronic 'envelope' (with addressing details) and contents. The contents are a header, which will contain several fields (such as From, To, CC and acknowledge receipt) and a body which may consist of several parts, not necessarily of the same type. When you login to a system it warns you if you have mail lying in your mailbox. Running the mail system allows you to see how much mail you have, who it is from and the subjects. You can then select a message to read.

Each individual has a 'user agent' which is a computer program permitting the sending and receiving of electronic mail, which can be on their personal computer or on a remote computer or server, accessed using a network. The user agent provides all the facilities necessary for creating, sending, reading and storing mail. Access to the user agent requires identification of the user by username and at least one password. The user agent communicates with another piece of software called the message transfer agent which acts as an 'electronic postman'; collecting, routing and delivering electronic mail for all the users in a system. In the simplest case, the user agent and the message transfer agent are on the same computer. In most organisations, there will be a number of different message transfer agents in different departments and sites, for example, sales office in Amsterdam and production management in Munich.

In order to facilitate the interconnection of computer systems, most vendors developed proprietary electronic mail 'standards' and these have now been consolidated into an international standard known as CCITT X.400. All public services and many private services are gradually converting to this standard or are developing a gateway allowing interconnection with X.400-based services. Gateways from electronic mail are possible to other services, for example, to telex and to conventional 'physical' mail. It is a relatively simple matter to print out an electronic mail message and, if required, to insert it in an envelope and arrange to have it delivered by conventional post or courier.

Case: Digital Equipment Corporation EasyNet

Scenario: In order to improve internal communications in Digital Equipment Corporation and to be seen to be using its own technology, EasyNet was established to link all DEC staff worldwide.

Perhaps the best known network outside the academic community is that of Digital Equipment Corporation, extending to all parts of the Corporation worldwide.

One of the uses is to allow technical and sales staff in different parts of the world to communicate. Thus, if someone in technical sales in Germany has a client with a particular requirement which cannot immediately be met, it is possible to put out a general question to equivalent staff all over the world. In a matter or hours or in a day or two at most it will be possible to find someone who has either a solution or has a client operating a solution. The clear benefit to Digital is the sharing of expertise throughout the corporation.

The benefits of electronic mail come from changes in working patterns: faster response times, fewer interruptions and from the removal of the frustrating delays of conventional communications. These gains can be translated into time freed for other activities and may make possible completely new work. The benefits of electronic mail can be categorised as follows:

INTERRUPTIONS
Electronic mail does not usually interrupt work; it is up to users to check their mailboxes, unlike the telephone.

TELEPHONE TAG
A well-known problem of telephoning busy people is that they are not in their office and when they try to call you back you are out, a process which can go on for days on end.

PERSON-TO-PERSON
Electronic mail is generally person-to-person unlike telex and facsimile which are machine-to-machine, avoiding the delays of slow local distribution or failure to deliver.

GEOGRAPHICAL INDEPENDENCE
Access to a mailbox is possible from a terminal or personal computer anywhere, always provided that the telecommunications link can be made.

TIME INDEPENDENCE
Since the sender and recipient do not need to interact with each other at the same time it is easy to communicate by electronic mail across time zones.

SPEED
Electronic mail is usually extremely rapid in transmission.

MULTIPLE COPIES
The marginal cost and time of sending a second or third copy is generally very small.

DISTRIBUTION LISTS
A document can be mailed to a single name which distributes the mail a number of recipients, often at different sites.

As with all new forms of communication, it is necessary for people to learn how to behave with electronic mail. They require to learn how many messages it is acceptable to send, about which subjects, how often and to whom. For example, it would be intolerable for the principal or vice-chancellor of a university, if, every day, every student were to send him one electronic mail message. The benefits of adding physical delivery (that is delivery of printed copies of mail) is that it allows users to have extended coverage, beyond the users of the purely electronic system. The disadvantage is that it allows non-users to avoid adopting electronic mail.

Case: Joint Academic Network

Scenario: In order to facilitate research, universities in the UK have access to facilities on a joint network.

The UK academic community of universities and research establishments is served by the Joint Academic Network (JANET).

In order to meet the requirements of communication between users on a very varied collection of equipment, the Joint Network Team had to develop its own protocol for electronic mail. The 'Grey Book' mail protocol was specified in the early 1980's and software was written by a number of universities to run on the necessary range of equipment.

JANET has 'gateways' to a number of research networks including: USENET (Unix), National Science Foundation Network (NSFNET). This allows the exchange of electronic mail messages with most countries in Europe, North America and most developed parts of the world.

JANET is gradually converting from the 'Grey Book' protocol to the international standard, CCITT X.400. This should allow users of JANET to take advantage of software which is commercially produced and supported, avoiding some of the problems of relying on software produced by university departments.

SuperJANET is an upgraded version of the existing JANET network, with the main links raised from 64 kilobits to two Megabits per second. The intention remains to provide an advanced communications service to support education and research in the United Kingdom. At the proposal of the Department of Trade and Industry, SuperJANET is also to be used as a testbed for research in communications and distributed systems. A combination of SuperJANET and high speed Local Area Networks on individual university campuses is intended to provide high quality networking at the leading edge of technology.

As a support for electronic mail, a Directory Service has proved absolutely essential; the equivalent of an on-line telephone directory. The addressing systems for electronic mail are so unbelievably complex as to make it almost unusable. Consequently, a standard was devised for a directory service which would find the mail addresses of users both locally and at remote sites. This is being introduced as quickly as the development of the software and the entering of the data allows. An experimental JANET Directory Service became operational in 1990. For example, the Directory Service entries for the authors are:

Mailbox	es@forth.stirling.ac.uk
Telephone	+44 786-6-7320
Surname	Sutherland
CommonName	Ewan Sutherland
Description	Business Studies

```
Mailbox        jrb@gdr.bath.ac.uk
Telephone      +44 225-82-6742
Surname        Beaumont
CommonName     Prof John R Beaumont
CommonName     John Beaumont
Description     Management
```

Groupware

The terms 'groupware' or Computer Supported Cooperative Work (CSCW) refer to systems for collaborative work; working as a group is explicit in the software and accentuated, as distinct from merely multi-user, where individuals are generally sealed off from one another. As most people appreciate, they do not work in isolation, a fact largely ignored by ICT vendors until recently. Groupware includes:

COMMUNICATION
Primarily electronic mail systems, with addition of some software to help filter messages, and some systems based on video-conferencing.

PROBLEM SOLVING
Computer support for critical path methods.

WRITING
Systems to help in the processes of writing, editing, incorporating comments and making revisions.

The software is all limited, often failing to address the complexities of the work being undertaken. The development of these tools has frequently failed to give sufficient attention to the social processes; there requires to be a mutual adaptation of the social and the technical systems. If the systems are successfully adopted then the individuals in the group should not only become dependent on each other, but they should also become dependent on the software to achieve their goals.

The diverse nature of work groups, their size and structure, the types of task they perform and the assignment of tasks all require to be addressed. The tasks involved in collaborative work include:

- writing and editing;
- planning;
- monitoring;

- negotiating;
- decision-making.

These tasks range from the very general (for example, writing a proposal) to the very specific (for example, developing customer profiles).

Case: Electronic meeting systems at IBM

Scenario: An experimental electronic meeting support system developed at a university was introduced into a commercial environment.

The University of Arizona, USA, developed an Electronic Meeting System (EMS) which it field-tested by use in several of IBM's sites from 1987 to 1989. A number of rooms were converted to include a u-shaped table for ten people, with a networked microcomputer at each place, a Barco video-projector, two conventional whiteboards and a place for a human 'facilitator'. A back-room facility allowed support including printing of results.

The facilities provided in the EMS room were aimed at supporting a wide range of different activities which occur in meetings, including:

- electronic brainstorming support tool;
- issue analyzer;
- voting tool;
- policy formulation tool;
- idea organiser;
- questionnaire tool;
- topic commentator;
- file reader;
- group dictionary.

Over thirty EMS facilities had been installed by the end of 1989 at IBM sites and over the three year period had been used by over 15,000 participants, from line workers to executive staff, addressing a broad range of problems. The lessons learned from these experiments included:

- anonymity is particularly beneficial;
- the number of people in a meeting who could be effective participants increased;
- the level of participation increased;
- fewer meetings over less time were required;
- the focus of participants remained on the topic;
- pre-planning of meetings is more important;
- post-meeting distribution of results is crucial;

> - low levels of computer competence did no deter effective use;
> - the meeting room environment should match the characteristics of the group;
> - software must be flexible;
> - an infrastructure of staff for the EMS is essential;
> - an EMS provides structure and control mechanisms for the meeting;
> - there was a propensity to use the EMS.
>
> Source: Grohowski, 1990.

At present there is no single technology which adequately supports group work, like office information systems, groups must rely on a range of tools, from more than one supplier. Adoption is heavily reliant on local expertise, which although not recognised by management, has the attraction of understanding the tasks being undertaken as well as knowledge of the tools being used.

5.4 Decision support systems

Computer-based information systems have a track record of either overburdening the user with complex tasks or forcing them to operate with unfriendly and difficult pieces of software. Decision Support Systems (DSS) are:

> ... computer-based systems that help decision makers confront ill-structured problems through direct interaction with data and analysis models. (Sprague and Watson, 1989, pages 1-2.)

One of the most important considerations in the creation of DSS is the recognition of 'information overload', caused by the indiscriminate supply of excessive data and information to managers. Instead of merely pumping data at managers, it is more sensible to allow decision makers to select the data they needed and to allow them to incorporate the data into models.

Decision Support Systems (DSS) have a diversity of uses in the analysis of problems and the modelling of solutions, always provided they are sufficiently easy-to-use and that managers know what and why they are doing something. DSS are focused on the decisions to be made by managers, requiring an emphasis on flexibility, adaptability and responsiveness. They must support many different types of decision-making:

- different individual styles;
- individual and group decision-making;
- simple and complex problems;

- semi-structured and unstructured problems;
- consultation and implementation.

If the introduction and use of DSS are to achieve the objectives set for them, the process must be initiated and controlled by the users. DSS should not be seen as a tool to permit managers to abdicate their decision making responsibilities.

Decision Support Systems have arisen from the revolution brought about by:

- the introduction and relatively enthusiastic adoption of the personal computer;
- the improved capabilities of telecommunications;
- the availability of commercial databases;
- the growth of end-user computing.

Individual systems vary in the relative emphasis given to each of the following DSS capabilities (see figure 5.3):

- interface;
- database;
- decision models;
- analysis.

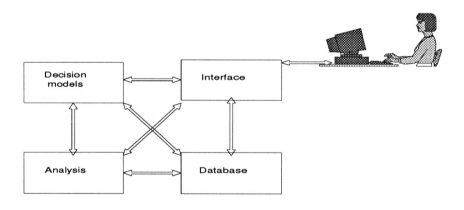

Figure 5.3 *Characteristics of a decision support system*

Although it is appropriate to discuss these capabilities separately, it is also helpful to consider them together. By emphasising different capabilities or combinations of capabilities, it is possible to begin to understand the different types of decision-making that can be supported by a DSS.

In the business world, spreadsheets are a particularly common type of DSS, combining the basic characteristics: 'decision models' and 'interface'. Spreadsheets are a matrix of rows and columns that can be used to undertake calculations on the cells. The primary 'decision' application areas are financial modelling, budgeting and planning. A spreadsheet model is defined in terms of interrelated variables and automatic recalculation facilities which permit sensitivity analyses. The ability to create graphs and to generate reports are also important for presentation of results. There are usually only limited database facilities and they do not have the straightforward capability for *ad hoc* analyses. Even with the availability of macros (the ability to run automatically a sequence of previously specified commands), only simple mathematical and statistical analyses can be performed, usually in a rather contrived manner. Recent versions have begun to extend and enhance the capabilities, for example, Microsoft Excel and Lotus '1-2-3 for Windows' make use of the 'user-friendly' MS-Windows environment.

The benefits which arise from the use of DSS relate mainly to the range of alternatives which can be considered by a manager. The use of a DSS allows the 'safe' testing of hypotheses against a number of models in a very short period of time to evaluate the potential implications of alternative decisions. Thus, managers can try out more options than they could previously cope with and in doing so they learn more about the model, if not necessarily the real world, providing them with more insight and generating more options to be tested. The use of a DSS makes *ad hoc* analyses much easier to undertake.

Executive information systems

In the mid-1980's, the first Executive Information Systems (EIS) appeared. Since then over twenty products have been announced and an EIS front-end has become an almost obligatory feature of Decision Support Systems and some other packages. As usually occurs with the latest ICT product or service, EIS have been 'hyped' by vendors; the term has been used to describe any user-friendly interface to a database or modelling system. The key benefits could be, and in some instances were, obtained by the mid-1980's. Yet many organisations are investing large sums of money to achieve no discernible advantage.

The key characteristics of an EIS are derived from how it is used (Bittlestone, 1990):

- personally by senior managers, including the executive directors;
- as a general tool, rather than a specific tool, covering several functions and extracting data from several sources;
- by senior managers whose main role is in managing other managers and developing the strategic direction of the organisation, rather than in an operational capacity;
- to provide insights into corporate data.

There is a wide range of possible types of data that can be provided using an EIS which include:

- internal and external data;
- evaluation of historical performance and forecasts of future activity;

- financial measures and physical indicators such as production volumes;
- numeric data and text commentary.

However, the main focus on applications is on well-organised and routine data coming from management accounts, including:

- routine management reporting;
- year-end preview;
- control and review of major projects;
- budget preparation and review;
- strategic planning;
- executive committee and board meetings;
- acquisition and competitor analysis;
- review of economic outlook.

Each of these tasks requires specific tools and manners of presentation in order to ensure that they can be carried out effectively and the results understood. Routine management reporting usually involves the automatic generation of standard sequences of images followed by the production of paper copies through 'exporting' data and charts into desk-top publishing software to provide a report including text, charts and tables.

The core of an EIS is a corporate model, which holds essential information about the organisation: its consolidation hierarchy, performance indicators, reporting cycles and so on. This is linked to a dedicated database which contains the underlying data. The nature of this link is the distinguishing feature between an EIS and a graphics front-end to a database. An effective EIS incorporates the rules and conventions determining the best treatment of different types of information, for example, how to derive year-to-date figures best practice for presentations. These determine how effectively the information will be presented and removes the need for the executive to define how information should be displayed.

A set of maintenance tools allows the system administrator to change the corporate model, to define the rules for processes and to specify the views that different users are given of the system. An EIS is 'fed' from a variety of specialist sources to meet the needs of the reporting functions: finance, marketing, production, personnel and so on. There will also be external sources including market research studies, on-line databases and CD-ROM databases (such as free text retrieval of newspaper articles and company reports).

The principal role of an EIS is to support group decision-making. The users are not directly responsible for the operational decisions, these are delegated to subordinates, therefore an effective EIS should address the delegation and involvement of their subordinate managers. The importance of group involvement has many implications for design, in particular the need to deliver the full functionality of the system in the boardroom for board and executive committee meetings, or in an executive office to support small meetings. Group use of the system necessitates a very close link between exploratory use with access to the underlying databases and a presentation style for looking at pre-recorded images.

Case: Financial control

Scenario: Many large organisations have a range of recurrent problems from using management accounting as their primary control instruments.

Financial and management control techniques were devised primarily to tackle the problem of a single firm. The increasing complexities of today's business environment has meant that many commentators have argued for a critical re-evaluation of management accounting as the primary control instrument within large corporate groups. By taking a broader perspective with management accounting in an overall information framework, it is possible to see a need for updating and maintaining an Executive Information System.

Robert Bittlestone (1990, page 12) provides examples of the difficulties:

- Management accounts present only the month or the year-to-date picture; the trend is lost.
- Centralised standard forms stamp out the crucial details; the subsidiaries' own product sales margin and expense analyses are what really matter.
- Comparisons with budget are meaningless; everything has changed since the month we put the budgets to bed.
- We have 70 subsidiaries in this group; we can't look at every number every month.
- The year-end forecasts are a sham; they depend on the optimism or pessimism of the forecasters.
- The accounts are impenetrable; financial details swamp all the useful management indicators.

Moreover, the existing systems cannot cope with the scale and rate of change required. For instance, the requirements for information on branch profitability may be changes to product profitability, or divisional results may become meaningless as developments through merger and acquisition occur.

A good Executive Information System can solve such problems, because, through its storage of corporate data, irrespective of how the data were entered, immediate analyses can be obtained for any cross-section of interest. The system itself can explore data series and highlight unusual trends or specific performance levels.

	Internal		External	
	Past	*Future*	*Past*	*Present*
Numeric	Management Accounting	Budgets & Forecast	Competitors' results	Brokers' forecasts
Financial Text	Results Narrative	5-year plan framework	Brokers' review	Press opinion
Numeric	Operation Performance	Capacity planning	Market share	Market research
Physical Text	Performance commentary	Strategic goals	Trade media coverage	Technology forecasts

Source: Bittlestone, 1990.

5.5 Knowledge-based systems

Computers are often viewed as 'bright' or 'intelligent'. However, all this does is to force us to define what we mean by intelligent; what is 'artificial intelligence'? In 1950, Alan Turing published his idea for a test, a 'thought experiment', to assess whether a computer could think. An observer was to be put in a room with a teletype terminal connected to two other rooms, in one of which was a person and in the other a computer. By asking questions, the observer had to determine which was the human and which was the computer. The rather more complex 'Chinese Room' Problem was formulated by John Searle to draw out the issues. An individual sits in a room into which is passed a sequence of Chinese characters, which the individual looks up in a book, indicating how to respond by passing a second sequence of characters out of the room. To outward appearances this might suggest that the Room 'understands' Chinese, when all that is being done is to look up tables. Although these problems are very interesting, they neither resolve the issue of what it is to think nor do they help in finding business applications.

The term Artificial Intelligence (AI) was first used in 1956 by John McCarthy at a conference in Dartmouth College, Connecticut. Although some of the early work was on general-purpose problem solvers, it soon became clear that much more progress could be made in more limited problem areas, initially on programs to play chess and draughts (checkers). Disappointingly, the progress in artificial intelligence has been much less than forecast, though the techniques have been taken up in other areas of information technology and have contributed to progress in other types of computer-based information systems.

Most computer-based information systems show the activities at which computers have proved very successful, mainly repetitive and usually arithmetical calculations. Computers are, on the whole, poor at:

- seeing;
- hearing;

- touching;
- displaying common sense;
- exercising judgment.

Considerable efforts have been poured into overcoming these limitations, in areas such as:

EXPERT SYSTEMS

Programs which offer the same advice as would a human expert given the same data, usually in a well-defined problem area.

NATURAL LANGUAGE PROCESSING

The ability to understand languages such as English and German, rather than the much more limited computer programming languages. In its most advanced form this includes speech input.

In 1981, artificial intelligence was given a political impetus by the Japanese government when they launched their programme for Fifth Generation Computer Systems. This caused little short of panic in Europe and the USA; Japan was seen to be trying to commercialise artificial intelligence. In 1982, the UK launched the Alvey Programme and in 1983 the European Community followed with the European Strategic Programme for Information Technology (ESPRIT). The political initiative soon fell away and developments were left to the normal academic and commercial forces.

Expert systems

One of the many definitions of an Expert System is:

A program which embodies some significant fraction of the knowledge characteristic of an expert in a specialised area and which can use that knowledge to suggest the same type of conclusions as an expert would. (Campbell, 1983.)

The constituent parts of a generalised Expert System are shown in figure 5.4. The inference engine is independent of the knowledge base and the problem being addressed, that is it can be used for many different problem areas by changing the knowledge base. The 'engine' induces or infers conclusions from the knowledge base with the information provided by the user. The knowledge base contains knowledge extracted and codified from human experts. Unlike conventional information systems, expert Systems can manipulate information which is: inconsistent, incomplete and non-numeric.

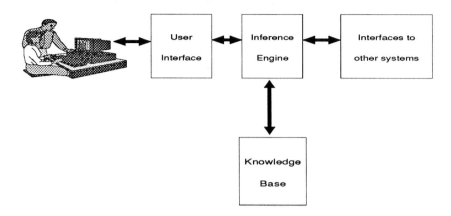

Figure 5.4 *Components of an expert system*

The business reasons for wanting an Expert System are generally in order to codify expertise to overcome problems such as:

- need to have expertise available at sites which are geographically remote or dispersed;
- scarcity of expertise;
- corporate 'memory' is likely to leave or retire;
- absence of exact methods to solve complex problems which rely on experience and evaluation.

A key consideration for the success of a project is the availability of experts. Moreover, the experts must be willing to help and they need to be able to explain the reasoning they use. Initial projects need to be selected carefully, too many have failed because the scale has been too grand; modesty helps. Once built, it is important that the user group is willing to accept the system. It goes without saying that management support is essential.

The type of applications of Expert Systems include:

- advisory;
- diagnostic;
- analysis of designs;
- scheduling;
- monitoring.

In common with other classifications, the distinction between Expert Systems and Decision Support Systems are diminishing. However, some differences are shown in table 5.3.

Table 5.3 *Difference between DSS and expert systems*

	DSS	*Expert System*
Objective	Assist management	Replace management
Who makes the decision?	Manager	Computer
Orientation	Decision-making	Transfer of experience
Applications	Functional areas	Specific problems
Database	Factual	Factual and procedural

With a few notable exceptions, positive progress on business and management applications of Expert Systems has not been as forthcoming as in other application areas, especially medicine and engineering. This can be explained primarily by the inherent nature of management applications, which are not technical; management problems are usually very complicated, or, at least, very difficult to define precisely for implementation. The process of 'knowledge acquisition' is the most difficult in building Expert Systems. Extracting and formalising human expertise has proved extremely difficult, primarily because so much of our knowledge is implicit.

Case: XCON

Scenario: Digital Equipment Corporation wanted to develop applications of Expert Systems within the corporation.

In 1978, Digital Equipment Corporation (DEC) and Carnegie Mellon University (CMU) began work on what was then known as R1, an Expert System which was to configure minicomputers. The system became operational in 1980 and development work has continued. XCON was used in the USA and in plants in Ireland and Scotland.

The task of configuring a computer involves the specification of the different components required to create a computer system. The need for this arises because DEC offers a wide range of products which are customised to the requirements of particular clients.

XCON took over the work of technical editors and engineers in developing the configuration plans for Digital VAX minicomputers. It could not manage all configurations, leaving the more complex and interesting configurations to be developed by the staff. The functions performed by XCON include:

• checking the customer's order;
• laying out the processor in cabinets;

> • placing boxes in the input-output cabinets and placing components in these boxes;
> • placing panels in the input-output cabinets;
> • laying out the floor plan;
> • designing the cabling.
>
> Rule example from XCON:
>
> IF
>   the context is layout and assigning a power supply
>   there is an available power supply
> THEN
>   put the power supply in the cabinet in the available space
>
> The most obvious measure of success was the acceptance by the technical staff of XCON. The business gains for DEC were mainly through cost avoidance. The process of configuration was a bottleneck in their production of computers, requiring more staff in an activity requiring considerable skills which are difficult to find.
>
> While XCON was of considerable benefit to the manufacturing part of DEC's operations it identified a number of errors in meeting customers' needs which occurred at the point of sale. Thus DEC followed this up with XSEL, an expert system to help their people when selling computers. XSEL selects the set of components required to assemble a particular configuration. Initially it was little more than a customer front-end to XCON, but was subsequently developed into a complex piece of software..
>
> Source: Mumford, 1989.

Natural language processing

The main applications of natural language processing include:

- user interfaces to systems;
- machine translation;
- understanding documents;
- speech generation.

The problems with natural language processing have emerged as being formidable. People are quite remarkably clever in their ability to cope with difficulties such as:

- poorly constructed sentences;
- incomplete sentences;
- ellipsis;
- metaphors;
- malapropisms;
- literary references;
- emotion;
- humour;
- homonyms.

For many applications it is necessary to use speech input, which must be converted into digital form from the sound waves generated by a human being. From this the phonemes can be derived, from which the words can be built, from which the sentences, and so on. One of the problems is that ambiguities arise. For example, the two phrases 'this new display' and 'this nudist play' sound identical or very nearly so. The only way to determine which is the more probable is from contextual knowledge; by knowing that the speech is part of a talk on the theatre and not from one on retailing. Nonetheless, there always remains an element of uncertainty.

Case: Machine translation

Scenario: Managers' decision-making involves handling textual data, and, with the growing internationalisation of business, an increasing proportion of this data is in a 'foreign' language. An enormous and growing amount of translation work is now undertaken by professional translators, and there is a developing use of computers in this process.

It must be stressed that, with the current state-of-the-art, machine translation software complements, rather than replaces, professional translators. However, good machine translation software with extensive data dictionaries can enhance significantly the efficiency of a trained translator.

In some respects, machine translation can be viewed as a specific extension to word processing. However, it would be misleading to see computer-based translation as a simple automatic process that involves looking up words in a data dictionary and presenting them in the correct order.

Assuming that the basic requisite linguistic skills have been developed, information is the key to high-quality technical translation: information in the form of subject and background knowledge and documentation, terminological information, reference materials and precedent. (Mayorcas-Cohen, 1986, page 61.)

5.6 Inter-organisational systems

The computer-based information systems described so far in this chapter have increasingly generally operated within the confines of an organisation or within a department. As organisations have developed their activities into 'global webs' their information systems have extended beyond organisational boundaries to clients, to suppliers and even to competitors, introducing elements of competitive strategy, supply chain management and newer and wider games of power politics. In some cases the benefits have been expressed in terms of efficiency, but they have also involved improvements to products and services and new ways of doing business, including: installation, delivery, service, maintenance, warranty, styling, packaging and so on. The customer 'sees' an efficient ordering process which allows more flexibility and more accurate information, thus giving a competitive advantage to the supplier. Successful implementation of such inter-organisational systems requires, for example, flexible manufacturing and automated warehousing systems and generally greater process integration.

Case: Otisline

Scenario: The use of ICTs to improve customer service.

The Otis Elevator Company manufactures and services elevators. The company developed a service known as Otisline, in which users were given a freephone telephone number allowing them to call a national reporting centre.

The Otisline service allows Otis to gather data on faults as they are reported. This can be analysed in many different ways, allowing Otis to identify which components are failing, which lift designs need to be revised and even which engineers need to given more training. Bringing the data together from throughout the continental USA allowed a much larger dataset to be made available for analysis.

In order to ensure that customers do not receive a lower level of service, despite moving from a local to a national service, it was essential to ensure that engineers could be easily contacted from the national centre. After completing a repair engineers telephone in with details of the repairs made (which are added to the database) and are assigned a new job. Service engineers are also given radio-pagers in case they are required more urgently.

The ultimate aim of Otis is avoid all call-outs by customers; that the customer sees only a set of elevators which always work. To do this the Otisline service allows Otis to be and to be seen to be efficient and, more importantly, to be better informed about its business.

It is important to consider some of the problems found in the introduction of Inter-Organisational Systems (IOS) and some of the factors which lead to their successful implementation. These include:

- a 'critical mass' of participants;
- a 'champion' and top management support;
- cost estimates;
- security;
- standards.

The real benefits of inter-organisational systems are often realised through a community of suppliers and customers; by successfully establishing such a community an organisation can alter the competitive environment. Suppliers or customers can provide electronic links to their partners which facilitate trade, making it less likely that they will turn to new partners. As industry-wide systems and standards develop, this advantage is wanes, but with increased product differentiation and 'tailoring' of products, good buyer-seller relationships become more important. Once good IOS have been set up for trading, it becomes a major decision to switch suppliers, knowing your customers expect rapid delivery of tailor-made products.

Other things being equal, the larger the community of users the greater the potential benefits. Yet, there is something of *Catch-22* about the process. To join, organisations want to see the benefits, yet the real benefits are realised only if everyone or at least a substantial minority joins. There are some exceptions, where, for example, the basis for competition is the level of use of information technology, there is little likelihood of building a community amongst competitors and 'closed' community groups around each supplier may arise.

The biggest obstacle to the widespread use of inter-organisational systems has been the problem of compatibility between the computer-based information systems of the senders and the receivers. To communicate, the rules and data language for the flow of information, must use the same syntax, message, standards and protocols. Hence there is a tremendous effort in setting up standards at international, national and industry levels. Considerable progress has been made, particularly at an industry level, for example, the financial community has already achieved a wide measure of compatibility. National standards and industry standards are gaining acceptance, and in some cases replacing standards established by major organisations such as the Ford Motor Company's Fordnet. As such standards become established, fears about incompatibility of systems diminish, encouraging wider adoption.

Electronic data interchange

Electronic Data Interchange (EDI) is the electronic transfer of orders, invoices, acknowledgements between trading organisations based on agreed standards (see figure 5.5). The more often data are communicated by EDI, the less you have to re-key data, and the less frequent are errors. With EDI it is possible to have speed at lower cost and, most importantly, an enhanced capability to handle increased and fluctuating volumes of business.

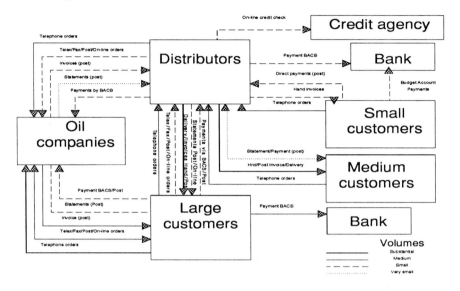

Figure 5.5 *Electronic Data Interchange*
(Source: DTI, 1988.)

The use of EDI enables organisations to develop new manufacturing and corporate strategies. New ways of organising production, such as Just-in-Time (JIT), can work more effectively if trading partners are linked by EDI. The benefit to the organisation stems directly from the introduction of the JIT system, which becomes effective because suppliers can get information concerning changes to schedules in real-time through EDI.

The form of savings include:

EFFICIENCY
Replacement of paper-based documents with electronic, improved speed and accuracy and the elimination of errors.

MANAGEMENT TIME
Elimination of time spent chasing transcription errors in orders. Savings in personnel have to be matched against the (discounted) cost of purchasing the hardware and software, maintenance, training and so on.

MARKETING INFORMATION
Information to evaluate sales promotions, competitive strategies, improved payment systems and so on, in order to improve information for decision-making.

Not only are there savings and increased efficiency in what organisations do at present, but also much greater potential for what could be done as the community of users grows and their electronic links become deeper.

5.7 Conclusion

This chapter has shown some of the great diversity of computer-based information systems found in organisations. The boundaries between the classes are never easy to justify, they change over time and the successes of one area are soon copied in another. Hybrid systems are commonly developed and, where they are not, marketing people often claim they have been.

The computer-based information systems environment for the 1990's is characterised by:

- improved development environment allowing reduced 'time-to-market';
- increased availability of off-the-shelf solutions;
- high levels of availability and performance at low cost;
- fully distributed;
- integration with DSS, EIS, OIS and IOS.

Diffusion by copying has been one of the main means by which innovations in ICTs have spread. The key to benefitting from the technology platform, lies in use of the information.

Today, the big thing to learn is not how to use the computer, or even how to organize information, but how to organize one's own work in the information-based organisation. This idea is something that we are just beginning to nibble on. (Drucker, 1990, page 73.)

Review questions

1   Which information systems do you currently use? Rate their relative importance with other sources of data not supplied through a computer-based information system.

2   Why has the 'paperless office' never been achieved.

3   Are there opportunities to explore inter-organisational linkages that do not exist in your organisation?

4   In which ways are you cleverer than a computer?

Study questions

1 Discuss the significance and implications of Document Image Processing (DIP).

2 Critically assess the success and failures of knowledge-based systems.

3 Discuss how the advances in data capture techniques have revolutionised data processing.

4 How can ICTs be used to support methods of communication which are not presently in machine-readable form?

5 Using examples, critically evaluate the role of commercial on-line databases for managerial decision-making.

6 Using examples, discuss the potential usefulness of ISDN for business.

Further reading

Journals: Network, Infomatics, Electronic Trader, International Journal of Information Resource Management, Management Information Systems Quarterly, Journal of Management Information Systems and the Journal of Information Technology.

Date, Chris "An Introduction to Database Systems, Volume 1" Third Edition, Addison-Wesley, 1989.

A good, if slightly technical, introduction to data bases.

DTI "Expert System Opportunities; Guidelines for the introduction of expert systems technology" HMSO, 1990

A pack of twelve cases, overall guidelines and video covering some of the cases. The cases are: real-time process control, legislative regulations, fault-recovery management, fault diagnosis and recovery, personnel selection screening, retirement pensions forecasting, precious metals leasing, product design appraisal and optimisation, complex uncertain diseases, corporate meetings planner.

DTI Vanguard "Electronic Trading Case Studies" HMSO, 1990.

A number of cases which can be photocopied for teaching purposes, covering a broad area of value-added services in the UK. Cases include: Analysis, Devon Ambulance, Highlands and Islands Development Board, Interlink, London Insurance market, Lucas Industries, National Bingo Game, Reuters, Tescos and Trebor Mints. Includes a video.

Ellis, Clarence and Najah Naffah "Design of Office Information Systems" Springer-Verlag, 1987.

A comprehensive and classic, even if slightly dated, view of office information systems.

Emery, James C "Management Information Systems: the critical strategic resource" Oxford University Press, New York , 1987.

A clear, balanced introduction for managers wishing to understand and exploit the potential business benefits of computer-based information systems. It is part of the Wharton Executive Library and satisfies the objectives of the series, that each volume is:

- *uptodate — reflects the latest and best research;*
- *authoritative — authors are experts are experts in their fields;*
- *brief — can be read reasonably quickly;*
- *non-technical — avoids unnecessary jargon and methodology;*
- *practical — includes many examples and applications of the concepts discussed;*
- *compact — can be carried easily in briefcases on business travel.*

Sprague, Ralph and Hugh Watson "Decision Support Systems: putting theory into practice" Prentice-Hall, 1989.

A useful volume compiled from the work of a number of authors giving helpful insights into DSS.

6

Information systems; strategy and implementation

Learning objectives:

- to understand the issues concerning infrastructure and the overall planning of computer-based information systems;

- to be aware of the methodologies, techniques and tools used to create information systems;

- to understand the role of the individual user and the organisation *vis-à-vis* the DP/IS Department and the specification and management of information systems.

6.1 Introduction

It is necessary to elicit the information requirements of the organisation as a basis for the design, development and implementation of computer-based information systems. It is essential to meet the needs of the organisational units and individual managers as well as the requirements and direction of the corporate strategy. These demands are diverse and often conflicting, requiring a wide variety of methods, tools and techniques and an ability to prioritise.

Clearly, there are lessons to be learned from the practice of strategic management and, to a lesser extent, from the literature. The distinction between formulation and implementation is now recognised to be artificial; the two must go hand-in-hand. Moreover, a growing emphasis has been put on organisational learning, the ability to utilise and exploit the expertise in the organisation.

A key constraint is money; it is all too easy to spend your way to bankruptcy building a complex infrastructure of information and communications systems which proves to be either obsolete or irrelevant. The following view from the early 1970's, indicates the attitudes of the period when the aim was to bring information systems under financial control through the imposition of economic and financial indicators:

The computer resource exists solely to help staff offices and operating units to execute their responsibilities better through cheaper processing of data, more efficient organisation of information systems, and procurement and deployment of information that is too expensive to obtain otherwise. The resource has no reason for existing except to provide such services, and these services should result in greater profits. In short the resource has a purely economic purpose. (Dearden and Nolan, 1973, pages 68-69.)

Over the years it has proved extraordinarily difficult to present decisions to managers in the simple economic terms implied by Richard Nolan. Often the solution to this problem, at least to get things to happen, has been to be economical with the truth, that is to lie! (See Chapter 8.) The other constraints are:

- management of transformation;
- availability of expertise;
- attention of top managers;
- management of ICTs.

An information systems strategy needs to be prepared by the Data Processing/Information Systems Department in consultation with the organisation as a whole. The strategy should provide:

- a strategic direction for use of ICTs;
- a utilisation of the capabilities of the ICT marketplace;
- a matched use of ICTs with the needs of the organisation.

It is essential to establish a partnership between the information systems and communications function and senior executives. The DP/IS Department must have a competent and talented team if it is to deliver what it promises and if it is to keep the business in the manner and style to which it should be accustomed or has reason to expect. Thus, for example, the DP/IS Department must both be aware of 'strategic' opportunities and make use of fast and evolutionary approaches to building information systems, while simultaneously managing a technology infrastructure which grows ever more complex.

In this discussion, categories of processes include:

INFORMATION SYSTEMS PLANNING
Strategy and overall coordination of existing and future information systems.

INFORMATION SYSTEMS DESIGN
Specification of the systems which the organisation requires to be built.

END USER COMPUTING
The least controlled of the areas, which is characterised by a considerable measure of *ad hoc* activity by individual managers and departments.

SECURITY
Action which can be taken to minimise or avoid the risks from viruses, hackers and so on.

6.2 Information systems planning

Bill Olle *et al.* (1991, page 4) define information systems planning as:

> ... the strategic planning of computerised information systems. The planning is strategic in the sense that it identifies which information systems are needed, rather than planning in detail for any specific system.

It should be made clear that we are considering not just one information system but a population of information systems, some young and some old. At any one time it will be necessary to phase in new systems and to phase out old systems, while maintaining the others. For example, work on the much-cited American Airlines' SABRE customer reservation system, a vital part of that company's day-to-day operations, began in the late 1950's. An enormous and often seemingly disproportionate part of the effort of Data Processing/Information Systems Department's effort and budget goes, and has gone, into maintenance in most organisations.

There are a great number of methodologies and approaches for information systems planning which cannot all be described here because of the confines of space and the overlapping nature of the methodologies. Amongst the better known are:

BUSINESS SYSTEMS PLANNING
A method developed to create top-level commitment and aimed at improving the performance of the DP/IS Department. It is intended primarily to create an integrated corporate database.

STAGES OF GROWTH
This is not really a methodology, but a framework to review the developing sophistication of the use of information systems.

CRITICAL SUCCESS FACTORS
A means of determining the information needs of senior managers with a view to creating the information systems required to control the business. A number of methodologies have been derived from this approach.

PORTFOLIO APPROACH
An approach based on the application of financial or strategic portfolios to information systems.

By and large these methodologies have been *ad hoc* responses to the problems of managing DP/IS Departments. Data processing management has evolved from being a matter of largely technical control exercised over a few programmers and fewer machines into a major management task, spanning the whole organisation and reaching out to clients and suppliers. Ideas and practices have often been absorbed from the other functional areas of management, usually in a somewhat indiscriminate manner.

Business systems planning

Business Systems Planning (BSP) is a well-established methodology developed by IBM for private and public sector organisations. It is a structured approach to planning both short- and long-term information systems requirements, geared towards integrated databases which are intended to serve the organisation as a whole. BSP focuses on conceptualising and designing the overall database, shifting the emphasis from individual programs or suites of applications to data or information.

BSP was established by IBM as a recognised methodology in 1970, though modifications have been made since then. It was based on work carried out by IBM's own internal planning and control group, addressing a serious problem of coordination within 'Big Blue' itself:

> Until the control and planning department was established, IBM had little overall direction in the internal use of computers. In fact, little coordination took place between divisions; most data processing activities were confined to locations and unit within divisions. Consequently, each manufacturing plant and marketing region developed and operated its own system. Although the individual systems carried out similar functions, they differed in design and performance; they could not be used interchangeably and could not communicate with each other. (IBM, 1984, page 2.)

Business Systems Planning is intended to produce a plan which both supports the needs of managers and is related to the overall corporate strategy. It provides a formal and supposedly objective method by which management can establish priorities. The systems which are developed from the plan are intended to have a long life, because they are based on the corporate plan and the needs of business processes and are intended to be relatively insulated from changes to the organisational structure. The aim of using BSP has been to improve the management of resources within the DP/IS Department. If these are well managed then this is likely to increase the confidence with which top managers view their DP/IS Department. If they also meet the needs of middle managers for data for decision-making this will help.

Under the BSP approach, data become a corporate resource which is planned, managed and controlled and is made available to everyone rather than being held exclusively by individuals or departments. This has significant implications in terms of organisational politics in persuading managers to release control of data which might otherwise be seen exclusively as personal or departmental, because it makes a department much more transparent to others.

The stages of the BSP methodology are as follows (though the first two stages are not formally part of the approach):

- gaining the commitment;
- preparing for the study;
- starting the study;
- defining business processes;
- defining business data;
- defining information architecture;
- analysing current systems support;
- interviewing executives;
- defining findings and conclusions;
- determining architecture priorities;
- reviewing information resource management;
- developing recommendations;
- reporting results.

The BSP methodology is aimed at creating an overall information architecture within an organisation, principally intended to take advantage of database technology, as such, it is data-orientated. It is well documented and is presented by IBM in a way in which it can be implemented. However, in some senses BSP is idealistic, in that it assumes that an organisation can build a vast and integrated corporate database. In reality such an effort would have to be gradual and incremental. Reflecting its origins in IBM, BSP is designed for centralised and standardised environments. There is little in the original methodology to help an organisation if its computing resource has become organisationally or physically decentralised; in an age of growing decentralisation, this is a severe limitation.

Stages of growth

The 'stages of growth' framework was developed to help communication between DP/IS managers and top managers (see also Chapter 4). It was originally intended to have a predictive value:

> Here is a convenient categorisation for placing the life crises of the EDP department in perspective, for developing the management techniques necessary or useful at various points, and for managing the human issues involved. (Gibson & Nolan, 1974, page 76.)

The stages of growth model was to help improve the management of the function through a categorisation of activities on an S-shaped learning curve. S-shaped curves have become commonplace as representations of learning or at least sequential development in management. The 'turning points' on the curve represent 'crises' in the DP department which signalled shifts in the way the computer resource was used. The characteristics of the original four stages were believed to have distinctive organisational processes, requiring particular styles of management and a particular set of staff skills.

COST-REDUCTION
Accounting applications such as payroll, sales and purchase ledgers, billing, etc.

PROLIFERATION
Expansion into all functional areas such as general ledger, budgeting, forecasting, personnel and stock.

MORATORIUM
Emphasis on control of new applications.

DATABASE
Integration of data into databases and on-line systems for query and data entry.

After the four stages, it was believed more, as yet unknown, stages would follow. In 1979, Richard Nolan published a revised version with a six stage model. One important change was that the vertical axis of the diagram was now labelled 'expenditure on data processing'. The stages were:

- initiation;
- contagion;
- control;
- integration;
- data administration;
- maturity.

Nolan identified one particularly important transition in the new set of stages:

Sometimes in stage three, therefore, one can observe a basic shift in orientation from management of the computer to management of the company's data resources. This shift in orientation is a direct result of analyses about how-to put more emphasis, in expanding DP activities, on the needs of management control and planning as opposed to the needs of consolidation and coordination in the DP activities themselves. (Nolan, 1979, page 118.)

Guidelines were formulated for action based on the model. The first was to recognise the fundamental organisational transformation from the management of computers to 'data resource management', in which the technologies are seen as 'enablers' and their value recognised as such.

The model was not intended to imply that an organisation is at a single point on the curve. In a large organisation, the various divisions are likely to be at different points. Recognising this fact, it is necessary to manage them accordingly; though this did not imply attempting to level them up or down. Nolan formulated guidelines for action:

- recognise the fundamental organisation transformation from computer management to data resource management;
- appreciate the importance of the enabling technologies;
- identify the stages of the company's operating units to help keep data processing activities on track;
- develop a multi-level strategy and plan;
- make the steering committee work.

Richard Nolan faced difficulties in sustaining and adapting his model with a growing diversity of technologies and applications. While the data processing world still comprised only mainframe computers everything was potentially manageable. However, as minicomputers, personal computers, workstations and other systems proliferated, his model simply could not be modified to cope. Perhaps the most serious undermining of the model came from the changes in management, many business units and departments began to manage their own DP/IS resources and so created their own learning curves, which could not easily be related to the core of corporate learning in the DP/IS Department.

Critical success factors

The Critical Success Factors (CSFs) methodology was devised by John Rockart of the Sloan School of Management at Massachusetts Institute of Technology (MIT) and was first published in 1979. This methodology was originally intended for use by information systems managers in responding to the needs of top managers, by addressing the problems encountered with the approaches then in use, which were categorised as:

NULL APPROACH

Acceptance of the diverse, changing and unpredictable needs of CEOs followed by capitulation — doing nothing.

BY-PRODUCT

Information for managers was generated as a by-product of transaction processing with little attention to information needs, illustrated by the traditional long computer printout.

TOTAL STUDY

The reverse of the by-product approach, a comprehensive approach to identify information needs, for example, Business Systems Planning.

KEY INDICATOR
The use of information systems to generate exception reports on specified key performance indicators.

The CSFs approach enables senior managers to express their needs in terms of the few factors that were absolutely critical to the performance of their jobs. Rockart defines Critical Success Factors as:

... for any business, the limited number of areas in which results, if they are satisfactory, will ensure successful competitive performance for the organisation. They are the few areas where 'things must go right' for the business to flourish. (Rockart, 1979, page 85.)

CSFs are derived from the considerations of strategic management: the industry structure, competitive strategy, industry position, business environment and so on. The information systems manager could use the CSFs to propose information systems which would meet the needs of the senior manager.

Let me stress that the CSF approach does not attempt to deal with information needs for strategic planning. Data needs for this management role are almost impossible to preplan. The CSF method centres, rather, on information needs for management control where data needed to monitor and improve existing areas of business can be more readily defined. (Rockart, 1979, page 88.)

The CSFs methodology was necessary because of the recognition of the chasm between 'general' managers in a business and managers in the DP/IS Department, which could be represented as follows:

Managers	DP/IS Managers
Little knowledge of IS	Little knowledge of business
Limited ability to express requirements	Need for detailed specifications
Business orientation	Technical orientation

CSFs are intended to give guidance and not to provide detailed development plans. To succeed, the Critical Success Factors which are identified should be:

- intelligible to senior executives;
- intelligible to IS/DP managers;
- possible to act on.

The CSFs methodology was subsequently extended to cover the more general task of planning all the information systems for an organisation and even used to assess the job of as DP/IS manager.

Case: CSFs for a business school

Scenario: Faced with increasing competition it is essential for Business Schools to identify and act on their Critical Success Factors.

The increasing competition in the provision of management education and development means that the nature of business schools has changed dramatically during the 1980's and this trend is likely to continue through the 1990's. What are the fundamental requirements, Critical Success Factors, that are essential for business schools?

As Head of a School of Management with an international reputation for management education and development, one of the authors has the responsibility to ensure its continued development. The Bath School of Management exists to advance the understanding of management in all types of organisations and to enhance the managerial effectiveness of organisations and their people. To be recognised by academics and business people as a global leader, the Bath School of Management pursues excellence both in innovative applied research and in useful, relevant and thorough teaching. Bath's School of Management:

- is positioned as an international leader in management education and development;
- is recognised as research-led;
- is known for innovation and quality;
- works with major organisations world-wide in partnerships for mutual development;
- operates efficiently and effectively to ensure the future of its customers and our own people.

Critical Success Factors, which can be thought of as a business strategy tool, must be linked to the School's objectives (which can and do change over time). There should not be too many CSFs for each objective, and a number may recur with different objectives.

The following Critical Success Factors are important:

- retaining, attracting and developing high-quality people;
- maintaining and improving customer service;
- ensuring effective management of the School in the wider context of the University;
- developing long-term partnerships with a range of organisations.

> As Dr Samuel Johnson remarked,
>
> Let me counsel you not to waste your health in inappropriate sorrow, but go to Bath and endeavour to prolong your life.

Portfolio approach

The Portfolio Approach was adapted by Warren McFarlan from the use of financial portfolios, with the intention of spreading the risks in information systems projects. It addresses the problems caused by the historical failure of DP/IS managers to assess the risks associated with individual projects and the aggregate risks of their complete set of projects, considering how the risk of different projects should be managed based on the nature of the risk involved.

The risks which arise from information systems projects are:

- failure to obtain forecast benefits;
- costs vastly over planned expenditure;
- implementation time greatly exceeded;
- technical performance significantly below expectation;
- incompatibility with existing hardware and software
- neglect of training requirements.

The extent of these risks are a function of the size of the project, the experience of the team working on the project and the structure of the work. In theory, the risk of a project declines as the project proceeds (assuming professional project management). Given that any project has a risk of complete or partial failure, the key question is whether the benefits outweigh the risks. If development of the system fails, how significantly will the organisation be affected?

> In addition to determining relative risk for single projects, a company should develop an aggregate risk profile of the portfolio of systems and programming projects. While there is no such thing as a correct risk profile in the abstract, there are appropriate risk profiles for different type of companies and strategies. (McFarlan, 1981, page 144.)

The keys to project management which McFarlan identifies are:

EXTERNAL INTEGRATION
To communicate between the project team and the user management and user community.

INTERNAL INTEGRATION
To ensure teamwork.

FORMAL PLANNING
To provide a structure and sequence to the tasks, including the allocation of resources.

FORMAL CONTROL
To measure the success or failure of progress.

6.3 Information systems design

Having decided in general what information is needed, it is necessary to translate these requirements into a set of design specifications which can be handed over to the 'builders'. The construction of information systems is amongst the largest and most complex tasks undertaken in business and has come to rival large-scale civil engineering projects for its record of running over time and over budget, which is often aggravated by delivering something markedly different from what the customer expected. These problems arise from the complexity and expense of information systems projects, together with the poor productivity of DP/IS Departments. The real solution lies in organisational learning, rather than yet more technology, through the development of methodologies formalising knowledge and experience from previous projects. Methodologies help in the division of labour and to provide a mechanism for quality control. The methodologies used in information systems design can be grouped as follows:

- programming development;
- software engineering;
- systems analysis and design;
- human computer interaction.

Information engineering is a term increasingly being used to describe the activities of building and maintaining information systems reflecting the fact that the practices have become formalised. Information engineering ought to be the application of 'information science', but in the absence of that, it relies on codification of empirical knowledge, which places it in the craft tradition.

The traditional view of managing software development has been of a 'life-cycle' model comprising a number of stages. These models have evolved over the years through the following:

- code and fix;
- waterfall model;
- evolutionary development;
- formal specification.

By the mid-1950's, it was realised that the 'code and fix' approach was impractical for projects of any size, it was just too complicated to delve back into machine code or assembler written by someone else and modify it. This led to models based on stages of development, such as the waterfall model, dating from 1970, shown in figure 6.1. A later modification of this approach was based on a spiral (see figure 6.2) which allowed for the iterative nature of the software production process.

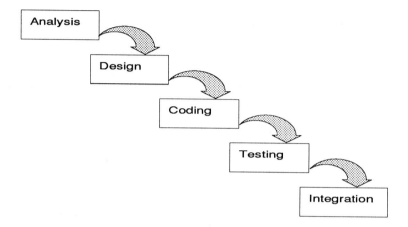

Figure 6.1 *The waterfall model of the software life cycle*

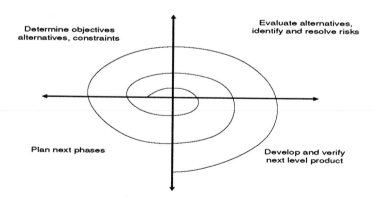

Figure 6.2 *The spiral model of the software life cycle*

By describing a linear model, it is to be inferred that each process is complete and discrete, that is when one stage is finished the output is fed to the next stage and so on. However, the waterfall and spiral life-cycle approaches contain a number of misleading or wrong assumptions which:

- give a false sense of certainty and do not adequately represent the high level of changes;
- imply a uniform and orderly sequence of activities;
- cannot easily accommodate rapid prototyping and the use of advanced languages;
- provide insufficient detail to allow optimisation of the process.

The development of software is not a simple unidirectional process. Implementation will always have effects on the design, if it does not, then there is no learning going on. By adopting an inappropriate model for the development of software, management of the processes will be wrong and the planning and tracking will be biased and misleading.

The idea of 'evolutionary development' introduced improved development tools, such as fourth generation languages (4GL's), to tackle the problem of users being unable to specify exactly what they wanted. The difficulty with the evolutionary process is that it is by no means certain to close; a final product may never emerge as users think up clever new ideas which they want incorporated into the system. Evolutionary development fails to address the root cause of vague user requirements, though it makes it easier to realise their changing wishes.

Prototyping was developed to allow the user to be shown the system being requested, within a short period of time, perhaps even immediately. Traditionally, analysts had gone away, written up a specification, had it coded and months or years could go by before the user saw the result. By that stage making any changes was difficult, expensive and slow. A rapidly produced prototype allows the user to see what is being specified and to revise the design interactively. Therefore, the design is more likely to be complete and less likely to contain facilities which are difficult to use. Table 6.1 lists some of the software tools used for prototyping.

Table 6.1 *Prototyping systems*

Language	Type	Applications
Smalltalk	Object-oriented	User interfaces
PROLOG	Logic	Symbolic processing
LISP	Functional	Symbolic processing
APL	Mathematical	Scientific
4GLs	Database	Business DP

'Formal specifications' were developed to avoid some of the problems with iterative software development. The specification could be developed iteratively, but it was to be converted automatically into runnable code. The growth in formal techniques has focused on ways of devising specifications which are provably correct, in some mathematical sense, using a language based on algebra. Examples of languages for formal specifications include Z (Oxford University) and IBM's VDM (Vienna Development Method). For each type of application a different formal specification language is likely to be appropriate, for example, LOTOS is used for communications systems. The objectives associated with the use of these techniques include:

- enabling the writing of unambiguous, clear and precise descriptions;
- allowing descriptions to be verified formally for consistency and correctness.

One of the main attractions of the formal specification approach is that it forces an analysis of the system requirements at a very early stage, thus avoiding alterations at later stages where modifications become more difficult and more expensive.

Object-Oriented Design (OOD) uses a model of software as collections of cooperating objects and complements Object-Oriented Programming (OOP). OOD decomposes a system into objects and messages, in a way which is intended to be incremental, rather than as a one-off monolithic approach of many other approaches.

Project management is a vital key to improving the development of systems and supporting software which will help in managing large software projects. Standalone software, such as Hoskyns' Project Manager Workbench, has been developed to support project management, using techniques such as Gantt charts, while project management software has also been integrated into most CASE tools. The techniques include:

- highlighting overloading and broken dependencies;
- what-if;
- automatic scheduling;
- costing;
- projects within projects;
- aggregation of multiple projects.

The key issues for the management of software development lie in optimising the process and in developing the ability of the organisation to learn. Adopting inappropriate models will simply lead to wrong expectations and so make the management of an already complex task more difficult. The cost of making alterations at the specification stage is much less than modifying the completed programs; it is also much more likely to satisfy the needs of users. Therefore developments in new specification techniques and software to support the development of software must be exploited. It also is important to remember that the training and socio-organisational costs of adopting these new techniques must not be forgotten.

Programming development

From the original 'hand-crafted' or do-it-yourself style of programming more systematic approaches have been developed. In order to improve the productivity and the reliability of the 'code' generated by programmers, more rigourous approaches were developed to programming languages and to the construction, layout and documentation of computer programs. The aim has to be to produce 'industrial-strength' software, which is an irreducibly complex task, especially when exhaustive testing is almost certainly impossible.

Computers operate by means of electronic switches with two positions, on and off, which can be seen as the mathematical symbols 1 and 0. In this way a computer can represent binary numbers and, by 'moving' the switches, can perform operations of addition, subtraction, multiplication and division. Initially programs and data had to be manipulated in binary, in what is known as machine language. However, working in binary is extremely tedious and a number of approaches to writing programming languages were developed. Five generations of programming languages are usually recognised:

FIRST GENERATION
Machine language in binary requires detailed knowledge of the design and operation of the chips and must be programmed in minute detail.

SECOND GENERATION
Converts from very basic and machine specific mnemonics into machine language. Assembler languages are still used for some work where machine efficiency is very important.

THIRD GENERATION
Programming with single statements converting into several instructions in machine language, using compilers. International standards were developed for FORTRAN, COBOL, Ada, and so on, making the programs less machine specific.

FOURTH GENERATION
Fourth Generation Languages (4GLs) continue the separation from the hardware, allowing the programmer to concentrate on the particular application. The operation is specified and not the details of how it is to be carried out. 4GLs allow faster development of applications software by the use of pseudo-English, for example, Informix and PowerHouse.

FIFTH GENERATION
Artificial intelligence, such as Lisp and Prolog. However, the definition is far from precise, having been the subject of considerable 'hyping'.

Over the years, there have been major changes in the appearance of programs. It is now recognised that programs are read more often than they are written, therefore, more attention is being paid to their readability. In the 1950's and 1960's the prime concern was to optimise the use of the computer, even at the expense of the time of programmers. From this a culture of writing machine efficient 'code' emerged, which was generally so terse as to be almost unreadable, at least by programmers not intimately involved with the particular application. In readable code, names are meaningful and are related to the real world entities they represent:

```
program Convert_Centigrade_To_Fahrenheit(input,output);
    var Fahrenheit, Centigrade : real;
begin
    read(Centigrade);
    Fahrenheit := Centigrade*9/5 + 32;
    write(Fahrenheit);
end.
```

Layout conventions are now standardised within departments and in particular on large scale projects; the particular details do not matter. Indentation, as in the above example, makes it clear how lines of the program are grouped together. Text annotation has been increased to help anyone trying to read the code, by explaining the purpose of operations and the names of variables.

Software quality is not significantly different from quality management in other areas of a business, from which a number of lessons can be learned (see, for example, Garvin, 1988). It is particularly difficult to spot 'bugs' in programs because of the complexity of software and the number of possible interactions between different pieces of software; faults often show up only intermittently or only after a particular sequence of operations have been performed. Nonetheless, quality management techniques are being applied successfully to the production of software. Like other forms of quality management, software quality is much more than verification and validation; it includes:

- maintainability;
- reliability;
- portability.

For each project particular attributes can be selected and performance measures set. The level of 'reliability' required is set out in the systems requirement specification, which might include:

- probability of failure on demand;
- rate of fault occurrence;
- mean time to failure;
- availability.

In real-time applications, there is an important requirement for high levels of reliability; a system absolutely must respond to external events, termed 'exceptions'. It is therefore essential that the handling of these exceptions is planned in the writing of the programs and not left to an operating system routine.

Object-Oriented Programming (OOP) was developed at Xerox's Palo Alto Research Center (PARC) in the form of the Smalltalk language. It is a method of implementation of in which programs are organised as a collection of cooperating objects, each representing an occurrence of a class, each class being a member of a hierarchy of classes, linked by inheritance relationships. An object is an occurrence of a class which has a state (a set of properties and their values), behaviour (how it reacts in terms of changes of state and passing messages) and identity (unique properties which distinguish it from all other objects). Messages are passed between objects which perform one or more of the permitted state changes and may pass a message to another object. The development of this hierarchy of classes is based on classification, in clustering together objects and processes. The most obvious attraction of object oriented programming languages, such as C++, is that objects can be retained and re-used in other programs.

Software portability is the ability to take software developed on one system and run it on another system. This can be achieved by the emulation of one system on another. For example, in the introduction of the ICL 2900 mainframe series in the early 1970's, the hardware allowed users to run applications developed on the earlier 1900 series. Emulation is only ever likely to be a temporary measure, to permit a move, which was not necessarily expected. If portability is to be designed into a program, then the program must be written in an abstract language which can be compiled on a number of machines. Ideally, the program should be self-contained, it should not rely on operations being performed directly by the operating system or hardware, however, complete independence is almost impossible to achieve. The more self-contained a piece of software is, the more easily it can be moved to another system. It will also be easier to adjust to the next version of the operating system and to any changes in the hardware.

The re-use of software has become important in recent years as it provides an effective way of containing costs and reducing the risks associated with software development. In the past, many of the basic operations, such as screen handling (for example, drawing forms on the screen), were rewritten for each program. The aims of re-use are:

- to increase overall systems reliability;
- to reduce overall project risk;
- to improve use of specialists;
- to embody organisational standards in re-usable components;
- to reduce software development time.

Of course, it is necessary to convince programmers to use libraries of software modules and programs, rather than write their own. This task may not be easy, because programmers often believe that they are better than their colleagues.

Systems analysis and design

Information systems methodologies are used to produce specifications or designs of systems which require to be built. The processes of analysis usually precede the design. Following the success of structured approaches in improving program quality, more rigourous approaches have been developed for systems analysis. Today, systems development is well supported by reliable and proven methodologies for investigation, analysis, design and implementation. These address issues such as overall planning, quality management and project management using well-established techniques including data flow diagrams and entity-relationship models. In a particular instance, a systems methodology is successful if the system produced is used as specified. It is judged a failure if it is:

- never delivered;
- abandoned;
- re-developed;
- delivered and never used;
- used only after modification.

The output of the design must be agreed by the designer with the user, either a group or an individual who represents a group of users. Responsibility for software management can be divided between a number of roles, not necessarily corresponding to individual members of staff, which would include:

RESPONSIBLE EXECUTIVE
The person responsible to the senior management for the successful progress and completion of overall information systems project.

DEVELOPMENT COORDINATOR
Coordination of the people and groups involved in the design and construction of the information system.

SYSTEMS ANALYST
A person responsible for all or elements of the analysis of the part(s) of the business for which the design is concerned.

DESIGNER
A person responsible for preparing the design specification.

USER'S ACCEPTOR
A representative of the users or the responsible executive who approves specifications, before construction begins.

USER
Someone who will use the information system once it is built.

RESOURCE MANAGER
A manager responsible for ensuring the necessary resources are available to ensure that the design process is performed properly.

At a level much lower than would be suitable for Critical Success Factors, it is necessary to elicit data and information regarding business processes. The following systems analysis techniques are commonly used, though they are not exclusive to systems analysis and are also found in many areas of research:

INTERVIEWS

These have the advantage of providing large amounts of information which can be of a high quality. However, this is eventually its downfall, it may provide too much information.

QUESTIONNAIRES

These can be a solution to obtaining opinions from large groups of individuals. Of course, it is not necessary to ask all the individuals concerned, since it is possible to construct representative samples.

DOCUMENT ANALYSIS

This is an important and relatively straightforward technique which involves looking at existing procedures through existing documents. However, on its own it can be very dangerous. Procedures change repeatedly and this is not always reflected in forms and reports. It is necessary to discuss with staff how they use the documents and how they would like the processes to be improved.

Three perspectives can be identified as providing the rationale for systems analysis methodologies:

- process-oriented;
- data-oriented;
- behaviour-oriented.

The process-oriented perspective was the first to be developed. It arose from the perception of computers as a cost effective way of performing well-defined business processes, for example, pay-rolls and sales ledgers. It was necessary to analyse how the task was performed in order to represent this in the programming languages available at the time, for example, assembler or COBOL. The intention was to reduce a business activity into a sequence of tasks which could be written as a computer program.

The data-oriented perspective arose as a result of the development of databases in the mid-1960's and in that sense it too was technology driven. It is 'opposed' to the process perspective, since it is argued that what is required is a complete and thorough analysis of the data and the relationships between the data. Originally, this was closely related to access paths in the software, but improvements in the technology have removed this constraint. It is prescriptive, but is independent of construction and performance; it provides a logical database design.

The behaviour-oriented perspective does not refer to human behaviour, but to the 'behaviour' of systems which respond to events in the real world. For example, a process control system must take into account events as they occur in the chemical plant. A behavioural approach is therefore one concerned with responding to stimuli, rather than the mere processing of data.

The aim of the design phase of a methodology is to produce a specification which is:

- specific;
- complete;
- unambiguous;
- non-contradictory;
- clear;
- concise.

For these purposes, English is too vague and ambiguous, while the more precise jargon and formal specification techniques of systems specialists are unintelligible to managers. The compromise is often to use two well-established techniques which overcome the problems of communication: data flow diagrams and entity-relationship models.

Data Flow Diagrams (DFDs) contain three categories of object in addition to data flows themselves:

EXTERNAL ENTITIES
Real world objects external to the system being modelled.

PROCESSES
Specific operations performed on data: arithmetic, sorting, logical and so on.

DATA STORES
Files where data are held pending processing.

Figure 6.3 shows the symbols used to represent data flows in one of the variety of representations commonly used. Data flow diagrams are closely related to the flow diagrams which have been used in programming for many years. DFDs are a mathematical language to represent the manipulation of data.

Figures 6.4 and 6.5 show an example for a conventional information system in customer order processing. One of the attractions of data flow diagrams is the ability to represent limited and controlled amounts of detail. For instance, in figure 6.5 we can see the overall picture of customer order processing and in figure 6.6 we see the order entry process in more detail.

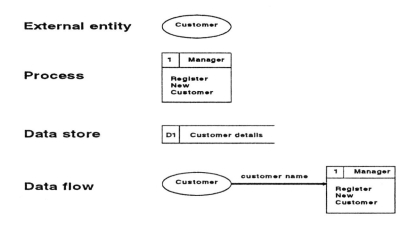

Figure 6.3 *Symbols used in data flow diagrams*

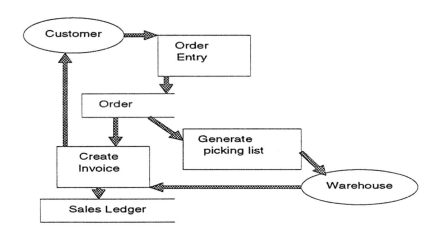

Figure 6.4 *Data flow diagram — level one*

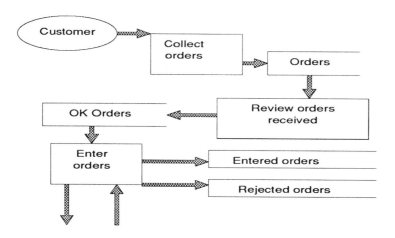

Figure 6.5 *Data flow diagram — level two*

In describing processes with DFDs, there is a problem of showing levels of details. The practice is to use 'functional decomposition', which is to use a number of levels of DFDs, so that at one level a process is represented by a single box, which at a lower level will be shown as a number of boxes. These levels are used to keep the detail in any one diagram within manageable and comprehensible limits, even if this results in unevenness in the number of levels used. The key consideration is that they be understandable by the user who is finally asked to 'sign off' the diagrams. Unfortunately there are no rules for functional decomposition, it is up to the participants to define the extent to which they divide up the details.

The second major technique used is the Entity-Relationship Model (ERM). An entity is a logical group of data items which have inter-relationships. An entity model reflects the logic of the data in the system and not the physical implementation of the data storage; entities are independent of current processing. These provide a system view of data structures and data relationships within the system. The following are examples of entities, students and books together with their attributes.

Three types of relationship are permitted between entities:

1:1	One-to-one	Student to ID Number
		Book to Registration Number
1:N	One-to-many	Student to addresses
		Book to Authors
N:M	Many-to-many	Students to Courses
		Books to Classifications

Table 6.2 *Examples of entity relationships*

Entity Type	Attribute List	Example
Student	Name	Millar, John
	Home Address	The Manse, Barra
	Term Address	MacBrayne Hall
	Telephone Number	041-339 8855
	Identification Number	92-0102036
	Degree Programme	BA Marketing
	Courses	4015, 45M5, 45E5
Book	Author	Smith, Adam
	Title	The Wealth of Nations
	Publisher	Strahan and Cadell
	Date	1776
	Size	22cm
	Classification	Economics
	Registration number	0121369

For the purposes of documentation a graphical representation of ERMs is used. Figure 6.7 shows part of a customer order system. There are a number of variations of the notation for ERMs, which are of significance only to the practitioner.

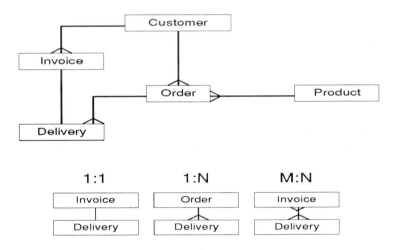

Figure 6.6 *Entity relationship diagram*

Entity-relationship models are used to complement Data Flow Diagrams. For example, in figure 6.6, the relationships between customers, orders and so on are shown. Data items can only be created and destroyed by events defined in an entity life histories. For example, figure 6.7 shows the entity life history of a customer account for a mortgage.

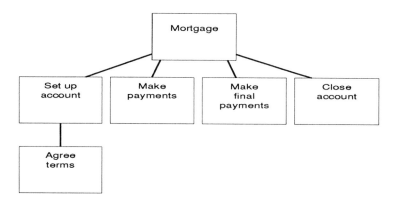

Figure 6.8 *An example of an entity life history*

Cross-references between the different models and their diagrams are extremely useful in verification tests. The final test of these diagrams comes in the walk-through which is the process of discussing with the users or their representatives. All the models and flow diagrams produced in the systems analysis process are presented and once agreed can be 'signed-off' by the users, allowing construction to commence.

SSADM

The Central Computer and Telecommunications Agency (CCTA), the UK Government's ICT consultants, has been responsible for the creation of a methodology known as Structured Systems Analysis and Design Methodology (SSADM). The intention behind the creation of SSADM was to provide a methodology for use in contracts with government and to make that methodology available to government, both central and local, and to businesses, in the hope that it would be widely adopted in commercial work. In order to increase the commercial adoption, the methodology was assigned to Learmonth and Burchett Management Systems (LBMS), a firm of management consultants, under contract to the government. Since its original launch in 1981, SSADM has undergone significant revision, again by consultants, and the fourth version was released in June 1990.

The reasons for wanting a methodology for systems analysis and design arose from serious problems in a number of government information systems projects. Although government seemed to be having more problems than commerce, the basic causes were the same:

- complexity;
- expense;
- overrun;

- poor productivity;
- failure of delivered systems to perform.

To counter this, SSADM was intended to provide:

- user involvement
- quality management
- separate logical and physical specifications.

Figure 6.8 shows the major stages of the SSADM methodology and makes clear the distinction between logical and physical design.

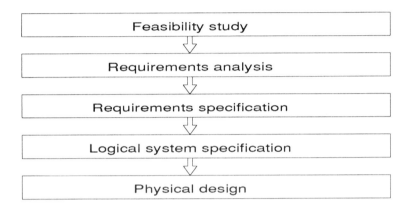

Figure 6.8 *The stages of SSADM*

SSADM is a fairly conventional systems analysis and design methodology. It is widely recognised as a good compromise between the data-oriented approach and the process-oriented approach. The multiple views it incorporates allow cross-checks to made on the validity of the analysis. SSADM is very well supported by books and courses. (Ashworth and Goodland, 1990.)

Software engineering

As early as 1968 the term 'software engineering' had been coined to describe the introduction of engineering techniques which were adopted in order to improve productivity, maintainability and reliability while optimising the use of system resources. 'Bugs', errors in computer programs, are always present, perhaps fifty or sixty serious bugs in every 1000 lines of computer program. (In the very early days, a computer comprised an open framework of components, allowing insects to enter and lodge in the circuitry. A bug short-circuited one of the early mainframe computers and the name has stuck!)

A major factor in the drive for improved productivity has been the shortage of people and particularly skilled people, especially in the face of a seemingly endless growth in demand for computer programs.

Considerable successes have been achieved through the use of Computer Aided Software Engineering or Systems Engineering (CASE), a term coined in 1981. CASE tools automate and support the functions of a development team, for example, ICL Quickbuild and Oracle CASE*Designer. Given the concern for automation they focus, almost inevitably, on routine and prescriptive tasks. These computer programs allow:

- creation and editing of diagrams such as data flow diagrams;
- simultaneous manipulation of several diagrams in different windows;
- automatic verification of diagrams;
- data modelling from a data dictionary;
- generation of inputs into and sometimes drafts of subsequent parts of the design product (such as report layouts);
- links to software for project management, performance evaluation and so on.

In most CASE tools, it is possible to do some prototyping. An important attraction of CASE tools is in the management of the documentation process.

Case: Coopers and Lybrand: CASE Tools

Scenario: Coopers and Lybrand is an international management consulting practice which wanted to select CASE tools for its own work in developing information systems for clients.

Coopers and Lybrand is a large accountancy-based international management consultancy operating in the UK as Coopers and Lybrand Deloitte. A part of the consulting work undertaken by Coopers is in the area of information systems. They have two methodologies for information systems: SUMMIT-S for strategic planning and SUMMIT-D for systems delivery.

The reasons for wanting to use CASE tools were to improve:

- systems delivery capability;
- sales and marketing capability;
- target key industries;
- large project capability and capacity.

An international task force was established to evaluate over two hundred CASE tools based on a common set of evaluation objectives from the two methodologies.

Coopers were not only seeking products, but also a partnership with the supplier and therefore vendor characteristics were seen as important.

The supplier would have to be international, financially viable and credible with Coopers' largest clients. In addition to a good product, they would have to possess the ability to develop that product over a number of years, requiring both vision and expenditure on research and development.

The features used for the evaluations included:

- quality of output and documentation;
- ease of 'navigation';
- speed of processing;
- levels of integration;
- modelling and graphics capability;
- security features;
- productivity;
- analysis and functional completeness;
- workgroup support
- maintainability of generated code;
- overall ease-of-use;
- learning curves;
- documentation.

From the 200 candidates, a list of twenty potential systems was drawn up. A process of interviews and assessment reduced this to a short-list of four vendors who were invited to attend a five day laboratory session at East Windsor in New Jersey.

An important issue for a large consulting group such as Coopers is its ability to meet the requirements of customers to use methods approved by IBM. Thus any CASE tool had to be able to support IBM's Application Development Cycle (AD/Cycle), or the supplier had to be willing to commit to developing such support.

The CASE marketplace and the products tested in 1989 were felt to be immature, but that enormous progress was being made in terms of product integration and re-engineering.

Source: Glen Strange in Spurr and Layzell, 1990.

The productivity improvements which CASE offers, arise from an ability to:

- motivate people;
- make steps more efficient;
- eliminate steps;
- eliminate re-work;
- build simpler products;
- use bigger components.

However, there are significant organisational issues which must be addressed if these benefits are to be achieved. CASE tools are not a miracle cure, they need to be planned and implemented systematically, taking into account the changes they imply for the organisation and for the people who must work with them. As a minimum, they imply a significant shift in the skills required in DP/IS Departments and in the attitudes of the staff.

Case: First Direct

Scenario: Management Information Systems were required to support a new strategic thrust in banking.

Midland Bank identified a 'niche' in the market for banking without bank branches, one which operated by means of telephone, post and Automatic Teller Machines (ATMs), which required to be supported by new computer-based information systems:

... customers are paying for the people and the bricks and mortar of the branch even though they hardly use the services of the branch at all.

The intention of creating First Direct was to minimise cost both by eliminating branches and by reducing costs in processing information. The bank is a single 'branch', which creates problems of data handling, for example, the daily print-out of overdraft information is of a scale unknown to branch managers.

The information systems were expected to change regularly, therefore a development environment was required which would allow the applications to be reviewed and modified:

The key for us was to be able to make application changes as quickly as possible without jeopardising the other fundamental parts of the operation. (Kevin Newman, IT and Banking Operations Director.)

This was necessary because the number of customers would expand and new ways of handling accounts would be found. Analysis of data patterns would be important to developing new services and new practices. Changes in economic patterns would cause the banking behaviours of clients to alter and would require changes in decision making and/or products and services:

> The system was in use for only two weeks and we had already identified 14 ways to improve it.
>
> First Direct chose KnowledgeWare's Information Engineering Workbench (IEW) as its CASE tool. This allowed staff to go into the information systems, locate where the change had to be made and improve the system very quickly using a personal computer. The person changing the system could fully understand the knock-on effects of the change being made.
>
> There has been an important change in staff behaviour; they are now encouraged to suggest changes. This became practicable, because they can be implemented rapidly.
>
> First Direct has an IBM central database using CICS, DB2 and COBOL with a transaction processing systems from Unisys and a telephone support system from Sequoia.
>
> The company was able to recruit staff both through financial packages and through the opportunity to work with the latest CASE technology.
>
> At the end of 1990, the system comprised 36 batch programs, ranging in size from 5,000 to 40,000 lines and 24 on-line programs. All the code was either generated directly from IEW or from information generated by IEW. There were very few problems because of the high quality of the analysis which IEW supported and the programs generated.
>
> Source: KnowledgeWare Application Profile.

The idea of the Integrated Project System Environment (IPSE) came from the work on the Ada programming language, for example, BIS/IPSE and ESPRIT PCTE (Portable Common Tools Environment). IPSEs are intended to cover an entire project rather than just a single activity, supporting:

- systems life-cycle;
- complete projects;
- whole teams.

Re-engineering software

Re-engineering is the authorised logical conversion of assembler source code or other older programs to a contemporary and commercial compiler-based language. The need for such reconstruction arises from the vast numbers of existing programs, which require constantly to be maintained and upgraded. For example, it is estimated that there are over 75 billion lines of COBOL programs in use worldwide. Many of the existing programs are poorly documented or not documented at all. The need for re-engineering is generally recognised for code which is:

- over seven years old;
- overly complex;
- written for a previous generation of hardware;
- contains hard-coded parameters;
- contains very large modules.

Case: Federal Aviation Administration

Scenario: In 1986-87 a system was re-engineered from one originally written in the 1960's in assembler language.

As part of a plan to upgrade the air traffic control systems in the USA, the Federal Aviation Administration (FAA) issued a contract for the upgrading of the real-time terminal approach and control system (TRACON). The original TRACON system had been written in the 1960's in 16-bit ULTRA assembler code to run on a UNIVAC computer. Ultra offered neither macro facilities nor did it support structured programming. TRACON was to be documented and converted into a compiler language with the resultant code functionally identical and directly traceable to the pre-existing code. It was to eliminate customised system components and the new code was to be reliable and to be easy to modify and extend.

53,000 lines of source code were converted into 83,000 lines of Pascal, of which 62% were comments, representing 340 Pascal procedures. This comprised 8,000 lines for the tracker system, 7,000 for the workstations, 3,000 for the operational database, 13,000 for support software and 22,000 lines for database specifications and the database containing site information.

The system was specified in Ada process design language and written in Pascal running on an IBM System/370 mainframe running the MVS operating system. The tools used included an interactive editor and library manager, executive software, a relational database management system (SQL) and an automated document preparation package. Pascal was chosen in preference to Ada, the FAA specified language for large projects, because the team had experience of Pascal but not of Ada (the languages are similar in many respects). Three teams undertook the work, comprising a total of twenty-five people.

Source: Britcher, 1990.

Facilities management

The section on Information Systems Design implied that the organisation requiring an information system would identify the need, build the system, then use and maintain it. Clearly, this is not always the case, since the organisation has to consider the classic economic question of whether to make or buy. As an alternative to operating and maintaining all of its own ICT systems an organisation can use 'Facilities Management' (FM), that is to contract out the provision of information and communications services. With the ready availability of high quality telecommunications links, the location of the computer hardware is of little significance, making such arrangement much easier. (More grandly, the Americans refer to the use of external services as 'outsourcing'.)

Contracts for FM specify the levels of service required in terms of day-to-day performance of computer-based information systems and in the development of new systems. It is often necessary to determine the existing service levels and then to apply them or to modify them for the FM contract. Equally it is vital to ensure that penalty clauses are included in the contract to ensure that the supplier maintains the required level of service. One attraction of facilities management is that it can provide access to higher levels of experience in technical areas, especially when staff are scarce.

There are risks of things going wrong, if ICT service are viewed as a resource which can be bought; the appeal to the CEO is often one of cutting costs. Clearly, if ICTs is an area which is directly related to the competitiveness of the organisation, it is dangerous to subcontract it (or at least to lose direct control).

Case: Introduction of the community charge

Scenario: Changes in the tax for local government required the building of many new information systems, presenting major challenges to local government in the United Kingdom.

For a variety of political reasons, the UK Government decided to abolish the 'rates' which was a form of housing tax used to fund local government. The rates had been based on a valuation of each house and was payable by the occupier. The replacement for this became known as the 'Poll Tax', although it was officially called the Community Charge. The Poll Tax was to be paid by every citizen over eighteen years of age, with special reductions for certain categories including students and the poor. In the face of intolerable political opposition, the Government scrapped the Poll Tax and reverted to a form of property tax, known as the Council Tax. To add to the already confusing picture, central government indicated its intention to force local government to put computer services out to tender.

In a relatively short period of time local authorities had to abandon their well-established information systems for the collection of rates and

---

replace them with new systems to support the collection of the Poll Tax. Given the diversity of computer systems in use in local government, many different systems had to be built and run in parallel with previous systems.

The Poll Tax posed special problems, since it required the local authorities to track individuals as they moved around the country. This was aggravated by the legal requirement not to link the registers to existing databases, such as the electoral register or library membership lists. Changes in house ownership are less common than movements of individuals, for example, students moving to and from university. The consequence was that local authorities had, for the first time, to exchange data to reconcile movements.

The new council tax meant that existing investments in on-going efforts had to be scrapped.

Local government in the UK currently spends £800 million annually and this figure is rising. One problem is that with fixed and relatively low salary scales local government finds it difficult to recruit and retain staff, especially in London and the South East of England. Faced with the massive amounts of work necessary to implement the new tax systems, a number of councils put the business out to FM suppliers. The use of shared capacity both to develop new systems and in the overlap periods between the different systems proved particularly helpful.

One of the consequences was that local government recognised the value of collaboration and facilities management in a way they had not do before. In the light of the experience over conversion to the community charge, central government and local government realised the value in developing a single 'national' specification for would be very similar information systems.

6.3 End user computing

The distinguishing feature of End User Computing (EUC) is that it is performed directly with or by end users, hands-on and not by remote IS specialists. The factors encouraging the rapid and seemingly limitless growth of EUC have been:

- availability of high quality easy-to-use software;
- improvements in hardware;
- growing familiarity of the user population;
- use of computers in schools, colleges and universities;
- diffusion from opinion formers;
- increased need for analysis;
- growing backlog of conventional IS projects.

EUC helps fill the gaps left by conventional DP/IS Departments. For example, the ability to take data from the tables of a relational database for insertion into spreadsheets, reports, business graphics and ultimately into documents produced with word processing or desk top publishing software. The categories of use of EUC include:

- accounting, reporting and calculating;
- writing;
- search and retrieval;
- communications;
- presentation;
- planning, scheduling and monitoring;
- analysis;
- remembering;
- processing records;
- learning;
- developing new programs;
- decision-making.
- isolated dedicated workstation;
- extension to a comprehensive DP/IS system;
- integral component of a comprehensive DP/IS system;
- communications computer;
- development computer;
- small, general purpose computer.

One of the problems which arises from EUC is that the benefits often occur in places quite different from the costs and not necessarily related to overall business objectives and the business strategy (see table 6.3).

Table 6.3 *Benefit versus beneficiary*

	Individual	*Organisation*
Effectiveness	Role enhancement	Product/service innovation
Efficiency	Task support	Process automation

(Adapted from Porter in Jarke, 1986, page 63.)

End User Computing can be viewed from a number of different perspectives, including:

IMPLEMENTATION
It is possible to increase the uptake of new technology through support and education.

MARKETING

The user has accepted the idea of the application, the task is steering people towards desirable hardware and software.

OPERATIONAL

Centralised planning and an advisory DP/IS role with more formal standards and cost benefit analyses.

ECONOMIC

Moving from supply to demand for information, where benefits outweigh costs and efficiency criteria.

EUC is a challenge to traditional DP/IS managers, more in an organisational than in a technical sense. There is a considerable loss of control as anybody in the organisation can buy and use computer systems. There is a wider challenge in the organisation from individuals who have access to information and DSS which allow them to interpret data and act on their interpretations. A major issue which arises for policy makers is to ensure control over resources, which inevitably raises political issues. The exclusive control over the purchase of hardware was largely lost years ago, as managers with even the most modest of budgets began to buy PCs and printers. Nonetheless, proliferation needs to be brought under control for reasons of maintenance, support and back-up. Similarly, software needs some degree of control, if only for reasons of training and support. More contentious is the question of ownership of data, duplication of data and, worse still, of inaccurate data, is a significant problem.

Serious risks of errors occur with the adoption of End User Computing. These arise from failures to carry out security measures or other checks which have been built into data processing methodologies. For example, it are uncommon to audit spreadsheets to ensure that the data is accurate and the processing is correct. Equally, it is quite common for users to develop valuable databases and spreadsheet models of which no copies are kept. Despite several decades of adverse comments on the quality of documentation, applications developed by individual users often lack any documentation at all.

One of the themes in the recent general management literature has been an invocation to get out of the office and find out what is happening by meeting customers and by visiting the factory floor. This goes under the term Management By Walking About (MBWA), though it need not be as unsystematic as the title might suggest. The Information Centre is the embodiment of this idea for the IS function, units out in the field, meeting customers and fulfilling their requirements.

An important technical advance has been the availability of software which allows the interactive querying of databases and the generation of reports. This contrasts with the former requirements for a program to be written or modified in order to obtain information from the database.

Case: Helpdesks

Scenario: To support end users, many organisations have developed a 'helpdesk' function.

The strategic significance of (total) customer service is being appreciated increasingly by managers in a range of different organisations. To provide a 'service' requires management, with all its components of leadership, strategy, human resources, infrastructure and monitoring. The 'best' information and communications technologies are no more than a burden on the 'bottom-line', if their users are not supported.

The fundamental purpose of a Help Desk is to resolve efficiently and effectively end-user information system problems to ensure management remains productive. While a Help Desk is established to service colleagues, it is important that the managers are perceived as 'customers'. The Help Desk is a phenomenon of the 1980's, and different organisations are at different stages in their development and use.

A recent survey undertaken by one of the authors on behalf of the British Helpdesk User Group (HUG) provides a summary of the existing Help Desk environment, primarily in large organisations. The majority of the organisations surveyed had operated a Help Desk for over three years, and recurrent factors behind their establishment include:

• centralise problem resolution;
• change to a service image;
• co-ordinate problem tracking.

It is interesting to note that, given a Help Desk exists for end users, the involvement of users in the specification and development of the Help Desk only occurred in a third of the organisations. The evidence indicates that Help Desks comprise a variety of hardware and software; the use of generic software is important, and the internal development of bespoke software by many organisations is also significant. (There appears to be some interest in recent technological developments, such as artificial intelligence and voice recognition.)

The majority of respondents (who were Help Desk managers) believed the existing manning levels were 'adequate', 'good', or 'very good'. Figure 6.9 summarises the weekly and diurnal patterns for Help Desk manning. The vast majority of organisations believed the number of calls was increasing. Over 80 percent of incoming calls are logged (with only about a third of outgoing calls logged), with, on average, over half of the problems being solved immediately.

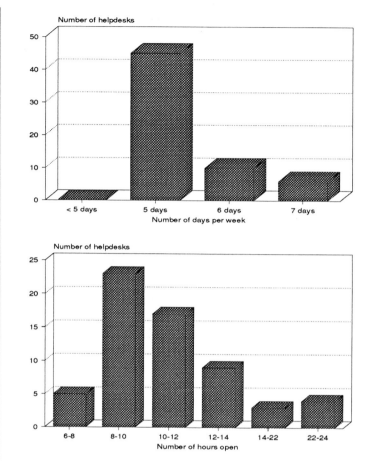

Figure 6.9 *Days and hours when help desks are open*

Four themes, all consistent with the practice of information resource management, were identified as ways of improving the Help Desk service:

- a clearer definition of the roles and responsibilities of a Help Desk and its people, with the associated problems of lack of service monitoring and, therefore, an inability to state truthfully whether the situation is 'good' or 'bad';
- a need for a 'pro-active' approach and improved communications between Help Desk people and their customers;
- the development of the knowledge and experience of Help Desk staff, with improvements mentioned regarding technical and business details and an improved understanding of customers' work and the extensive variety of many organisations' hardware and software. These points are developed more specifically in terms of human resources management of the Help Desk, such as scheduling,

flexibility (including shift operations), training, opportunities to share knowledge and experiences, and recruitment;
- the investment in a variety of systems including, call management systems and on-line documentation.

6.4 Security

Organisations have come increasingly to rely on their information and communications systems for day-to-day operations and for future strategic performance. How long would an organisation be able to continue trading without its information and communications systems, for example, Sainsbury's supermarkets with their Electronic Point of Sales (EPoS) systems or Barclay's Bank branches with their Automatic Teller Machines (ATMs)? Indeed, any organisation that uses on-line ICTs must accept that security and network management problems can and probably will affect their business adversely.

The systems are exposed to a large number of risks, which include:

- power failures;
- disc crashes;
- incompatibility of software;
- bugs in software;
- poorly or wrongly trained staff;
- staff influenced by alcohol and other drugs;
- fire, smoke and fumes;
- flood;
- animals;
- explosions;
- legal actions;
- bankruptcies;
- strikes;
- sabotage;
- espionage;
- fraud;
- theft;
- malice.

Counter-measures against the adverse effects of these risks include:

- transfer the risk;
- reduce the probability of a risk;
- reduce the vulnerability;
- detect the occurrence;
- enable recovery.

Case: CRAMM

Scenario: The UK Government has developed a methodology to help in the assessment and management of risk.

The Central Computer and Telecommunications Agency (CCTA), the ICT consultancy wing of the UK Government, has developed the CCTA Risk Assessment and Management Methodology (CRAMM) for use in reviewing the security of computer systems. Government is much more concerned about security risks than private industry with items of genuine national security and details about private individuals and the dangers of parliamentary scrutiny. It comprises three stages:

• Identification and valuation of system assets;
• Identification of threats and vulnerabilities;
• Identifying counter-measures.

The first stage determines the boundaries of the system and the nature of the components within the system. Hardware and other physical assets are valued on the basis of replacement or re-construction costs. Responsibility for the hardware, software and data is identified, together with the user communities and the manner in which they use the system. Such information is obtained mainly by means of interviewing staff. Valuation of the effects of a complete or partial failure of a system is made in terms of:

• organisational embarrassment;
• loss of commercial confidentiality;
• infringement of personal privacy;
• personal safety hazards;
• failure to meet legal obligations;
• financial loss;
• disruption to activities.

The second stage involves the evaluation of the dependence of the system on groups of assets, completing an assessment of the threats and vulnerability, calculating levels of risks and reviewing the findings.

The third stage identifies how the security risks are to be managed. Appropriate and justifiable counter-measures must be identified as must any existing unjustified counter-measures.

Source: CCTA, 1990.

A corporate security policy comprises a set of rules and practices governing how assets including sensitive information are managed, protected and distributed within an organisation. Specific security measures are necessary to protect data, software and hardware. Organisations need to identify and quantify risks, then accept, minimise or eliminate the risks.

Failures in the assessment of security are commonplace, arising from:

- incomplete coverage;
- false sense of security;
- addressing only the obvious points;
- inconsistent across the range of systems;
- no justification for expenditure on counter-measures.

The most likely time to make an assessment of security is after an incident, when it is too late!

Amongst the more commonly considered threats are natural disasters such as fire and flood. Fire can be minimised by the use of manual and automatic fire alarms and extinguisher systems, which involve filling machine rooms with an inert halon gas. Flooding, which can be caused by fighting fires in other parts of the building, can be avoided by the use of waterproof ceilings and floors together with the provision of adequate drainage should any water enter the room. In a rather too well publicised fire at the Open University a portable office was burnt down including a computer, causing several years work to be lost. In the absence of a back-up, it was necessary to have DEC attempt to recover the data from the charred and buckled disc drives. Some natural disasters, such as flooding and earthquakes, are generally related to location, so that the selection of primary and back-up sites should take this into account. For example, San Fransisco is associated with earthquakes and Hong Kong with typhoons, while parts of Central London could conceivably be flooded.

Insurance has been a means of tackling risks for centuries. Lloyd's of London will insure anything against any risk. It is difficult for insurance companies to cover information systems and their associated technology platform, since new threats arise all the time.

The following topics are considered below in more detail:

VIRUSES

The identification and elimination of computer programs which spread themselves between computers.

PIRACY

The illegal copying of software and data.

HACKING AND ACCESS CONTROL

Setting and maintaining appropriate levels of security together with the related management techniques.

Viruses

A virus is a computer program which spreads itself from one computer system to another reproducing itself independently of the original copy. The following are examples:

CASCADE
Characters fall down and form a heap at the bottom of the screen.

ITALIAN
A ping-pong ball bounces across the screen.

DARK AVENGER
Once it enters a system it copies itself into every executable file which is opened, hence it is prolific, and the damage cannot be undone.

The first counter-measure is to ensure that staff are aware of viruses and the threats they pose to their data and equipment, and through these the risks to the organisation. The use of floppy discs from any source outside the organisation can result in the introduction of viruses. To avoid this, software should only be bought from reputable dealers and any discs should be checked on an isolated PC, that is, one not connected with any network, fitted with special software. In addition, it is sensible to have regular and/or random checks for viruses on PCs.

Virus checking software can be installed on PCs, but can only look for known viruses, leaving a possibility of intrusion of more recent viruses. Some viruses change their identities regularly making identification more difficult. A battle of wills exists between the people who devise the viruses and the security experts.

Piracy

The traditional view of pirates is exemplified by Long John Silver in *Treasure Island* and Captain Hook in *Peter Pan*. Today, the term has been extended to include the illegal copying and counter-feiting of software a lucrative activity if less glamourous and risky than seaborne piracy. Software is sold under the terms of a licence usually for single copies, a limited number of copies or site licences.

Case: Federation Against Software Theft
Scenario: In order to protect their investment, software companies have created an organisation to enforce their copyright.

The Federation Against Software Theft (FAST) represents the interests of over 140 software companies from around the world. The objective is to seek out illegal users of software and prosecute them so as to encourage others to buy the correct number of legal copies of software.

One of the FAST advertisements states that:

• 2.4 million PC users are guilty of breaking the UK Copyright Law;
• 55% of senior managers using PCs have run software illegally;
• 43% of senior managers are unaware of their organisation's formal policy on software use.

FAST estimate that over £300 million of revenue are lost each to software companies in the UK alone.

FAST also points out that since August 1989, directors of companies in the UK are responsible for illegal use of software in their companies and face up to two years in gaol.

By an unfortunate co-incidence, a team of thirty officials from FAST and the Business Software Alliance raided Mirror Group Newspapers (MGN) on 26th November 1990, shortly after the death its proprietor, Robert Maxwell. To add MGN's financial problems, FAST discovered 800 items of software of which only 97 were legal copies. A number of files had been erased at 09.30 on the morning of the raid, but could still be discovered using Norton Utilities. An initial estimate was that MGN would have to pay around £250,000 to make legal all the software found in the raid.

Hacking

Hacking is commonly associated with the criminal or malicious activities of electronic breaking and entering, technological hooliganism. Dialling up computer systems over the telephone and data communication networks then forcing an entry with attempted usernames and passwords. In 1984, for example, the mailbox of HRH the Duke of Edinburgh on British Telecom's PRESTEL system was found to have been 'hacked', though the mailbox had not been used for some months.

Case: The German spy

Scenario: One of the most sophisticated hacking stories to have been disclosed involves a German 'spy' found to have entered computer systems in the USA and Canada.

The hacker in question broke into a number of networks from a starting point in Germany. Use was made of 'holes' and 'bugs' in a number of operating systems, including Unix, together with a bug in EMACS, a popular text editor. The intrusion was not so much the result of faults in the operating systems, but rather blunders or 'human errors'.

The intrusion was detected by accounting inconsistencies at the Lawrence Berkeley Laboratory and by a failed attempt to break into a computer on the US military network from one of the Lawrence Berkeley Laboratory accounts. The intruder was led on by the Laboratory and followed. Alarms were put on accounts that were known to be compromised and print-outs made of every key-stroke allowing the identification of user IDs and passwords.

The hacker came into the Laboratory's computers by a number of different routes and similarly went out using many networks. Some connections were made using the public and academic data networks, while others used the telephone networks. The intruder, used both the telephone network and the international packet switched data network to gain entry to computers in two German universities and to the outbound modems of a US-based defence contractor and thus to the Lawrence Berkeley Laboratory. Using the connections between the academic and military networks, connections were made to computer systems belonging to universities in a number of states and in Canada, together with bases of the US Air Force, Army and Navy, plus a number of computer and networking firms.

In total, attempts were made to enter over four hundred computer systems with identifications such as: root, guest, system and field. Once on a Unix system it is possible to use the commands *who* and *finger* to identify other users on the system, their names and organisational roles. In some cases the default passwords for system managers and field service engineers had not been altered from those set in the factory. Password files were copied and decoded, allowing the intruder to return. Mail messages were read which sometimes contained instructions on how to log onto remote systems, including the user IDs and passwords. To reduce the chances of being spotted, the intruder disabled audit trails and accounting software.

The advice from the Lawrence Berkeley Laboratory is to:

- establish time expiry periods for passwords;
- monitor incoming traffic;
- establish alarms;
- educate users to keep and change passwords;
- regularly re-build system utilities.

They also hired a student to probe the strengths and weaknesses of their system.

Source: Stoll, 1988

In the USA a new form of hacking has been developed, namely hacking into private telecommunications networks. The aim of this is to use the out-bound telephone lines provided for company employees. For example, using an '800' freephone service intended for the company's dealers, hackers dialed into the network of an American machinery company and cracked the code for long-distance and international calls. Over one weekend calls to the value of several thousand dollars were made, including a twelve hour call to Asia.

Mitch Kapor, the founder of Lotus Development Corporation, and others have founded Electronic Frontier Foundation to lobby politicians and support lawyers defending clients facing certain charges of hacking. The aim is to encourage a debate on the freedom of speech issues involved in electronic communication.

Multiuser systems require a user to give their identity by means of a username and password, sometimes two different passwords. The password can be required to meet certain criteria, for example, more than six characters and contain at least one letter and one number. The system can also force users to change their password at regular intervals, though it tends not to stop users immediately resetting their password to the previous password. Passwords are often obvious, such as, the names of partners, children and pets or vehicle registration numbers.

It is possible to achieve much higher levels of protection by making physiological measurements of the user. For example, biometric devices can be attached to computers which read the retinal patterns of potential users; the pattern of blood vessels at the back of the eyes is extremely complex and unique. Thumbprints and voice patterns can also be used. Risks to hardware can be covered by:

- creating a duplicate computer system;
- installing a temporary replacement computer system;
- buying or leasing a building and fitting it with services (air-conditioning, wiring, etc) ready for computer operations;
- using a service run by a third party;
- having an *ad hoc* reciprocal arrangement with neighbouring companies using the same equipment.

Specialist service companies operate 'hot sites' which are bomb-proof computer centres containing a variety of computer systems, peripherals and the personnel to operate them. The need for personnel is crucial as the back-up system must be brought into use rapidly and in conditions of confusion. It is absolutely essential that back-up systems be compatible, it is too late to find out they are not fully compatible when they are called into operation. Copies of the most recent versions of data, programs and documentation should be stored off-site in a secure place and updated regularly.

6.5 Conclusion

This chapter has discussed the progress made in the management of the functional areas of ICTs and how information systems strategies can be implemented.

Considerable advances have been made and will continue to be made, though the focus has too often been technical rather than managerial or organisational.

Developments in methodologies for the design and construction of information systems have brought the DP/IS function under much greater control. Nonetheless, the continued growth and ever greater diversity of applications makes it a difficult area to manage, but leadership must come from the needs of the business.

Although quality has been recognised in other areas of management, it is still poorly addressed in the ICTs, though this is more for organisational reasons than for technical reasons. The classical dilemma of 'buy' or 'make' has shifted towards 'buy', after many years in which 'make' has dominated. This presents a different set of management challenges, in which the outcomes are, as yet, uncertain. To date, the recognition of the importance of users has been limited, with the concept of delivering a 'service' seldom admitted let alone achieved. There is much scope for improvement on all these dimensions; the successful organisation will act accordingly.

Given the reliance of businesses on their ICT systems it is essential that they be given the necessary security and back-up. This is not simply the traditional back-up facilities for the large computer rooms, it must also extend to the departmental fileservers and LANs and the all too easily stolen laptop computers carried by executives.

Review questions

1 Why might an organisation select a particular systems methodology?

2 Discuss the roles and responsibilities of different people in the formulation and implementation of an information systems strategy in an organisation you know.

3 Draw a data flow diagram for a car reservation system.

  4 Discuss the limitation of Critical Success Factors.

Study questions

1 How safe is your own work? If all your computer system disappeared now, could you recover the position?

2 For an information systems need, specify the way you would approach its design and implementation.

Further reading

Journals: Sloan Management Review, International Journal of Information Resource Management, Management Information Systems Quarterly (MISQ), Communications of the ACM, Computer Journal, Computers and Security, IEEE Computer, Journal of Information Technology and the Journal of Management Information Systems.

Ashworth, Caroline & Mike Goodland "SSADM; a practical approach" McGraw-Hill, 1990.

> *One of the better of a great many volumes on SSADM, though for a more substantial and definitive version, the NCC is probably the best.*

Brooks, Frederick P "The Mythical Man Month" Addison-Wesley, Wokingham, 1975

> *A real classic, addressing many of the early problems of managing COBOL shops.*

Cohen, Bernard; W T Harwood and M I Jackson "The Specification of Complex Systems" Addison-Wesley, Wokingham, 1986.

> *A first class introduction to formal specifications. A times it is a bit complex for those whose algebra is rusty.*

Garvin, David "Quality Management" Free Press, New York, 1988.

> *A book on quality management which is both fashionable and good.*

Madnick, Stuart (editor) "The Strategic Use of Information Technology" Oxford University Press, 1988.

> *A collection of 'classic' articles from the Sloan Management Review covering methodologies for the building and use of information systems. Includes papers on critical success factors.*

Marciniak, John and Donald Reifer "Software Acquisition Management" John Wiley and Sons, 1990.

> *A detailed guide to the purchase of customised software from software houses. Geared to the procurement procedures of the US Government.*

Olle, T William; Jacques Hagelstein, Ian Macdonald, Colette Rolland, Henk Sol, Franc van Assche and Alexander Verrijn-Stuart "Information Systems Methodologies" Addison-Wesley, Second Edition, 1991.

The definitive book on methodologies for information systems; it represents the boiling down of a number of conferences and many years of experience. A bit dull.

Sommerville, Ian "Software Engineering" Third Edition, Addison-Wesley, Wokingham, 1989.

A standard computing science text, though quite useful for reference and occasionally to read.

Can we cope?

Learning objectives:

- to be aware of the reasons for the growth of human resources management and the major areas of activity:
    - influence of people;
    - human resource flow;
    - reward systems;
    - work systems;

- to recognise the importance of intellectual capital to the current and future success of organisations;

- to be aware of the siginificance of organisational culture in the management of transformation;

- to understand the role of leadership in management;

- to appreciate the human, personal and social factors which affect the implementation of information and communications technologies.

7.1 Introduction

This chapter provides an understanding of the social, cultural and organisational issues related to the successful selection, adoption and diffusion of information and communications technologies. These issues are of growing importance with much more than purely technical significance and need to be set in the context of organisational policies for Human Resources Management (HRM). That an information system works, in some technical sense, is a necessary, but not a sufficient condition; real success can only be achieved in business terms. Ultimately, that success depends on the attitudes, skills and experience of the people involved in the design and use of the systems. Like other assets, human managerial expertise is essential to maximise the value of ICTs; it is the people in an organisation who identify the problems, determine how to solve them and implement the necessary actions.

The relationships between business strategy, the use of ICTs and the organisation are shown in figure 7.1. Positioned at the top of the triangle is the business strategy, the importance of which was discussed in Chapter 2. An organisation 'interacts' with the business strategy both in the sense that the organisation must deliver the results of the strategy and the organisation evolves the strategy. An organisation also interacts with the use of ICTs, through the specification of the set of technologies to be used and then in the use or misuse of those technologies. The logical connection between these three areas lies in the vision of where the business is going and how it is to get there.

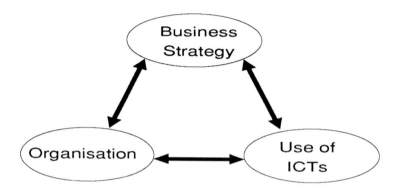

Figure 7.1 *The 'strategic' triangle*

This chapter includes the following topics:

HUMAN RESOURCES MANAGEMENT
The management decisions which affect relationships between an organisation and its people.

ORGANISATIONAL CULTURE
The patterns of assumptions which guide the people in an organisation in their behaviour.

LEADERSHIP
How an organisation can be modified by dynamic leadership.

IMPLEMENTATION
How our knowledge of an organisation and of the technologies can be used to increase the chances of success in the implementation of computer-based information systems to support the business strategy and facilitate decision-making.

The failure either to adopt ICTs or to achieve successful implementation can significantly impair the performance of an organisation. In extreme cases, it can make it more difficult for the organisation to recover, leading to a downward spiral in performance. However, this is not to suggest a technological imperative. Although technology can be very beguiling, it is seldom either the key to success or the area where the real challenges lie; the technology is simply more visible and so more diverting. Like the iceberg in figure 7.2, the real dangers lie deeper in non-technical issues, concerning social, organisational and cultural matters.

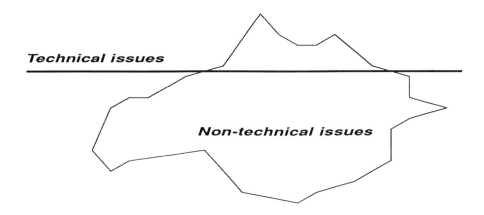

Figure 7.2 *The iceberg model*
(Source: Mortensen, 1983.)

Jobs and skills

The use of information and communications technologies changes jobs and consequently the skills required of individuals and groups. However, the effects are much more complex than this, rather simplistic, statement might suggest. Changes can be observed at each of the following levels:

- individual;
- work group;
- organisation;
- economy;
- society.

The traditional view of information and communications technologies was as a substitution of capital for labour, allowing an organisation to achieve higher levels of efficiency. The results of this type of automation are often lower unit costs which can lead to increased demand for a product, creating new opportunities for employment.

However, the new job opportunities generally arise in areas of the organisation such as sales and after-sales servicing, rather than in manufacturing. The net effect for the organisation may not be a significant change in numbers employed, but for the individuals concerned it it is certainly not easy and may not be possible to switch from a factory-floor job to a service position with the requirement to meet the customer in person.

Robert Reich (1991) divides work into three categories:

- routine production;
- in-person service;
- symbolic analysis.

He sees a growing divergence in the earning power of the symbolic analysts (such as business strategists and consultants) and in-person service providers (such as burger bar sales staff). Competition for in-person service jobs now comes from those who have worked or who would otherwise have worked in the routine production jobs in manufacturing (such as car assembly). The education needs of the first two categories are low, while the needs of the symbolic analysts are high:

> The middle manager of the core American corporation at mid-century was not, by most standards, a rugged individualist. Indeed, his tendency toward conformity was the subject of considerable comment at the time. ... But conformity and tractability were perfectly consistent with the standardized, high-volume system of production he oversaw. The system neither required nor rewarded much in the way of original thought. (Reich, 1991, page 54.)

The net effect on employment of the diffusion of ICTs is very difficult to calculate. In part, it depends on the labour market and on the ability of individuals and organisations to adjust by training and re-training and by deploying their people effectively.

7.2 Human resources management

In recent years, Human Resources Management (HRM) has become one of the most important of the 'topical' areas in business, along with 'total quality management', 'excellence' and so on. This development has been fuelled, in part, by business and management books of the kind sold in airport bookstalls. Nonetheless, there are real business issues which have pushed HRM to strategic importance:

- increasing global competition;
- increasing size and complexity of organisations;
- growing demands for career and life-style satisfaction;
- changes in workforce profile (age, nationality, sex and skills);
- more legislation.

HRM is now seen to be a vital component of an organisation's strategy. Changes in the business environment and in the way in which managers perceive their organisations have raised HRM to a level of importance which was never achieved by either personnel management or industrial relations. This section includes a discussion of:

NETWORK ORGANISATIONS
How the new organisational structures, which go beyond conventional organisational boundaries, affect HRM.

INTELLECTUAL CAPITAL
How the knowledge within an organisation can be used to create differential advantage in the marketplace.

EDUCATION AND TRAINING
How the abilities of the people in an organisation can be developed.

One of the better definitions of human resources management is provided by Michael Beer et al. (1984, page 1):

Human resource management involves all management decisions and actions that affect the nature of the relationship between the organisation and employees — its human resources

HRM is much, much more than personnel management and industrial relations. Personnel management can conjure up images of second rate managers sent somewhere where they 'can do no harm', checking superannuation details or completing government statistical returns, while industrial relations can suggest the bizarre rigmaroles of collective bargaining which precede acquiescing to the petty tyrannies of trades unions and the loss of yet more international competitiveness. It is interesting to note complaints from students in both the UK and the USA, that industrial relations is taught as case law, that is, what you are legally allowed and forbidden to do, while what should be done is to identify best practice.
Michael Beer et al. (1984) subdivide HRM into:

INFLUENCE OF PEOPLE
Employees are 'stakeholders' with interests in the organisation which are important in considering how an organisation functions; these range from salary and other financial rewards to dignity, satisfaction and status.

HUMAN RESOURCE FLOW

The 'flow' of people in, through and out of an organisation must be managed to produce the right mix of knowledge and skills, if the organisation is to meet its strategic objectives.

REWARD SYSTEMS

Rewards are important to attract, motivate and retain staff. Questions which arise include remuneration for individuals or groups, for example, should there be profit sharing and how should non-cash rewards be used: status, goods and services?

fat cats offers bonus incentives to all employees.

WORK SYSTEMS

The definition and design of work. The role of ICTs can be vital, used properly they can empower people, used badly they can reduce them to little more than automata.

If these four areas of HRM policy are effective, then the benefits should be found in terms of:

COMMITMENT

People should share and be committed to their colleagues and to the clearly stated and well understood goals of the organisation.

COMPETENCE

People should have the levels of attitudes, skills and knowledge necessary to carry out their specific tasks and more generally to carry out the mission of the organisation.

COST-EFFECTIVENESS

The overall cost of the people should be close to the lowest possible cost commensurate with achieving the corporate mission and without causing unnecessary problems.

Sadly, a large part of the industrial relations effort in the UK has been directed into formal negotiations with trades unions which have been characterised by confrontation. Frequently, the only contact between management and workforce ('them' and 'us') has been through meetings with officials of the trades unions in which both sides are deeply embedded in a culture of mistrust. In the years after World War II, the result was to grind management down to a point of near passivity, allowing the trades unions to walk all over them. This view is seen in the adoption of ICTs by the insistence of trades unions that staff receive additional payments or be regraded simply for the use of the systems, or in extreme cases, that previous staffing levels be retained.

In the 1980's this situation was countered by a 'right to manage' school, which called for aggressive action to break up the power of the trades unions, if not the unions themselves. This school was aided by the Thatcher Administration (1979-1990) which wanted to end the power of the trades unions, rather as the Romans ended the revolt of the slaves led by Spartacus, with the crucified bodies of the trades unionists lining the road from the Doncaster to Downing Street. A number of parliamentary acts were introduced to curb the powers of the trades unions with the intention of changing the changing the balance in industrial relations in Britain.

Case: Miners' strike

Scenario: In 1984 the National Union of Mineworkers declared a strike against the National Coal Board, which developed into the bitterest dispute in the UK since the General Strike of 1926.

Harold Macmillan (British Prime Minister 1957-1963) declared that there were three institutions not to be challenged by man: the Brigade of Guards, the Roman Catholic Church and the National Union of Mineworkers (NUM). The NUM had been the driving force behind the 1926 General Strike and had a major industrial dispute with the Labour Government in 1947. Disregarding his predecessor's advice, Ted Heath's Government, faced up to NUM strikes in the winters of 1972 and 1974. The result was that when Heath called an election on the 'right to govern' issue he lost, leaving the Conservative Party with a considerable dislike of the NUM, if not outright animosity.

In 1983 Ian MacGregor was transferred from British Steel to be Chairman of the National Coal Board (NCB). A Scot by birth, MacGregor, had gained most of his management practice in the USA where he had considerable experience of taking on and defeating strikers. With the support of Mrs Thatcher, he challenged the NUM in what was fully intended to be a major confrontation. Unlike in 1972 and 1974, the NCB was fully prepared; coal stocks had been built up to unprecedented levels both at the pit heads and at the electricity power stations.

The dispute arose because the NCB wanted to close a number of pits where the costs of production were particularly high. The NUM insisted that pits be kept open, almost regardless of cost. Mining jobs were characterised as being hereditary; miners had no right to accept redundancy payments because the jobs lost really belonged to the children and grandchildren of today's miners. The strike had a slow start, initially it was only a ban on maintenance at weekends. The NUM held a special delegate conference in April 1984 to authorise a national strike, thus avoiding a national ballot. The strike was characterised by mass action involving, on occasions, thousands of pickets, sometimes leading to riots. Once tightly-knit mining communities were riven with pro- and anti-strike factions. A rival Union of Democratic Mineworkers was set up, which attracted considerable regional support. In order to move funds out of the reach of the British Courts, where the NUM faced sequestration, NUM officials transferred money to obscure banks in Luxembourg and Liechtenstein. Legal actions against the NUM were brought by strikers, individual NUM members, demanding the right to go to work without fear of intimidation. The NUM received limited support from other unions, not least because of the legal penalties they would have been liable to pay.

The miners' leader, Arthur Scargill, had come to national prominence by devising the highly effective 'flying pickets' of the early 1970's. His style, especially his oratory, was confrontational, casting him in the role of war leader. Scargill never seemed, then or since, to compromise or to acquiesce. The strike ended with a drift back to work. Eventually, the other NUM leaders capitulated and organised a march back to work with banners and brass bands; an unusual way of acknowledging defeat.

The overall effect, from the point of view of the National Coal Board, now British Coal, was of a successful breaking of the power of the NUM. The NCB could manage individual pits and even close them down much more effectively than in the past, when whole coalfields or the entire NUM could and would come out on strike.

Source: MacGregor, 1986.

The attitudes of both British managers and trades unionists are in contrast to those found in most of continental Europe and Japan, though they have certain similarities to those in the USA. In Germany, there has been successful co-determination by management and trades unions for decades. Nonetheless the 1980's saw a shift in the power balance towards management, through increased unemployment and reorganisation of work to develop the flexibility necessary to exploit the new technologies. The German government has funded significant initiatives in training of young people, for re-training of the unemployed and for further training of those in work.

Reflecting the attitudes of its continental members, the European Community's Social Charter guarantees (other than in the United Kingdom):

- freedom of movement within the Community with equal rights in employment, working conditions and social welfare;
- freedom to choose and engage in an occupation, which shall be fairly remunerated;
- minimum rights for part-time and temporary workers, including rest periods and annual paid leave;
- right to adequate social protection;
- right of access to life-long vocational training;

- right of equal treatment for men and women, especially in access to employment, pay, working conditions, education and training and career development;
- right to information, consultation and participation for employees, particularly in conditions of technological change, restructuring, redundancies and for cross-border workers;
- right to health protection and safety at the workplace, including training, information, consultation and participation for employees;
- rights of children and adolescents including minimum working age;
- right for the elderly to a reasonable standard of living after retirement;
- right of people with disabilities to programmes to help them in their social and professional lifes.

Case: Toshiba in the United Kingdom

Scenario: In 1981, Toshiba took over a failing television factory in the UK and made it into a success through non-traditional management techniques.

On 28 October 1986, Toshiba Consumer Products celebrated the production of its one millionth television set from its plant at Plymouth in South-West England. The plant had been opened in the late 1940's by Bush to manufacture radios. In 1972 it passed to the Rank Organisation, a UK-based conglomerate which is a financial partner in Rank Xerox. A joint venture with Toshiba, the Japanese electronics giant, was established in 1978. The failure of the joint venture in early 1981 allowed the Japanese to takeover the plant. The blame lay largely with Rank, which had not adopted any Japanese or American management ideas and had consequently failed to exploit the technology made available from Toshiba. While Rank wanted to produce television sets which were easy to maintain, Toshiba had aimed to produce television sets which did not require any maintenance at all.

The new Japanese operation was markedly different from the joint venture:

- four factories cut to one;
- 2,600 'workers' cut to 300 'members';
- seven trades unions cut to one.
- sixty-two models cut to eight;
- circuit boards used in a TV, cut from twelve to three;
- manufacturing time cut by 40%;
- output increased from 300 sets per day to 2,000;
- video cassette recorders and microwave ovens added to production.

These changes were possible as a result of the crisis caused by the closure of the original operation, they were certainly not incremental. The 'new' factory was consciously different from the old one. However, the management practices were not strictly Japanese and they were certainly not magical:

- select and train 'members' for flexible working;
- focus production on television sets;
- develop new relationships with suppliers emphasising quality, pricing and timing of delivery;
- introduce single status employment contracts;
- introduce single union agreement with 'pendulum arbitration';
- create a Company Advisory Board (COAB) to discuss all aspects of company performance with 'members'.

The plant operated without job descriptions and 'personnel' functions were the responsibility of line management. The single status of 'members' meant that:

- all 'members' wore similar blue company 'coats' with Toshiba badges;
- there was a single staff restaurant;
- there was a single open-plan office for all staff, including the managing director;
- all staff were paid monthly.

From the start, Toshiba Consumer Products operated as part of Toshiba's worldwide operations, integrating into its sales and marketing networks.

Source: Trevor, 1988.

In the autumn of 1991, the Trades Union Congress condemned the introduction of 'alien' work practices by Japanese companies.

Network organisations

In our discussion of competition and business strategy in Chapter 2 and in the examples given in Chapter 3, we have shown how some organisations now operate through 'global webs'. No longer do these organisations rely on simple contracts for purchases and sales, they have developed complex partnerships, collaborating in joint projects. In such networks, inter-relationships between individuals became much more significant than the formal structure of the organisation which officially govern the links. Jack Rockart and Jim Short (Scott Morton, 1991, pages 189-219) identify the key attributes of a successful networked organisation as being the sharing of:

- goals;
- experience;
- decision-making
- responsibility;
- accountability;
- trust;
- timing;
- work;
- recognition;
- rewards.

This new multiplicity of networks achieves business goals in non-traditional ways, which presents challenges in terms of managing the collaboration and interdependence of the individuals, business units and separate companies to achieve the overall corporate strategic objectives. A critical capability is provided by the technology platform which can allow the coordination of the many individuals and different business networks. Networked organisations need to find new measures of performance which take into account the diffuse and cooperative nature of business, addressing the particular problems for assessing the performance of individuals.

Intellectual capital

As organisations struggle to compete they have been forced to realise that the most important way in which they can increase their competitiveness is through the effective utilisation of the people they employ. This can be termed 'intellectual capital', which Hugh Macdonald of International Computers Limited, defines as:

> ... knowledge that exists in an organisation that can be used to create differential advantage.

Organisations which use their 'intellectual capital' more effectively than others are able to realise competitive advantage through their ability to achieve differentiation not once, but repeatedly and regularly. Competitive edge comes from applying the knowledge and skills of individuals in the organisation in order to achieve intangibles such as being perceived as being 'talented', in terms of:

- research;
- development;
- design;
- tailoring.

The concepts of managing intellectual capital and its practice are still in their infancy. Clearly it is necessary to reward and retain those who possess the individual building blocks of intellectual capital if the organisation is to utilise their abilities. Intellectual capital depreciates and must be renewed not only through new people entering the organisation, but also through those already there learning through new activities. Intellectual capital must be identified and fully exploited; a key consideration is the ability to carry new ideas through into practice.

Education and training

If an organisation is to survive and prosper it must ensure that its people have the attitudes, knowledge and skills necessary to carry out its corporate mission. It must also be possible to develop a new mission and to carry that out. The development of people's attitudes, knowledge and skills in the organisation is essential to allow it to exploit business opportunities.

Debates on education have been undertaken in most European countries and in the USA and Japan. Each country believes itself disadvantaged and is striving to improve its national system, usually by copying features of another (see Chapter 1). In Europe, there is also a slow drift towards a single system as mobility of students and managers increases.

However well educated people are on their recruitment to an organisation, it is vital for organisations to develop their talents. Here, Japanese companies are recognised as the leaders, with extensive programmes for staff development. Looking at the in-company training of organisations in the UK, Coopers and Lybrand concluded:

> Most companies agreed that Britain did under-train compared with its main overseas competitors, but also thought that the amount of training they themselves undertook was about right. This lack of concern might be regarded as reflecting confidence; we think it would be more realistic to regard it as reflecting complacency.
>
> This complacency was reinforced by a widespread ignorance among top management of how their company's performance in training compared with that of their competitors — even those in the UK, let alone overseas. (Coopers and Lybrand, 1985, page 4.)

One of the main reasons why organisations will not train their people is because they are afraid that other organisations will poach them. So in order to acquire the necessary knowledge and skills, they poach people from other organisations, creating a vicious circle. A more positive way of thinking would be to create an attractive and stimulating working environment to ensure an organisation retained its people with their skills and knowledge.

ICT-related courses were slow to develop and too much inclined to hands-on and technical issues, while too many courses on strategic ICT are of the 'magic bullet' variety. Managers need to be brought face-to-face with the issues addressed in this book, covering a broad range of strategic and organisational issues, as well as some basic understanding of trends in technology.

Case: ICL Senior Executive Programme

Scenario: As part of an effort to support its customers, ICL offers a one day course for senior executives.

International Computers Limited (ICL) offers a wide variety of courses, one of which is for senior managers and directors of organisations which are customers or potential customers. These courses are generally held at Hedsor House, a country house in Berkshire, 'next door' to Cliveden and Chequers.

The aim of this twenty-four hour course is to provide senior executives with some of the current thinking on the business uses of information technology in business. Over the period a number of experienced ICL staff and an outside speaker will cover many of the issues raised in this book, in particular the lessons from the 'Management in the Nineties' Research Program. Prior to the course every 'student' is interviewed by one of the course staff to identify the issues which most concern them and to identify what they hope to gain from the course.

The course is not purely a business event, there is a strong social element. The standard of the food and wine is high and intentionally so. The people on the course are all of an equivalent level in their organisations and gain much by meeting each other and having the opportunity to discuss these issues.

7.3 Organisational culture

A number of ideas from the social sciences have been brought into organisation theory and a few have even made the transition into management practice. Of these ideas, organisational culture is one of the most useful, though it remains difficult to grasp. Organisational culture is seen as a combination of deep-set beliefs about the way work should be organised, the way authority should be exercised and the ways in which people should be, and are, rewarded:

A pattern of basic assumptions — invented, discovered by a given group as it learns to cope with its problems of external adaptation and internal integration — that has worked well enough to be considered valid and, therefore, to be taught to new members as the correct way to perceive, think and feel in relation to those problems. (Schein, 1985, page 9.)

Organisational culture is a way of looking at organisations in terms distinct from their structures, processes and procedures. The use of organisational culture allows us to go beyond a hierarchical or a bureaucratic view, it allows us to consider social interactions in management processes. The culture is how values are transmitted to members of the organisation, for example, how hard and how long we should work: should we stay late, take work home and come into the office at weekends:

> Consider breakfast, for instance. You'll never see IBM salespeople along with the hordes of others congregating at Howard Johnson's every morning, because IBMers are encouraged to see their time as too valuable to waste in a roadside diner. When IBMers want coffee they will share it with a client or colleague. The point is for IBMers to begin the day not discussing baseball or the price of steak but to get a head start by focusing on the company, the industry, and their habits as professionals. (Deal and Kennedy, 1988, page 60.)

Organisational culture can be seen at three levels:

ARTIFACTS AND CREATIONS
These objects include technology, art and patterns of behaviour.

VALUES
These are testable in both physical and social environments.

BASIC ASSUMPTIONS
These concern the organisation and its relationships with the business environment, people and so on.

Although certain aspects of the organisational culture can be seen, they are often difficult to decipher, while the basic assumptions are taken for granted and cannot easily be tested. Simple considerations such as standards of dress are often the most noticeable. For example, academic staff in universities can dress very much as they like, idiosyncrasy is almost encouraged, whereas in companies such as IBM relatively strict rules have long been in operation requiring male staff to wear conservative suits, white shirts and striped ties. Similarly, the appearance of offices can be very revealing. In the UK Civil Service, offices have a degree of uniformity which is almost unknown in the private sector. Office furniture and equipment is purchased nationally and distributed as needed. Each grade of officer knows what he or she is entitled to, in terms of carpet or linoleum, number of chairs and so on. Thus on entering the office of civil servant whether in the Treasury in Whitehall or in the Scottish Office in Edinburgh one finds offices which are almost identical, down to the same pattern of chair covers. It is possible to tell the grade of the official one is meeting by a quick scan of the office.

Internally the Treasury contrives to display something of the appearance of a Victorian poorhouse. Tiles and lino constitute the prevailing decor. The atmosphere is one of earnest frugality, which seems perfectly appropriate to the Treasury's *métier*. (Bruce-Gardyne, 1986, page 32.)

The most impressive and potent artifact in the whole of the UK Government is the portrait which sits in the office of the Minister of State in the Foreign and Commonwealth Office; it is of George III, the monarch who lost the United States of America.

Whilst such patterns are interesting, the real question is what they tell us and what might we do as a result of such knowledge. Japanese companies, such as Toshiba, require all staff, including managers, to wear uniform jackets so that they cannot readily be distinguished, making the single status of staff evident to all. This acts to break the social and organisational distance between manager and worker so common in American and European organisations which so often leads to aloofness and insensitivity.

The organisational culture contains values and basic assumptions, information about what the organisation is, about its mission and its *raison d'être*. These values and assumptions indicate how the organisation operates with respect to other organisations in the business environment in terms which can be grouped together as business ethics and environmental care. The attitudes towards its staff, its shareholders, its customers, its suppliers as well as towards the community in which it operates.

Anthony O'Reilly of Heinz, opened his Chairman's Statement, 'Year in View', in the 1991 Annual Report by stating:

The last year has been one of change and challenge. In trading terms, the recession has caused reduced consumer demand but the company has contrived to perform strongly.

On the legislative and regulatory front there has been considerable activity both in the UK and within Europe. A new Food Safety Act has been enacted, an Environmental Protection Act has added to the statute books a wide ranging White Paper on the environment published. European legislation awaits in the form of Eco-labelling and packaging directives, food labelling proposals and discussion on formalising environmental audits.

Overall environmental issues have remained high on the agenda, and the public's consciousness of environmental matters has matured with a more discerning attitude being taken by some consumers. ...

In May 1990 an Environmental Audit was conducted across the Company. As a result, an Environmental Team was set up with senior representatives from all functions with the brief to execute a detailed Company-wide environment strategy for the company.

Stories, jokes and myths are important ingredients of the culture of organisations, transforming events in an organisation's history into a valued heritage and a source of shared meanings. They also turn bureaucracies into more human places, offering a break from the daily routine and permitting the display of emotions such as amusement, pride, bitterness, relief or worry. Myths and jokes also provide a way of expressing hard truths which might otherwise go unheard. For this reason, they can open windows into organizational life reveal unnoticed aspects. One of the key ways in which an organisational culture is passed on is through stories, which often identify heroes within the organisations.

Case: University of Stirling, Scotland

Scenario: A relatively new university was established on a green field site at Stirling, Scotland, in 1967; slowly an organisational culture has developed.

The organisational culture of a university is very different from that of commercial organisations, not least because it contains three cultures, those of the students and of the staff (academic and non-academic). As former members of academic staff, the authors, can only really describe the culture of the academic staff.

The University of Stirling is a relatively new institution, having been founded in the late 1960's. Some of the staff have been there since the very early days and so carry with them many of the stories contributing to the culture. The buildings are modern, constructed in concrete and breeze block, with an occasional piece of modern art on the walls. Stirling lacks the appearance of an ancient university such as St Andrews (founded 1411) and some of the buildings are commonly believed to be based on the design of a Swedish prison. It has the advantage over many universities of being set in rural Scotland and in a very attractive eighteenth century estate, including a small, if artificial, loch.

Being a campus University on the edge of a relatively small town, the atmosphere can feel at times claustrophobic and incestuous. The staff not only work close together, they generally live nearby, meeting each other socially and even when out shopping or at the cinema. Husbands and wives and members of less formal partnerships often both work in the university, though generally in different departments. Even part-time and summer jobs frequently go to children of staff. Thus information and gossip passes around extremely rapidly; for example, a secretary expressing surprise at finding a lecturer in a particularly seedy disco. The local atmosphere is the academic equivalent of a mining or pit village, certainly, it requires circumspection in the behaviour of staff.

Strangely, there is no Senior Common Room where staff meet and talk, instead they have coffee in their own offices and departments. They must join the madding throng of students for lunch in the MacRobert Centre, where they huddle together at 'separate' tables for marketing, computing science, economics and so on. There is no staff bar, requiring staff either to use bars shared with students or to drink in solitude. On the occasions when the conversation deals with work, the preference is for research rather than teaching. Staff find research interesting and worthy of debate, whereas teaching is the subject of complaint, second, of course to administration. To compliment people for their administration or teaching is considered inappropriate, research is what counts. Like all universities there is a fairly high level of back-biting and back-stabbing amongst the staff. Individual departments are little fiefdoms, much like the Scottish clans before the Battle of Culloden.

Personalities can have an important, albeit transient effect. For example, the former Department of Business and Management was created by Professor Tom Cannon, a colourful character who certainly led from the front. Tom had, at all times, a clear, albeit not necessarily consensual, vision which was communicated directly to the people in the Department. Since his departure for the Manchester Business School life has been less colourful and the developments less positive and progressive. A rumour that Tom was to return as Principal and Vice-Chancellor sent a shudder through the more conservative parts of the University of Stirling. Moreover, staff have left as opportunities elsewhere seem more attractive. At least the Tom Cannon Trophy remains, for the annual MBA staff-student football challenge.

One of the many ways in which it has been suggested that managers might improve their organisations is through changes in the organisational culture. Populist authors such as Tom Peters have suggested that the organisational culture can be engineered, in the belief that particular cultures are better suited to particular fields of activity. One of the most difficult things to achieve in an organisation is innovation, which Peters and Waterman (1982, page 120) tried to show to a client by visiting 3M to see how they go about problem solving:

Our friends at 3M were tolerant of the excursion, and we observed all sorts of strange goings-on. There were a score or more casual meetings in progress with salespeople, marketing people, manufacturing people, engineering people, R&D people — even accounting people — sitting around, chattering about new-product problems. We happened in on a session where a 3M customer had come to talk informally with about fifteen people from four divisions on how better to serve his company. None of it seemed rehearsed. We didn't see a single structured presentation. It went on all day — people meeting in a seemingly random way.

The ideas of quality and service, which have so dominated management thinking in recent years, have important implications for the organisational culture and place significant demands on it. Looking to the transport sector in the UK, one sees the need for change, not only in investment but also in changing the attitudes of staff who have often lacked courtesy and have frequently seemed to view passengers as at best a nuisance. To change such deep-seated attitudes requires a shift in organisational culture. While British Airways (BA) is now less frequently known as 'Bloody Awful', its counterpart, British Rail, is still trying to get there.

Organisational culture is very difficult to change; by comparison it is easy to change a business strategy and relatively easy, if expensive, to change the technology platform. On a superficial level, one can issue new dress codes and, if necessary, appear in jeans and t-shirt or even in white tie and tails. The real challenge is how to change values.

For the average European manager, the books on organisational culture may have a lot to say about organisations, but rather less about what they perceive to be 'culture'. Many of the examples from American organisations appear to be ghastly excesses of 'hoop-la', causing the European reader to cringe. Whether because Europeans see themselves as more refined or because they are more conservative, it is inconceivable to imagine typical French, German or Scottish managers behaving in ways which their North American counterparts would regard as quite acceptable. Nonetheless, after toning down, the American message is valid. Culture is changed by group activities, by coming together to do things and to celebrate things.

The key is to shape the organisational culture in such a way as to empower people to use the new vision. In the first instance, this is done by asking questions which empower 'what should we do?' and 'how can I help you?'. The celebration of success is a major opportunity to reward people who have acted in a way which fits with the new culture. The important factor is to generate concrete actions to support the vision.

One important use of the organisational culture is to overcome the failings of the structures and procedures of the organisation, which also, unfortunately, often drive or at least constrain strategy. That is, to have a culture which tells people not to adhere to the rules and procedures so rigidly that it is going to hurt or upset the customer. This is in complete contrast to the bureaucratic approach which is to embed the rules in a manual and does not recognise the ability of the individual to override those rules.

Case: Générale de Service Informatique

Scenario: Générale de Service Informatique has achieved considerable growth while retaining an unusual organisational style which leaves considerable responsibilities with individual managers and business units.

Générale de Service Informatique (GSI) was launched in 1971 initially to provide a computer bureau service. It expanded rapidly through the enthusiasm of a group of individualists who refused to conform to the traditional norms of large organisations.

The main sectors of GSI's activity are: management, motor trade, transport and tourism, marketing information, banking, facilities management, advanced technology, payroll and human resources management. GSI uses very simple organisational structures and procedures with autonomous operational units. Despite many problems, GSI has been able to succeed with its non-bureaucratic system. Perhaps the most important feature of GSI is that its organisational culture is sufficiently strong to correct the adverse effects of the rules and the structure (or the lack of them).

In a traditional hierarchical organisation, decisions must be referred upwards. This means that a manager cannot always make decisions for his staff which, in effect, emasculates the manager. GSI devolves power to managers to avoid this problem. In terms of organisational structure, GSI has no personnel department; responsibility for personnel lies with managers.

In terms of organisational culture, individuals at GSI are encouraged to value their colleagues, for example, to listen where once they would have talked.

The overall aim of GSI's HRM policies is to create a set of conditions which are favourable to individuals, which allows them to develop and to use their abilities to the full. People work as teams and develop habits of thinking and acting in common. The role of a manager is to:

- listen;
- inform;
- delegate;
- facilitate.

This is reflected in the criteria used for assessing managers:

- have you obtained the best from your colleagues?
- how have you conducted yourself *vis-à-vis* your peers?
- how have you helped your boss?

Source: Crozier, 1990.

The attitude of many individuals and organisations in the past has been to criticise people who made mistakes or at best to hide the mistakes. Today, the attitude needs to be to learn from mistakes and to ensure that the knowledge is passed on. It is from mistakes that we learn, both as individuals and as organisations.

Organisational culture and information and communications technologies

Organisational cultures contain attitudes about the use of ICTs, whether they are a good or a bad thing and about how, by whom and on which tasks they should be used. To confuse matters, the use of ICTs changes the culture in a number of ways, including attitudes to their use.

Looking at the area of accounting information systems, Macintosh coined the phrase 'social software' to encompass how accounting information systems are seen to interact with organisations:

> It is concerned with how these systems influence and are influenced by personal attributes, group dynamics, and impersonal forces in the organisation ... (Macintosh, 1985, page 3.)

Accounting information systems are generally seen by managers as biased and unhelpful. The measures used in such financial controls are often set by others and do not necessarily reflect the measures of competitive performance which the managers themselves would have chosen to reflect the actions and opinions of the marketplace. The process of setting budgets establishes patterns of budget-orientated behaviours, both in their establishment and in measuring subsequent performance against budgets. In some senses, budgets can become self-fulfilling. Similar responses to this can be seen to information and communications technologies, where behaviour is modified to achieve the targets set. If people participate in setting the goals, it seems that they are more likely to feel ownership of the project and to achieve the targets.

The culture of a group is related to the artifacts it uses, as is all too obvious in our consumer society, with its designer clothes and accessories. Information and communication technologies bring a substantial and very rich set of new artifacts (a mixture of hardware, software, datasets and telecommunications facilities) into the culture of organisations and their presence and use result in the displacement of older artifacts, including older ICT-related artifacts. On one level the artifacts can be seen as output such as desktop publishing or colour transparencies for overhead projectors and as notebook computers and mobile telephones used on planes and trains. While at another level, in terms of behaviour, cultural attitudes can be seen in views about, whether it is acceptable for managers to type their own short memos, electronic mail messages and so on.

Tools can only be used in certain ways, imposing the use of standardised methods and, in the case of ICTs, standard formats of results. One measure of user-friendliness is the extent to which people can continue to use familiar patterns of work. Whether friendly or hostile, a computer-based information system has to be used according to methods that were not previously in use in the organisation. The construction of computer-based information systems requires a complex process of systems analysis, which examines and makes explicit the operations of some part of the organisation. The result of this process will be that some aspects of the culture are embedded into the system, while others are omitted and some new factors added.

A range of responses to the challenges presented by the use of information and communications technologies can be seen in organisations. At one extreme is 'ICT Phobia', where few ICT proposals are made and fewer still are accepted. At the other extreme is 'ICT mania', where ICT proposals are made without sufficiently careful consideration of their importance to the organisation and where acceptance is almost unquestioning. How the management of an organisation decides that it needs a new computer-based information system is an important indication of its attitude towards

ICTs. In many large organisations, there will be important and powerful Data Processing or Information Systems Departments which control developments where and when developments are allowed, when they are maintained, expanded and replaced. There must be negotiation between individual operational departments and the DP/IS Department to achieve this, which will reflect power politics and organisational culture.

A proposal for a computer-based information system can be specified in many different ways. How this is done in practice reflects the organisational culture in such traditional factors as the degree of centralisation and the initiative which managers at different levels are expected and permitted to take. The most important factor is the understanding of the business needs of those specifying the system, to be able to state clearly the business objectives and to understand the business implications of different proposals. A key consideration is whether information and communications technologies are seen to be related to business strategy or whether they remain a simple source of efficiency gains.

The culture of an organisation helps to determine who is consulted in the implementation of ICTs. Some organisations work on the *Blitzkrieg* approach; soften them up with some short courses and parachute the computers in at dawn. At the other extreme, lies anarchic forms of end user computing. A combination of lower costs, enthusiastic salespeople and the growth of a nebulous beneficial feeling about ICTs has led to a proliferation of systems within organisations. In particular, the delays encountered with requests to DP/IS Departments, often as much as two or three years, provide an incentive for managers to 'go it alone' by buying off-the-shelf packages and systems.

The use of ICTs changes how work is performed in organisations. However, new standards and expectations do not develop evenly or simultaneously within an organisation. Some people and some units of the organisations modify their expectations and integrate the new information systems into their culture more rapidly than others. One of the main ways in which information and communication technologies change the way we work is through the increased flexibility it gives people, resulting in an inevitably interim character of work. No longer is a document ever finished, it is always possible to make adjustments to the text, the numbers or the illustrations up to the very last minute. The authors of this book, Beaumont and Sutherland, took advantage of this feature to try, not entirely successfully, to keep apace of events.

Case: Computer Stories

Scenario: In the past ten years, computers have become a rich source of stories and jokes in many organizations.

Computers help us, but they also threaten us: our jobs, our traditions, our pride and our intelligence. Their 'behaviour' can be dazzling or it can be erratic, unpredictable and temperamental. Minor computer failures can lead to huge 'cock-ups', scores of angry customers issued with the wrong tickets, hundreds of employees sitting idly for hours until the machine gets fixed, thousands of letters going to the wrong addresses and so on. Equally computers offer a ready and defenceless scapegoat for human and organizational errors. For such reasons, it seems almost natural that, even in a short period, computers have generated their own folklore. Listening to these stories can reveal how people feel about computers, how they have affected their lives and how well they have become assimilated in the organization.

One of the commonest types of computer story involve computer experts ridiculing the non-experts and vice versa. This story was recounted by a consultant for a small charity which requested a run of 20,000 labels for a mailshot. A few months later, the consultant visited the office and saw a clerk busy copying by hand from the labels onto envelopes. "You should have let us know that you wanted a second set of these", she said, "Oh no, we thought we'd do them by hand because we didn't trust the computer" came the answer.

Nowhere is the distinction between expert and non-expert clearer than over the mastery of the jargon. Two executives of a major computer company recounted with relish how they had made a long presentation to a government department, demonstrating a hardware and software system called DRS-PWS, colloquially referred to as Dorris Pughes. The presentation went very well and the officials said that they were very impressed with the system, only they could not understand who that woman Dorris Pughes was, whose name kept cropping up. This gave away the fact that they had understood very little indeed; a good deal was therefore on the cards.

Understanding of computers and their language is not only the trademark of the expert; it is also a symbol of modern management, generating an aura of competence, efficiency and success. The Director of a research and publishing organisation prided himself on his computer literacy, had four computers in his office and insisted on being the first to test new packages. In the researcher's presence, he severely reprimanded his personal secretary for typing the address on an envelope rather than having it printed off a program. Yet, one of his subordinates reported:

The great story about computers is the common belief that the Director doesn't really know anything about computers at all; one of my friends in the research department was always getting called into his office to sort things out in his computers, and she would say "You know, it was only a simple matter, and he pretends he knows all about it, but in fact he knows bugger all, and he's just showing off.' He had these computers as a symbol of how important he was and all that, but he actually didn't use them.

If experts enjoy a laugh or two at the expense of pretenders and non-experts, the latter enjoy stories in which the experts end up with egg on their faces. The non-expert celebrates computer failures with the same delight as the expert celebrates the naivete of the users. Some of the stories of computer failure reverse the classic scenario in which the god of the machine came to the rescue of the failing humans. In the library of a large manufacturing firm, they liked to tell the story of a director urgently requesting a copy of an article that had appeared in a newspaper. No amount of computer searches could identify the article until a seasoned librarian phoned up all the newspapers and eventually tracked down the article. It had been written by a free-lancer who held the copyright and could not be included on the computerized database.

One can pick up similar stories in many organizations, where workers have to fall back on their traditional skills and use their cunning and experience every time the computer crashes. Even in highly automated organizations, such stories seem to proclaim, the computer does not have the last word. People cannot and must not become mere servants of the computers; they must remain their masters and bosses. Such hopes may be little more than wishful thinking, for it may already be too late to reclaim control over the computers and those in the know. The Head of Information of a large manufacturing firm recounted a story that drove him 'round the twist':

It's the bloody computer-boys and their tricks again. In the old days the telephone system was mechanical and you couldn't do anything with it. Now, of course it is computerized. Put in the new telephone system and for the first ten days, it was going wrong all the time, and it was the computer guys trying to see if they can wreck it, you know, 'let's be clever', messing about with the software. We had things like the Chairman's phone got extended to a lift and oh!, they are absolute menaces.

Computers are powerful tools and those who control them have power. To control them, one needs to speak their language, or more precisely, the language concocted by those who designed them. Many people find these languages forbidding. Interviewing a hospital secretary, the researcher asked her if she had a special system for naming files on her PC:

"Oh, yes", she said, "I name them all Jackie". "Surely, every time you create a new file named Jackie, you delete the earlier one on the hard disc," I retorted. "I don't use the hard disc" came the answer, "Those files I will need later, I save them on floppy discs".

The researcher realized to his surprise that Jackie had an entire library of floppy discs, each containing a single file named Jackie. Interviewing several of her colleagues, it quickly transpired that many did not even

> know the name of the software which they used and that none had even a rudimentary knowledge of MS-DOS.
>
> Stephie, a MS-DOS veteran in a consultancy organisation, said:
>
> DOS is, I wouldn't say part of a conspiracy, people are not organized or intelligent enough to perpetrate such a large conspiracy, but I think that it conspires in a way that gives people power. Because it is difficult to operate, difficult to understand, difficult to work with, those people who can work with it have power, they have influence and they are respected for their knowledge. In this organization, DOS is the source of my and Nigel's power.
>
> Source: Primary research undertaken by Yiannis Gabriel at the University of Bath.

The culture of Data Processing and Information Systems Departments is visibly and perceptibly different from that of other departments in an organisation. It is almost always a physically separate department, with a super-abundance of computer, terminals, manuals and printouts. In particular, it will have a secure and air-conditioned 'machine room', the *sanctum sanctorum* of the DP/IS Department. The staff dress and behave differently, usually much more casually. Moreover, they talk a different language, with a particularly dense and obscure jargon, one which changes with frightening rapidity. Traditionally, there have been few, if any, staff movements between the DP/IS Department and the rest of the organisation, although some organisations second DP/IS staff to user departments for specific projects. These 'technical' staff see themselves as independent 'professionals' who move to their next job because of the technical challenges presented and generally expect that move to be to another organisation. Indeed, many technical magazines and newspapers are circulated free-of-charge on the basis of the advertising revenue for those jobs. The role of the DP/IS Department is seen to be independent and professional, providing a technical service.

It is inevitable that in any rich organisational culture there will be pockets of particularly strong local cultures, for instance in advertising. The culture of the DP/IS Department will overlap with that of the rest of the organisation. However, dangers arise when the culture of the data processing or information systems department causes it to respond in a different way from that expected by the rest of the organisation. The solution is not to force a uniformity of culture, which is neither desirable nor strictly necessary. What is required is that the DP/IS Department behaves as a member of the organisational team.

7.4 Leadership

It is no longer plausible to believe that business success can be achieved through the traditional hierarchy of authority, rules and procedures for coordination and the division of labour; the division of tasks into small parts and their specification in manuals (at one time the UK Post Office manual required over three metres of shelf space). The tasks organisations set cannot be specified simply in terms of actions, but require that we adhere to sets of values held in common with each other and with the organisation. Customer service, quality, process innovation and so on, cannot be achieved by direction alone, they require acceptance of certain common values.

Experience of management shows that people must be led:

> To manage is to lead, and to lead others requires that one enlist the emotions of others to share a vision as their own. (.Henry Boettinger, formerly Director of Corporate Planning, AT&T.)

> People cannot be managed. Inventories can be managed, but people must be led. (H Ross Perot, Founder, Electronic Data Systems.)

> Making it happen means involving the hearts and minds of those who have to execute and deliver. It cannot be said often enough that these are not the people at the top of the organisation, but those at the bottom. (Sir John Harvey-Jones, formerly Chairman, Imperial Chemical Industries.)

Nowadays, we are all leaders, whether we lead from 'below' or from 'above'. We must identify and develop change in our own organisations and must help and encourage our colleagues, clients, suppliers and partners to do the same. We must encourage those who are practising change and, most importantly, we must welcome change ourselves. There is nothing worse than for people to know that they can sit out your current fad.

Case: Jan Carlzon

Scenario: At a relatively early age, Jan Carlzon was given control of travel and airline businesses, in which he developed an unusual and very successful management style.

At the age of 32, Jan Carlzon was made President of Vingressor, the package holiday subsidiary of Scandinavian Airline Systems (SAS). He started off managing by edict and was known in the company as 'ego boy', after a racehorse of the time. Gradually he learned to pull back, that you should not command, but rather convince.

In 1978, he was made head of Linjeflyg, the Swedish internal airline, where his first act was to call all the staff into a hangar and ask them to help him to save the firm. He asked people for ideas and encouraged them to go around any blockages.

Carlzon became the Chief Executive Officer of Scandinavian Airline Systems (SAS) in 1981 at the age of 39. He was responsible for a major turnaround of the company, through the development of EuroClass with attention to service for the business traveller.

He believes that for a service-based business to succeed it is vital to devolve responsibility to those people closest to the customer. To achieve this, it is essential to provide the necessary information, to allow people to see the fuller picture. Of course, this results in a loss of control at the top, but that is essential if the necessary creativity and risk-taking is to be unleashed:

The ability to understand and direct change is crucial for effective leadership. Today's business leader must manage not only finances, production, technology, and the like but also human resources. By defining clear goals and strategies and them communicating them to his employees and training them to take responsibility for reaching these goals, the leader can create a secure working environment that fosters flexibility and innovation. Thus, the new leader is a listener, communicator, and educator — an emotionally expressive and inspiring person who can create the right atmosphere rather than make all the decisions himself. (Carlzon, 1987, page 35.)

Jan Carlzon has focused on people, both customers and staff, rather than on planes, technology or money.

Source: Carlzon, 1987.

The manager as consultant

The role of the manager as described in this book is dramatically different from the traditional view. He or she is now called upon to play roles such as:

- coach;
- counsellor;
- leader;
- mentor;
- problem finder;
- problem solver.

The old-fashioned roles of the manager were as an expert and commander, telling people what to do and providing solutions. Today, it is unlikely that this role will succeed or even be possible. By comparison, the traditional role of the consultant has been to appear, ask a few questions then write a report with definitive conclusions. It is increasingly likely that the consultant will be required to stay around and implement the solution. The problem is how to arm ourselves with ideas and methodologies to increase the likelihood of helping and to reduce or even eliminate the likelihood of an unsuccessful outcome.

Ed Schein has developed a 'process consultancy' model which is more complex than traditional views, attempting to fit consulting activity explicitly with real problems:

> Process consultation is a set of activities on the part of the consultant that help the client to perceive, understand, and act upon the process events that occur in the clients' environment. (Schein, volume 2, 1987, page 34.)

The focus is on how things are done, rather than on the things being done. This is in contrast to traditional models such as the purchase of expertise or the doctor-patient relationship in both of which the clients abdicates at least some of their responsibility. The manager-consultant must be willing to sit and listen, rather than to issue commands, similar to the approach known as Management By Walking About (MBWA).

It is assumed that the client does not necessarily understand the source of the perceived problem, though they will generally be able to describe the symptoms of the problem. The client may be aware of some of the types of help which are available, but is unlikely to know about all of them or how they might be applied to solve the problem. The aim of process consultation is therefore to help the client to learn to diagnose problems and that this is achieved, in part, through participation in the process of diagnosis. To achieve this there must be a constructive relationship between the client and the consultant:

> When individual colleagues or students came to me with problems, I found that the best stance was to keep asking questions that would clarify how the person was seeing the problem and, more important, to ask what the person had already tried to do about it. New ideas usually emerged that could be implemented. I found myself to me most effective and helpful if I took a task process orientation unless I had specific information that needed to be shared, in which case I would, of course, share it. (Schein, volume 2, 1987, page 59.)

There a problem of the observer interfering with what he is observing; people behave differently for outsiders. Likewise it is essential to avoid traps, to identify possible reasons for failing to see the real problems:

- cultural assumptions;
- personal defensive filters and biases;
- expectations based on previous experiences.

To do this you must identify your own biases and your own cultural assumptions and how they might affect your judgment and reason. Institute systematic checking procedures: spirit of enquiry

Organisational politics

In every organisation there are 'political' and 'personal' battles fought to win resources or to be recognised as successful, collectively known as organisational politics. Sadly, as in real politics, organisational politics sometimes degenerate into warfare, fought for its own sake or for sheer vindictiveness. Some people would like to have a severed head on a pole outside their offices as a reminder and a warning to their staff or would wish the motto 'In victory vengeance, in defeat malice.' However, the Machiavellian School of Management, with its daggers and poisons, is by no means the most certain route to success. There are no recipes for success in organisational politics, the winners are those with the personal qualities to succeed. Different people survive with different abilities. By and large, nice people get trodden on and people gang up on the real villains. Almost everybody uses networks of friends and colleagues to influence decision-making; people who are under some obligation to help. Sometimes the attitudes displayed by individuals are empire building, which can verge on megalomania. It is vital to recognise the abilities and limitations of yourself and others, preferably in the context of what would be good for the organisation.

One of the main areas over which political battles are fought is resources. Is it possible for someone or some department to get more resources or more money than opponents? Large technology-related projects and the budgets for DP/IS Departments are, therefore, inherently political, a fact which must be recognised and taken into account by the 'actors'. Appropriate political methods should be used to supplement or supplant the traditional and apparently strictly rational judgements made in terms of, say, return-on-investment (see Chapter 8).

The other major area of organisational politics lies in attributing blame or success. Success does not have to be real, you need only to be seen to be successful, either by stealing the success of others or passing off onto others the blame for your own failures. The 'Teflon factor' is named after the non-stick coating on pots and pans; reflecting the ability of some people to emerge unscathed from circumstances in which other people would be blamed.

7.5 Implementation

Seen from the point of view of the purchaser, computers are now little more than commodities. However, this must not be allowed to reduce the importance of managing their implementation, it is in this that many organisations fall down. The skills and knowledge required to ensure the successful adoption and diffusion of ICTs are very far from being commodities.

The introduction and operation of information and communications technologies require very significant expenditure in staff development and training, if organisations are to change the attitudes and ways in which people work. All too often this is neglected, usually through 'penny-pinching', in order to achieve 'hurdle' rates of payback. Investments in ICTs have long since ceased to be the simple capital substitution of labour, they require intellectual capital to maximise the benefit.

It is difficult, if not impossible, to arrange for the use of technology in advance of its adoption in everyday work, too often new uses are found which were quite unintended and unexpected. Consequently, a considerable measure of experimentation is necessary which requires a temporary lifting of tight limits on measuring performance and a willingness to adapt. This is not to suggest that high levels of training should not be undertaken prior to the introduction of the new systems. Continuous learning both formal and informal are needed, if progress is to be made up the learning curve.

The organisational reforms which are necessary if new technology is to be properly utilised, include:

- participation;
- flexible assignment patterns;
- multiple skilling;
- self-supervision;
- quality problem-solving groups.

All of these are aimed at empowering staff, through:

MOTIVATION
Can job redesign be used to motivate people to achieve improved levels of performance?

COMPETENCE
Can the levels of competence be increased through the use of ICTs?

COORDINATION
Can the coordination between functions be improved?

Only when there is innovation in the design of work do we find significant improvements in performance asociated with the introduction of new technology. The problems which must be faced include the design of:

- jobs with sufficient breadth and flexibility to allow people to understand all or large parts of the system;
- connections between those who share responsibility, in order to improve collaboration and the management of interdependence;
- jobs that generate high-levels of motivation;

- jobs that promote learning about the system and about the business tasks themselves.

The manner in which, for example, a workstation arrives on your desk and the ways in which you are introduced to the facilities are important determinants of how ICT will be perceived and how it will be used. The nature of this implementation phase appears to be dependent upon a number of features of the organisational culture, for example, the degree of decentralisation of decision making and the pace of organisational life. Although participation by end users in decision making processes is well recognised as being beneficial to the implementation of ICT, it is less widely practised. The timescales over which people are expected to return to and exceed their previous level of efficiency are major factors in the pressure under which staff operate.

7.6 Conclusion

The issue for managers is not whether they can cope with change, but how; for there is no alternative. The first thing to do is to set an example. An important aspect of leading is the ability to empower, not simply to delegate the dirty or the dull jobs but to take the risk of a subordinate proving that he or she is better than you are!

Managing change cannot be separated from the organisational culture, which contains within it many of the determinants of success and failure. Consequently, we must look carefully at the processes being used to consult, to manage and to implement. They must take into account the culture of the organisation, both because the processes should reflect how things are done in the organisation and because they should also warn us when the culture must be altered.

The introduction of ICTs provides an opportunity to achieve change; 'leverage'. However, they must not be used as an instrument of terror, as was the guillotine during the French Revolution.

Recognising that the success an organisation, especially in the longer term, depends on the abilities of people, whether it is termed intellectual capital or core competencies, it is essential that recruitment is meticulous and that people are subsequently trained extensively. It is important to build links to other organisations whose intellectual capital is of value, for example, consultancies, advertising agencies and research laboratories. Information and communications technologies can provide an important support for maximising theuse made of intellectual capital.

The overall aim is to create a 'learning organisation'; an organisation which can learn faster and better than its rivals and which can turn that knowledge into products or services or improvements in product or service characteristics which will win competitively. Such an organisation creates change and adapts to the change created by others.

Review questions

1 How would you communicate an organisation's vision or mission?

2 How do you expect ICTs to change the ways in which managers will operate in the next five to ten years? What skills and knowledge will you need to acquire as a consequence of these changes?

3 What are the advantages of process consultancy over more traditional forms of consultancy?

4 Consider the differences between 'management' and 'leadership'?

Study questions

1 How can an organisation where ICTs are seen as an administrative expense be persuaded to look for strategic advantages?

2 How would you make your organisation more customer-orientated? What specific measures would be necessary?

3 If a 'corporate raider' such as Lord Hanson or Sir James Goldsmith took over your organisation, how and why would he change the way it operated?

4 Discuss the following comment from Jack Welsh, CEO, General Electric.

"Neatness and orderliness are not what we are after. We are after getting information to people who can act on it."

Further reading

Beer, Michael, Bert Spector, Paul Lawrence, Quinn Mills and Richard Walton "Managing Human Assets" Free Press, New York, 1984.

A classic text from the Harvard Business School on human resource management. Although published in 1984, it remains as valuable today as when published, providing views which link HRM to the strategic management of organisations.

Belasco, James A "Teaching the Elephant to Dance" Hutchison Business Books, London, 1990.

This book is very useful for the practitioner. It is unlikely to be read from cover to cover, but can easily be dipped into either for specific issues, provocative questions or to find new and interesting ideas and, most importantly, suggestions about how to employ those ideas.

Buchanan, David A and James McCalman "High Performance Work Systems: the Digital experience" Routledge, London, 1989.

A case study of how work was changed at the Ayr Plant of the Digital Equipment Corporation, through the introduction of high performance work systems. It focuses on how to make better use of people, rather than on how to automate a factory manufacturing computers.

Crozier, Michel "L'Organisation à l'Ecoute" Les Editions d'Organisation, Paris, 1990.

In French. A leading French industrial sociologist's view of HRM. It demonstrates some of the differences between French management tradition and the Anglo-American approach.

Deal, Terrence E and Allen A Kennedy "Corporate Culture" Penguin Books, Harmondsworth, 1988.

One of the classic works on corporate culture (originally published in 1982). It contains many interesting stories, including some in which Tom Peters features as a consultant.

Huczinski, Andrzej and David A Buchanan "Organisational Behaviour" Second Edition, Prentice-Hall, London, 1991.

One of the best of the standard texts on organisational behaviour. It is practical and not overly concerned with theory. As good behaviouralists, the authors chose a bright yellow cover to attract attention.

Kanter, Rosabeth Moss, Barry A Stein and Todd D Jick "The Challenge of Organisational Change: how people experience it and manage it" Free Press, New York, 1991.

This book addresses a fundamental management issue for the 1990's of how to face change. Case studies are used to support the arguments and, interestingly, they show both how to introduce change and how not to introduce change.

Mills, D Quinn "Rebirth of the Corporation" John Wiley and Sons, New York, 1991.

With obvious linkages to total quality management, striving for continuous improvement, Quinn Mills argues for organisational transformation, replacing the hierarchical organisation by the cluster organisation. The orientation of the clusters' development are relationships with customers and suppliers and information requirements — that is strategy, rather than structure. An interesting example of successful clusters is provided by the information services of Du Pont Fibers. Simply stated, an excellent, thought-provoking volume.

Schein, Ed "Process Consulting" Two volumes. Addison-Wesley, Reading, 1987.

A very useful book for the consultant and practitioner alike. It identifies ways in which it is possible to work with groups of people and help them solve their own problems.

Schein, Ed "Organisational Culture and Leadership" Jossey-Bass, San Fransisco, 1989.

Rather heavier going than 'Process Consulting', this is the academic side of organisational culture, primarily for those interested in pursuing the theoretical basis of the ideas.

Scott Morton, Michael S (editor) "The Corporation of the 1990's" Oxford University Press, 1991.

Chapter 7 "The Networked Organisation" J F Rockart and J E Short.

Chapter 8 "The Impact of IT on Jobs and Skills" Paul Osterman.

Chapter 9 "Organisational Change" R B McKersie and R E Walton.

What is the payoff?

Learning objectives:

- to understand how to link investment in information and communications technologies with business strategy;

- to recognise the need to understand and, where necessary, to redesign business processes before making investments in information and communication technologies;

- to be able to identify appropriate measures for the appraisal and accounting of investments in information and communication technologies.

8.1 Introduction

One of the few statements which has remained true for information and communications technologies is that if you wait, then technical and market developments will make things cheaper, faster, smaller and generally 'better'. However, you should not necessarily delay investment; if it can be justified now, it should be made now:

> Investment in information technology is a business strategy designed to substitute information-technology capital for information-handling labour. Improved effectiveness may be realised through better quality, cost reduction, decreased uses of resources, enhanced use of employee talents, or improved customer service. (Strassmann, 1985, page 151.)

Investments in information and communications technologies are often very large and, given that the benefits of automation have usually been achieved, senior managers are increasingly asking 'what is the payoff?' For too long, investment decisions have been 'acts of faith', based on costs and benefits suggested by trusted senior managers. Moreover, these investments are too rarely followed up, as post-implementation reviews of costs and benefits are very seldom undertaken. When the expected returns fail to materialise it can be, and usually is, blamed on changing and unforeseen circumstances. The only reasonable conclusion is that the overall quality of the decision-making is poor.

Evaluation of the costs and benefits of an investment is not straightforward. The task of evaluating the strategic role of information resources is admittedly particularly difficult, but it needs to be done. To a certain extent, the problems can be linked directly to the absence of precise measurement techniques. The increasing concerns of managers about the absence of proper evaluation can be explained partly by the developing strategic role of ICT investments and partly by the continuing growth of expenditure on ICTs.

8.2 A cost or an investment?

Given current practices regarding ICT investment appraisal, our basic objective, in this chapter, is to raise neglected issues, rather than introduce and define a range of different techniques (see Further Reading for more details). The basic argument stresses the need for an explicit linkage with the overall business strategy and for careful practical consideration of measurement: what? and how? Paul Strassmann's concept of 'Return-on-Management' is discussed specifically:

> The firms that just survive in the information economy will be the ones that use information resources and computer technologies only as cost-displacement and labour-saving tools. The firms that compete effectively and flourish in the information economy will be the ones that use information technologies and information resources in strategic ways to manufacture new and better products, find new markets and enlarge their share of existing markets, and distribute products and services in creative ways. These will be the intelligent organisations of the future. (Marchand and Horton, 1986, page 293.)

It is important that there should not be a conflict between the financial and strategic justifications for information and communications technologies; management can, and should, justify investments on financial grounds. The financial appraisal must explicitly recognise the particular nature and attributes of the ICT investment, where, unfortunately, traditional cost-benefit analysis is generally inappropriate and inadequate. It is essential to be able to prioritise investment decisions because of the need to manage scarce resources, especially finance and ICT expertise. Peter Keen (1991, page 11) correctly identifies the problem:

> Much of business managers' discomfort with IT reflects the lack of a clear economic framework of judging IT investment options and payback. Even when the competitive benefits of IT are apparent, it has proven nearly impossible to measure the economic benefits.

As early as 1984, the management consultants A T Kearney produced a report for the British Department of Trade and Industry which identified that:

> The main barriers to the further use of information technology are the lack of appropriate cost-benefit techniques.

In an excellent discussion, Paul Strassmann (1985), argues that the 'payoff' will eventually come, but not from the technology alone. Success will be dependent on how managers at all levels in the organisation are organised, educated and trained. It is not the quantity of the investment that counts, but the way in which it is applied and managed — this is not a trivial task. If information and communications technologies are to be viewed as a strategic necessity, then the perspective taken must be that of their potential business benefits, rather than simply viewing ICTs as an administrative or business cost.

The 1987 Price Waterhouse/*Computing* Opinions Surveys found concern amongst senior managers that about one third of all ICT expenditure in UK companies would be authorised outside DP/IS Departmental budgets. A 1987 survey in the USA by the Diebold Group indicated that this so-called 'illegal' expenditure was, on average, approximately 50% of official DP/IS Departmental budgets. Investments in information and communications technologies remain the only major business area which is increasing at a rate substantially greater than economic growth and this can be expected to develop further as 'end-user' computing continues to expand.

The Price Waterhouse/*Computing* Opinions Survey (1990, page 5), highlighted changes in the rankings of top management problems:

> The (1988/89) Review reported the emergence of a business problem in the UK which was beginning to challenge some of the more technical issues which traditionally concern the IT executive. Integrating computer plans within overall corporate strategy appeared as the number three issue there, demonstrating that the drive to achieve competitive advantage through the use of information technology was beginning to be more widely recognised as a potential business weapon, and increasing numbers of IT managers were being asked to devise or implement appropriate systems.
>
> Now our survey reveals this to be the principal concern of executives in Australia, Denmark, Japan, Spain and the UK, and other concerns are pushed to the background while companies grapple with the principles involved. However, devising competitive strategies does not lead to elimination of the technical problems. On the contrary, new applications impose new deadlines and delivery problems, and meeting systems deadlines is still the main concern of respondents in Canada, France, Ireland and the USA, and is a good second in Australia, Spain and the UK. Another issue which causes some concern is that of predicting developments in technology, and rates second place in Canada, Denmark and France. The dilemma is presented of whether to take buying decisions on the basis of today's proven systems and possibly miss the opportunity of snatching a lead with emerging technology developments, or carry on with the obsolete system until the new technologies show that they are here to stay.

Costs and benefits must be considered for the organisation as a whole, rather than from the perspective of a DP/IS Department. However, the allocation of costs to individuals and departments is not a straightforward task. In practice, unrealistic and artificial mechanisms are often used which means that a true picture of performance is concealed:

> IS managers have no ready formula for allocating infrastructure costs fairly. Consider this representative sample of the questions they face. Should the first users of a telecommunications service carry the full burden, even though the marginal cost is low? Who should pay for the development of a customer master data base, an infinitely reusable resource that will eventually be of value to many business units? Where outside services are cheaper, should business units be allowed to use them and thereby reduce the customer base for the shared corporate resource. (Keen, 1991, page 148.)

The costs of ICTs need to be apportioned logically, otherwise they could be thought of as a 'free' resource. If the DP/IS Department acts as a 'profit centre', however, there are dangers of its objectives becoming inconsistent with servicing the overall business needs of the organisation. Where internal charging is used, there needs to be some direct relationship with the prices of external suppliers, while the internal costs of devising and implementing the financial allocation mechanisms should be kept to a minimum.

In any investment decision, it is obviously necessary to consider the existing ICT asset base. Indeed, against a backcloth of rising and/or understated system and project costs, developments are often funded as incremental additions to existing systems. This budgetary process, with authorised expenditure levels (often including head counts), can hide the real costs, especially implications for later in the system life-cycle. On the other hand, this approach can allow an organisation to continue to make ICT investments.

Case: 'Tradeable Information' — what price?

Scenario: In order to conduct a trade in information, it is essential to establish a price for the commodity.

'Tradeable information' is a phrase:

> … designed to create an awareness that information is a commodity which has value, can be bought and sold like any other, and that like most commodities, value can be added to the raw material at various stages of processing.
>
> Information is a particularly valuable commodity; almost uniquely it can be sold and retained at the same time. Information can have different values, different types of customers, and can be manipulated by the application of technology for very many different purposes. (Department of Trade and Industry, 1990, page 4.)

- what is the value of a database?
- what price should be charged for a database?

Economics is a social science concerned with the allocation of scarce resources and involves choices and values. Although information has value, databases do not possess value simply from their existence, it arises from their use in different areas of decision-making (although the value of a single database can vary by the distribution media: printed output, magnetic tape/floppy disk/CD-ROM, on-line access and so on, because of the ability of customers to handle the data). Value must be measured against the 'productivity' of management as it feeds into their decision-making. The value of information can be seen as linking means and ends (with their ratio often being defined as 'productivity'). A real difficulty exists because the value of information for the decision-making process has to be anticipated when databases are purchased; it can only really be known once the effects of decisions have been assessed. Thus, when establishing a database, the information really only possesses 'latent' value; the same information has different values for different organisations, different managers, different decisions and at different times.

The concept of information 'half-life' has been used to indicate how its value depreciates over time. Unfortunately, this seems rather simplistic and suggests constant, if exponential, decay over time. It does not allow for the elimination of databases through the introduction of new and better databases, which happens all the time. Neither does it allow for the power of computer-based information systems which:

- develops over time, as historic data series are built up to provide insights into trends;
- is dependent directly on the people designing and using the system.

Conventionally, economists argue that the price of a product should be closely related to the costs of providing that product. (If there is a large and continuing difference between these two measures, anti-trust and monopoly authorities may become involved.) However, for a single dataset, the production costs of the first copy are extremely large, whereas the costs of subsequent copies may be minimal. Moreover, the usual problems of expanding production into uneconomic levels, when diseconomies of scale occur, are not generally found with databases. Indeed, when data are provided, the original supplier does not lose possession of the product. Direct costs, therefore, provide little real indication for pricing. In fact, there is an argument to continue to expand the market for a database, although this strategy would be dependent on a suitable pricing policy.

Usually when goods are consumed they are destroyed, although there are other goods, such as motor cars, which can be 'reconsumed' (although eventually they become worn out). In contrast, for information, consumption and 'reconsumption' do not lead to destruction and, therefore, in setting prices, consideration must be given to expected frequency of use.

The complex and changing linkages between supply and demand are important. Pricing of databases is a non-trivial task, with account having to be taken of the different forces affecting the buyer-seller relationships, especially their relative bargaining power. For example, for the buyer:

- what are the anticipated benefits of the database?
- what costs (hardware, software and people) are incurred to be able to use the data?
- what are the 'switching' costs of changing supplier?
- what level of accuracy is required for decision-making?

For the seller:

- what are the real costs of collecting, maintaining, marketing and delivering the data?
- what distribution media should be provided?
- how many users can be expected?
- how to deal with the 'product life cycle' of a database?

Notwithstanding the above and other forces, pricing mechanisms are not straightforward. In practice, competing information products are often priced in 'categories' usually established by first entrants, even if their underlying costs are quite different. In addition, prices can relate to outright sales or leases over specified time periods, with some agreement for updating as appropriate.

Finally, it has been assumed that a database is a fixed unit for pricing. However, users generally want different subsets of a database, making it necessary to calculate direct or apportioned costings and pricings which can be extremely difficult, if not impossible (or, at least, cannot readily be justified because of the effort required).

Managers, who are concerned about their investments in information and communications technologies, often highlight project management difficulties such as cost overruns, implementation time delays and reduced functionalities (see also Chapter 6). While these are important considerations, this understandable focus of attention is on the input side of the investment, rather than on the business outputs. Moreover, in any overall evaluation, risk and uncertainty must be incorporated explicitly. In a consideration of 'information economics', Parker *et al.* (1989) differentiate between the following categories of risk and uncertainty:

STRATEGIC UNCERTAINTY
The likely success of an organisation's corporate business strategy.

ORGANISATIONAL RISK
The necessary management knowledge, skills and attitudes that are required for a successful ICT investment.

INFORMATION SYSTEM INFRASTRUCTURE RISK
Not only the technology, but also aspects of project management and the required support from the DP/IS Department.

DEFINITIONAL UNCERTAINTY
The extent to which the information needs of managers have been specified explicitly.

TECHNOLOGICAL UNCERTAINTY
The extent to which an ICT investment relies on new or unproven technology.

As Keen (1991, page 142) argues,

There are three issues in managing the economics of information capital: managing costs, managing benefits, and managing risk exposure.

8.3 Measurements

The promise of business returns from investments in information and communications technologies must be addressed explicitly. There is a need to consider both:

- investment criteria;
- performance indicators.

Management must examine the initial investment appraisal to determine whether a project should be implemented. Once agreed, management should monitor the outputs from their investments. Assessments can and should be undertaken at different stages, including evaluation of:

- the IS strategy to support the overall business strategy;
- particular IS projects, which must be prioritised with regard to other possible capital investments;

- the effects of the system over time, including a comparison of the actual and planned costs and benefits.

Kumar (1990) argues that organisations do not generally recognise and separate explicitly the different stages of appraisal, and this confusion can be further exacerbated by the different perspectives and different objectives taken by managers and ICT specialists.

Marchand and Horton (1986, page 212) stress that:

> ... no topic is more complex than the one of finding useful ways to measure the value of information ... Research in this area is still very limited, and there is substantial disagreement at both the theoretical and the applied levels.

It is necessary to start with basics, raising significant, theoretical and practical questions of measurement:

- what should be measured?
- how should it be measured?

Some people fail to answer, or even to ask, these fundamental questions. Instead, they view investments in information and communications technologies as part of the cost of doing business and lump them together into corporate overheads. Given the scale of these costs in most organisations (on average, one third to one half of capital expenditure), this cannot be justified. The alternative, to calculate the costs as some proportion of revenues, is not particularly helpful either to try to keep the proportion from increasing or to undertake comparisons with other organisations (as is done with advertising expenditures). Such 'boundary' values relate to aggregate expenditures and say nothing about individual projects. An organisation, for instance, may be spending well 'above average', either to 'stay ahead' or to 'catch up'. Moreover, these views fail to link the investments to the business in terms of either the way it operates or its strategic positioning.

As Peter Keen (1991, page 11) argues:

> Information technology must pay its way. It will do so if it is targeted at opportunities to improve the firm's profit structures — its 'top-line'. Profit is traditionally referred to as the bottom line, because that is where it appears on the profit and loss statement. The implicit business model is revenue-focused. If firms grow their revenue base and keep their costs under control, they will see a healthy bottom line. Profit now has to become a top-line consideration. With operating margins being remorselessly driven down by global competition, deregulation, and sophisticated consumers, growth is becoming a way to go broke! Firms must drastically change their cost structure and rethink the relationship between revenues and profits. They need to be able to monitor sales, costs, and margins on a day-to-day basis, so that they can be alerted to and respond to trends as they occur. They need new sources of revenues that provide healthy operating margins.

The traditional managerial emphasis on costs, specifically new materials, labour, plant and equipment, needs to be modified in at least two fundamental ways. First, new costs will increasingly need to be incurred, for instance those associated with enhancing quality and services. Second, attention must be given to revenue generation, rather than only cost-cutting. Keen (1991, page 14) argues that:

The top-line framework is the basis for an economic model of IT as a business resource.

Figure 8.1 *Top-line emphasis*
(Source: Keen, 1991, page 13.)

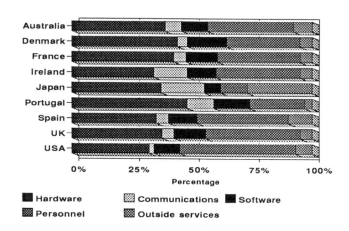

Figure 8.2 *Average IT department budget — fiscal year 1989/90*
(Source: Price Waterhouse, 1990.)

It is essential that a broad definition of information and communications technologies is adopted. Inclusion of hardware and software is not sufficient; databases and human resources must also be included. Human resources costs, for example, represent a significant proportion of the total ICT costs and this, often neglected, component continues to increase (see figure 8.2). Moreover, it should not be forgotten that any investment automatically incurs future 'maintenance' costs.

Questions of definitional scope raise issues regarding the capitalisation of software and databases, and the recognition that training and development should be accepted explicitly as an organisational asset, as 'intellectual capital'. In accounting terms, by treating such costs as expenses, it is very difficult to estimate the overall value of available software in an organisation because of inappropriate management accounting information. As indicated earlier, it is necessary to consider the costs incurred by the organisation as a whole, not just the costs incurred by the DP/IS Department.

Case: Creating the IT balance sheet

Scenario: Successful organisations understand their costs. Notwithstanding the difficulties of forecasting the business benefits and assessing the risks of any ICT investment, few organisations fully appreciate the real costs of such investments.

Peter Keen proposes the development of an IT asset balance sheet, and exemplifies his ideas through a description of a bank that spends $200 million per annum on IT:

The bank has long been aware of the most obvious capital item, hardware and equipment, but has overlooked the capital tied up in personal computers, departmental telecommunications, and small unit-cost items that together added up to several million dollars.

Top management had no idea that the bank had spent close to $500 million to create the software currently in use, nor that it was an information factory sitting on data that had cost well over $1 billion to create (this figure includes relevant fractions of the salaries of staff in the bank's operations and back-office unites). IT assets added up to over $2 billion. (Keen, 1991, page 143.)

The IT Balance Sheet could be summarised as:

ASSETS

(US$ millions) Commentary

Hardware:

Centrally managed   120 This is the most obvious computers
                                   component of the IT base and the one that

		accountants track; it is just 5% of this bank's real IT assets.
Distributed	84	Mainly personal computers. In many organisations, PCs, workstations, and departmental systems now account for more expenditures than do central expenditures.
Network equipment	105	Telecommunications facilities, often distributed across many different operating budgets.
Distributed telecommunications	59	Local area networks and departmental equipment
Total Hardware	368	
Facilities	92	Data Centre and operations
Software:		
Applications	420	Software development expenditures are expensed development. The bank had no idea how much it had spent to build the software in use, nor did the accounting system make it easy to find out.
Other	68	This and the figure for "other PC software software" are really educated guesses. It also ignores replacement costs, which the firm's IT planners estimate as at least $1.2 billion, three times the original cost.
Total Software	488	
Data Resources	1200	This is the estimated capital cost of the salaries, processing, and storage incurred in creating the on-line data resources that are the basis for the bank's products and services, which is an infinitely reusable asset. Data resources do not wear out as they are used.
Total Assets	2240	

Source: Keen (1991).

Can accountants help?

Considering the "rise and fall of management accounting", Johnson and Kaplan (1987, page 260) have argued that accounting has not stayed in touch with changing management needs and the new capabilities of ICTs to provide information:

> The obsolescence of management accounting systems has not occurred overnight. The systems, whose intellectual roots can be traced to events sixty to one hundred years ago, worked well for the times in which they were designed. We have speculated that the dominance of financial accounting procedures, both in education and in practice, has inhibited the dynamic adjustment of management accounting systems to the realities of the contemporary environment.
>
> If organisations' management accounting systems fail to provide useful signals for measuring the efficiency of processes and profitability of products, the ability of senior executives to manage ... will diminish
>
> Poor management accounting systems by themselves will not lead to organisational failure. Nor will excellent management accounting systems assure success. But they certainly can contribute to the decline or survival of organisations.

As indicated in Chapter 6, a range of approaches has been developed to conceptualise the development and implementation of computer-based information systems; the stages of growth models are supposed to provide qualitative indicators of the most appropriate form of investment for an organisation in its current state of development and Critical Success Factors have a behavioural focus on the qualitative factors which senior managers think are behind a successful business strategy implementation. The apparently detailed accuracies of quantified accounting-based investment appraisals are excluded in these approaches. Moreover, there is really no indication of business priorities and risks, or even apparent acceptance of the inherent uncertainties involved (technological, cost, skills, ...).

Traditional investment criteria, such as return on investment and net present value, have been proposed and occasionally used to justify ICT investments. Such measures of efficiency are only appropriate for 'automate' investment decisions. Interestingly, a recent study by Barbara Farbey et al. (1990) indicates that nearly half the projects studied were 'not justified' and that, of the 'justified' projects, the assessment was no more than some kind of 'rationalisation', yet all had been implemented.

Measurements must be linked to objectives and defined operationally in a simple form. Investments, for instance, in customer billing systems, can be driven by productivity considerations ('automate') which can be appraised by conventional methods. Efficiency gains can be achieved from cost reductions or avoidance and from improvements in people's productivity. If the return on investment approaches can be used, direct comparisons with other capital investments, which also compete for an organisation's scarce resources, become more straightforward.

However, where the object is not to 'automate', sound investments may not be supported because it proves impossible to quantify all the future business benefits as cash flows. Robert Malpas gave an example of the decision to build a new control room for British Petroleum's Grangemouth oil refinery. It was initially rejected because the payback was too low. Nonetheless, it was built and achieved the required payback rate by providing more information about the refinery, allowing it to be better managed. That is, the investment could not be justified for 'automate' reasons, but it could have been justified for 'informate' reasons.

The simple message is that to measure the business benefits of investments in information and communications technologies it is essential to differentiate alternative strategic objectives and to accept that different measurements and metrics are required. Different business objectives each have different associated measurements, however, new metrics should not be introduced specifically to make the case for particular ICT investments. For example, market share and market growth are useful in marketing, while for operations management, costs, inventory levels and quality are all relevant. Information and communications technologies can assist in achieving these business objectives, indeed certain functions are increasingly dependent on the capabilities of this infrastructural platform.

In terms of what should be measured, the emphasis is on business investments related to an organisation's corporate strategy. No consideration is given to other types of benefits, such as those that make people's working life less mundane. Business objectives can generally be defined in terms of profitability and market share and relate to customers and suppliers and to products and services. More specific underlying objectives include service levels, inventories, production costs, market penetration and so on.

As discussed in Chapter 4, it is important to appreciate the dynamics of the situation, rather than simply take a snap-shot at one point in time. Although many organisations set out to achieve automation, this orientation can evolve over time to more sophisticated views, such as 'informate' and 'transformate'. It is necessary to recognise that an investment in information and communications technologies can simultaneously achieve more than one of these objectives. For example, linkage with suppliers can improve customer service through bespoke product design, while reducing stocks gives direct financial benefits.

The satisfaction of multiple objectives could arise from *ad hoc* developments over time or from the initial design and implementation of an information system. Whatever the reason, multiple objectives can be appropriate and evaluation may require the use of multiple measurements. Multiple applications create new issues in evaluation; it is necessary to understand the underlying cost and benefit components, as well as the overall picture.

Neither evaluation of the initial investment (attempting to anticipate later developments) nor the continuing monitoring (attempting to relate to changing situations) is straightforward. Indeed, it is possible to argue that unforeseen benefits are likely to be achieved over time. Taking this further, some investments in information and communications technologies should be viewed as 'infrastructure' in that they can provide the foundation for 'leveraging' of future benefits as new applications are introduced. The level of such long-term investment varies by organisation, by industry and by country.

8.4 Information technology and information systems strategies

Investments in information and communications technologies can be made for a variety of reasons: 'automate', 'informate', 'empowerate' and 'transformate' (see Chapter 4). Measurement of the payoff must be consistent with the specific objectives of the corporate business strategy.

With appropriate use of information, an organisation can improve its profitability through better planning and control. Moreover, appropriate information can provide an opportunity to be innovative and responsive in the competitive business environment. Such statements are straightforward to present, but difficult to implement. How can we measure improvements from more informed decision-making, improved communications, competitive advantage?

Unfortunately, it is not possible to offer a simple checklist that can be employed to evaluate particular strategies. Current practices can be improved by having a clear understanding of the business objectives and appropriate performance indicators from the outset. For instance, the following measures are some of those that could be used in functional departments:

- procurement of raw materials
  - costs
  - quality
  - delivery scheduling
- manufacturing
  - costs
  - quality
  - work-in-progress
- sales
  - revenue
  - customer profitability
- marketing
  - market share
  - market expansion
- DP/IS
  - costs
  - functionality
  - time.

The metrics for such measurements can also vary; for example, 'quality' could be related to acceptance/rejection of a specific standard or to variation in the level of the standards. Ultimately, at least in the private sector, the chief executive and board are responsible to shareholders, who are interested in their earnings per share and equity growth.

As a simple illustration, many retailers have made large-scale investments in Electronic Point of Sales (EPoS) systems, primarily to 'automate' checkout operations and inventory management, linking branches through the warehouse and distribution system. However, data generated by this investment are proving to be useful to 'informate' managers about the vagaries and potential of their local catchment areas and to 'empowerate' local managers to make special offers on goods and arrange their management of staffing levels.

8.5 'Return-on-Management'

Moving away from the 'automate' rationale, the business benefits are achieved primarily from better management. Strassmann Inc. has a registered trademark, 'Return-on-Management' (Strassmann, 1990), which is defined as:

$$\text{Return-on-Management} \quad = \quad \frac{\text{Management Value-added}}{\text{Management Costs}}$$

As with all productivity performance measures, it is defined as a simple ratio, management output/management input. Paul Strassmann (1990, page 84) argues that management creates all surplus value:

> To attribute all surplus value to management instead of capital or labour, is a departure from classic economics. It is management that makes the investment and pricing decisions. It is management that motivates the employees. It is management that chooses products and markets. It is management that organises the suppliers and productions and delivery of goods to customers. Good management can get more of the capital it needs, at a lower interest, than poor management.

Management value-added is defined as the residual after all an organisation's inputs, costs and value-added from different resources, including capital, but excluding management (see figure 8.3). It is necessary to define what is meant by 'management' and what are the associated costs. In a functional sense, it is easier to highlight the 'non-management' operations areas (such as purchasing, production, distribution, sales and billing) and view management as the remainder, incorporating finance, personnel, legal, marketing, R&D and planning functions.

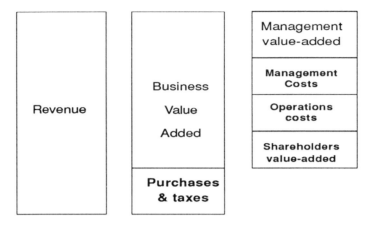

Figure 8.3 *The definition of management value-added (Source: Strassmann, 1991, page 89.)*

Strassmann (1990, pages 92-93) highlights a number of advantages of his Return-on-Management approach:

- it combines the effects of both Financial Statement and Balance Sheet entries;
- it is self-indexing. The numerator and the denominator are in terms of current costs which means that the ratio is indifferent to currency or inflation;
- it isolates the productivity of the critical business resource, which is managerial;
- it is particularly suitable for measuring service-based businesses, which use less capital to create revenue than manufacturing or utilities;
- it tracks performance during corporate restructuring when capital-intensive firms become increasingly dependent on purchased components and leased assets;
- it makes possible diagnostic evaluations, including cross-industry and international comparisons where there are major differences in vertical integration, debt-to-equity ratios and taxation.

A cogent argument for this focus on management productivity can be made because it is 'good' management which is the scarce resource, rather than information and communications technologies. While this approach calculates the returns as money values, clearly, at the initial appraisal stage, as with other techniques, the return-on-management must be estimated prior to making an investment.

8.6 Conclusion

It is no longer possible or desirable to avoid the evaluation of ICT investments. A range of approaches and techniques have been proposed by academics, consultants and practitioners. While the debate on their relative strengths and weaknesses will continue, a number of central messages can be highlighted, including the need:

- to link ICT investments to the corporate business strategy;
- to improve (or at least to examine) management practices before making any investments;
- to accept that conventional financial measures are generally inappropriate, but not to evade evaluation.

Although real difficulties exist about justifying any ICT investment, *ex post facto* evaluation, at least as a monitoring process, must be recognised as sound management practice. Unfortunately, there are no simple and unambiguous techniques that can be applied, which is not really surprising given the range of organisations, with their different information cultures and the range of applications, each with their different ICT needs.

However, there is now an increasing wealth of experience and sound advice. Paul Strassmann's (1990) findings and recommendations, for instance, include:

- there is no relation between spending on computers, profit or productivity;
- conventional analyses that apply revenue ratios or return-on-asset measures are unreliable;
- the published rankings of excellence in using computers do not relate to profitability;
- the effectiveness of information technology is difficult to evaluate because it mostly supports unmeasurable work;
- business 'over-achievers' do not spend more money on computers, they concentrate their information technology on business value-added;
- use business value-added to evaluate computer projects;
- propose business plans with or without added spending to measure the financial contributions of information technology;
- rely primarily on financial plans and controls for balancing the costs and benefits of computers;
- take advantage of the steady cost reductions available from advances in electronics;
- make the communication network the key to future productivity gains;
- have computer experts concentrate on the delivery of efficient computer applications;
- require that information resources management becomes every job.

The state-of-the-art of ICT investment appraisal has to improve. The complex evaluation processes may benefit from the use of information and communications technologies, such as knowledge-based systems that not only provide the assessment but also indicate the reasoning. Such an approach could incorporate all the stages of appraisal, with an explicit focus on the life-cycle of an ICT investment and, not only on direct effects, but also second-order effects. Unless better evaluation of potential ICT investments is made possible, the current myopic focus on the short-term will continue to undermine the necessary longer term perspective. Moreover, it must be appreciated that the ICTs are essentially enabling technologies, which means that direct returns may be difficult to identify, never mind quantify.

Ultimately, the board has the responsibility to their organisation. What will happen if they do nothing about ICT? The future prosperity of their organisation may depend on it.

Review questions

1 Why should an organisation invest in ICTs?

2 Discuss some of the difficulties in undertaking an ICT investment appraisal.

3 Comment on the strengths and weaknesses of the 'Return-on-Management' measure.

4 Discuss whether ICT investments too important to be left to the specialists.

Study questions

1 For a specific ICT investment, consider how you would attempt to justify it? (For example, the purchase of a laptop or palmtop computer for your own use.)

2 Using secondary data, such as annual reports and industry surveys, develop a picture of the scale of ICT investment across different industries and different organisations.

3 Consider some of the practical problems of an ICT investment once the 'go ahead' decision has been made — project management, availability of experienced staff and so on.

4 No ICT investment happens as planned. Using different illustrations, justify what trade-offs you would be willing to make with regard to increased costs, time delays and reduced functionality or capability.

Further reading

Buzzell, Robert D and Bradley T Gale "The PIMS Principles: linking strategy to performance" Free Press, New York, 1987.

A large-scale, longitudinal database that measures various business characteristics and outputs for a large sample of companies. Quantified relationships are explored in an attempt to understand causality.

Lincoln, Tom (editor) "Managing Information Systems for Profit" John Wiley, London, 1990.

As with most edited volumes, the chapters are uneven in both quality and depth. However, as a single recent volume, this book, which is written by past and present IBM consultants, provides a useful and relevant guide to the techniques and issues of managing information systems. Interestingly, the general conclusion is that IS management has been unsuccessful.

Meyer, N Dean and Mary E Boone "The Information Edge" McGraw-Hill, New York, 1987.

Documented cases are presented to illustrate the returns (up to 830,000 percent!) from investments in information and communications technologies. However, to assign directly all benefits to such investments is rather optimistic if not misleading. What about the impacts of enhanced management?

Strassmann, Paul A "Information Payoff" Free Press, New York, 1985.

A balanced account from an experienced IT professional that emphasises the fact that people ultimately determine the business value of IT investments. This focus on the demand side is a refreshing alternative to the large number of books which focus on the supply side of information and communications technologies per se.

Strassmann, Paul A "The Business Value of Computers" The Information Press, New Canaan, 1990.

A thorough, readable discussion aimed at executives, who must manage their organisation's investments. From empirical analyses, indicating that there is no relationship between IT expenditure and profitability, Strassmann provides insights into the requirements for business value from any investments and introduces the concept of management value-added, the Return-on-Management. Indeed, there is a clear message that it is necessary to enhance management, prior to automation or systemisation.

9

Information resources management

Learning objectives:

- to appreciate the importance of future developments in the possible uses of information;

- to understand the significance of developing intellectual capital in the knowledge platform;

- to recognise the limits to the importance of information resources management for the strategic performance of organisations.

- to be aware of the issue facing organisations in the information-based industries in the 1990's.

9.1 Introduction

As our knowledge-based society and economy develops, both individuals and organisations need to put a greater emphasis on learning. Shoshana Zuboff's (1988, page 375) 'informated' organisation suggests a growing symbiosis, with the individual and the organisation learning together in the face of ever greater complexity.

> The informated organisation is a learning institution, and one of its principal purposes is the expansion of knowledge — not knowledge for its own sake (as in academic pursuit) but knowledge that comes to reside at the core of what it means to be productive. Learning is not something that requires time out from being engaged in production activity; learning is the heart of productive activity; learning is the new form of labour.

Peter Drucker (1989, page 224), the management guru, has argued for a set of 'new realities':

> An economy in which knowledge is becoming the true capital and the premier wealth producing resource makes new and stringent demands ... Society dominated by knowledge workers makes even newer — and even more stringent — demands for social performance and social responsibility.

In this chapter, we consider a range of important issues and trends as they relate to society, organisations and individuals. The basic argument is founded on the belief that the key strategic asset for any organisation is its people. Therefore, it is essential for the organisation to develop and to utilise both knowledge and information, a requirement which raises questions about the management of the information function and the manager as an individual. Information and communications technologies are not panaceas and although information resources management has been seriously neglected, it should not now be elevated to a position that it does not merit. To finish, we highlight some of the dynamics of the information-based industries that will not only mean that they continue to be exciting and strategically significant, but also illustrate the types of developments that could further support management.

The knowledge platform

By now readers should be familiar with the ways in which ICTs can provide a flexible infrastructure or platform for an organisation and how this can be used to develop new ways to do business. To go a step further it is possible to view the 'intellectual capital', 'core competencies' and 'learning ability' of an organisation as a 'knowledge platform' on which an organisation can build its business. From this perspective, we can finally begin the proper development of the knowledge-worker in the knowledge-based organisation after so many years of talking about it.

In considering what will determine an organisation's competitive performance, Peter Drucker (1991, page 69) argues that:

> The single greatest challenge facing manager in the developed countries of the world is to raise the productivity of knowledge and service workers.

Following Frederick Taylor's idea of 'working smarter', Drucker highlights five steps:

- define the task (as productivity gains should follow from the removal of unnecessary activities);
- concentrate on the task;
- specify performance;
- involve the people in looking for productivity improvements;
- incorporate continuous learning, with the 'best' people being used as teachers.

The management of the knowledge platform becomes a new corporate function. The organisation must gather knowledge from wherever it can be found and, most importantly, know what to do with it. We must not forget Dr Johnson's distinction between knowing the answer and knowing where to find the answer. For instance, the transfer of technological knowledge may require the development of a university-industrial complex which can feed valuable knowledge gained from research into organisations, perhaps, involving government. Success is not, unfortunately, straightforward, it is a business environment illustrated by Silicon Valley in California.

Case: ICL version of the MIT90s findings

Scenario: International Computers Limited (ICL) sponsored and participated in the Management in the Nineties Programme at MIT. For the benefit of its clients and itself, it wanted to interpret and 'internalise' the results.

ICL had been one of a dozen organisations sponsoring (US$ 5,000,000 over five years) and participating in the Management in the Nineties (MIT90s) Research Program at the Sloan School of Management. ICL's aims were:

- improved public relations and image;
- connection with other sponsors;
- lessons for ICL management;
- lessons for ICL products and services.

One of the problems identified by Hugh Macdonald, who had acted as the main link between ICL and the MIT90s Programme, was how to manage academics and how to assimilate the knowledge gained from them.

The academic researchers are interested in extracting knowledge. The business men are interested in applying the knowledge to improve the efficiency and effectiveness of their businesses. Motivations and attitudes are different and it is necessary in any sponsored programme to understand these differences. If these differences are not understood and accepted, then the relationships will be unsatisfactory and both sides will become frustrated. (Macdonald, 1990, page 8.)

The 'deliverables' comprised a large pile of reports which were not particularly readable and of which one director joked that the most obvious use was to stand on top so that you could see further into the future. The real problem was that the material was not presented in a way which helped managers to see how to act. Appreciating the need for 'translation', Hugh Macdonald decided to identify ten key findings or 'crown jewels'. These were expressed in terms which could be understood by the people in ICL, its customers and suppliers:

1 Turbulence in the business environment will continue;
2 Improvements in IT capability will continue;
3 It is necessary to rethink the core of the business;
4 Integration provides the main opportunities for improving business effectiveness;
5 Flexible networked organisations need to be created;
6 Data and information will be a major problem area;
7 The nature of work is changing
8 Managers must be agents of change;
9 There are new roles for organisation leadership;
10 Line managers must take up roles of the leadership.

The MIT90s material proved to be intellectually difficult to digest, even a two and a half day executive course covering the main findings was found by many to be tough, if highly stimulating. In other settings, where less time was available, the messages were often over-simplified; people in ICL had learned that there was something in MIT90s and they reduced it to very simple stories, which were not always correct.

In order to succeed in diffusing the MIT90s material to the company as whole and to clients a considerable effort in education and training proved necessary. This comprised a summary card of key findings, a colour brochure, a series of half-day courses, a two and a half day course and a number of *ad hoc* events.

Sources: "A Window on the Future" ICL, 1990. Macdonald, 1990. Discussions with Hugh Macdonald.

The idea of in-company research, to look at the organisation itself, adds to the areas of possible collaboration. By bringing in researchers it is possible to gain access to advances in theories about business, but more importantly to exploit skills in analysis and synthesis and an openness to new ideas. In this way the organisation can provide itself with the tools necessary to learn about itself and to improve its ability to identify and exploit knowledge which it has but has not exploited. This is also in keeping with the suggestions recently made by Henry Mintzberg that the business schools should consider teaching organisations rather than individuals.

Ikujiro Nonaka, in a discussion of how knowledge is created at Japanese companies such as Honda and Matsushita, stresses that Western managers frequently define 'knowledge' too narrowly, usually restricting it to 'hard' (quantifiable) data. Nonaka correctly broadens the scope and argues that it is important to be able to tap people's ideals, insights and intuitions. This means that knowledge creation and development cannot be merely a mechanistic process.

... the knowledge-creating company is as much about ideals as it is about ideas. And that fact fuels innovation. The essence of innovation is to re-create the world according to a particular vision or ideal. To create new knowledge means quite literally to re-create the company and everyone in it in a non-stop process of personal and organisational self-renewal. In the knowledge-creating company, inventing new knowledge is not a specialised activity — the province of the R&D department or marketing or strategic planning. It is a way of behaving, indeed a way of being, in which everyone is a knowledge worker — that is to say, an entrepreneur. (Nonaka, 1991, page 97.)

In the 1950's and 1960's, organisations were staffed by the dull grey ranks of 'organisation man'. In the 1990's, we can already see the emergence of a different type of manager to suit a different age and a different style of organisation. Having ceased to be cogs in great machines, managers can increasingly assert their individuality, setting free both flair and talent. The roles in the organisation or organisations for which this individual works can be tailored to suit character, attitudes, skills and knowledge, both in recognition of individuality but also because it is the best way for the organisation to benefit. New skills and new attitudes are called for in inter-personal relationships and workings in groups. Increasingly, the contemporary human resources focus on 'how people can help the organisation' will be complemented by a consideration of 'how the organisation can help its individuals'.

At the extreme, we are entitled to question the continued existence of organisations at least in their traditional form. That individual must ask himself or herself why do I need to work for an organisation or should I work for myself?

Through the use of ICTs the manager has access to all the knowledge and information he requires, wherever the individual happens to be located. 1991 marked the end of the first decade of the Personal Computer (PC), the 1990's are the decade of another PC, Personal Communications, and also 'political correctness'.

9.2 The individual as information subject

Our concern as individuals for privacy remains strong. In most areas our rights are enshrined in international treaties, such as the Universal Declaration of Human Rights and the European Convention on Human Rights. In an era of instantaneous global access to information, it is necessary to consider both the right to privacy and the right of access to data. A cogent argument can be made that we should, at least, be able to demand redress for errors, equally it is argued that democracy can only work if the participants are fully informed or have the potential to be so informed.

Geodemographic data from customer databases are, for instance, increasingly being used to target small market niches, making offers to the wealthy, the healthy and the secure. The authors, Beaumont and Sutherland, both regularly receive targeted mailshots with offers based on their postcodes and their American Express cards. What happens if your are poor or live in an area which does not interest the marketers?

A potentially more frightening development is the unravelling of information about the human genetic code, DNA. This is likely to reveal, for example, your propensity to develop certain diseases and could be very useful in assessing applications for jobs and life assurance. In particular, organisations in the USA may wish to select employees who are not likely to become seriously ill, in order to reduce their medical insurance bills. Your employability may soon be influenced by the genes you inherited from your parents, yet there is nothing whatsoever you can do about it.

Where advances of occur which create discontinuities, there is great difficulty in developing pro-active legal reform. With rare exceptions, lawyers are content to wait for the problems to develop and then to seek ways to address them. The problems facing both lawyers and politicians, are increased enormously by the breakdown of the boundaries of national sovereignty, requiring international collaboration to make effective any legal rights and remedies.

Case: Electronic democracy

Scenario: The power of today's information and communications technologies means that large quantities of data, including specific information about millions of individuals, can now be handled both effectively and efficiently. While such technologies have helped highlight the significance of 'electronic democracy', the fundamental issue of 'How much are we allowed to know?' has been an issue for decades, even centuries.

Britain is often described as the most obsessively secretive state in the 'developed' world. Indeed, information disclosure (even outside the Official Secrets Act) remains a criminal offence. (Northmore (1990) provides an up-to-date account of the freedom of information in Britain with regard to individuals, companies, computers, central and local government, the law and the health service.)

The Prime Minister's mail is opened at about 9.00 a.m. A civil servant runs through it quickly to see if there are any documents that should be kept secret. The rest goes into a folder which is available for public inspection — anyone can go into the Prime Minister's office and demand to see it.

However, this Prime Minister's office is not located in 10 Downing Street, London, SW1, but at the Riksdag building in Stockholm. In Sweden, every citizen has a constitutional right to read official correspondence and documents under the Freedom of the Press Act. In Britain, there is no equivalent freedom of information law. (Northmore, 1990, page v.)

In the USA a Freedom of Information Act was passed to ensure access to governmental information. This has led to absurd positions in which citizens of foreign countries have had to go to the USA to obtain information about events in their own countries; in some cases possession of such freely available information is a criminal offence in their native country. However, there has recently been some adverse reaction in the USA to this degree of freedom on the grounds of cost.

Simply stated, the power of any information system is dependent directly on the data stored in it. Power has traditionally been associated with controlling access to data, with organisations, departments and individuals guarding their data jealously. However, there is increasingly, a recognition that 'power' stems from use and that data are being viewed increasingly by organisations as a collective resource. Issues concerned with the availability and accessibility of data raise significant questions about the value of data and the broader societal questions of democracy.

Any policy specification must be forward-looking, recognising that:

- users' requirements are changing;
- competing commercial databases are being established;
- information and communications technologies are evolving;
- trans-border data flows are increasing.

It is essential that the varied dimensions of electronic democracy are addressed as a matter of urgency. There needs to be a profound change in thinking in government and in business for our knowledge-based society and economy, paralleled by improved educated opinion.

9.3 Information-based industries

As Chapter 3 has demonstrated, the turbulent dynamics of the information-based industries mean that we must continue to expect significant structural changes. The globalisation of the information-based industries is continuing with an increase in the formation of international strategic alliances. For example, IBM and Apple Computer have joined forces to develop a new series of personal workstations using IBM's high speed RISC processor chips and Apple's user-friendly software to create a new and proprietary 'standard' for workstations, with Motorola being involved as a second source of the IBM RISC chip. At the same time, Apple Computer has subcontracted the manufacture of all its laptop computers to Sony.

After Fujitsu purchased a controlling interest in Britain's ICL, it was removed from one of the European research programmes, the JESSI (Joint European Submicron Silicon) initiative, although IBM was allowed to participate. Such decisions, allegedly based on sovereignty, are increasingly more difficult to make as most international organisations have R&D and manufacturing presences in many different countries.

Case: Hewlett-Packard Jaguar

Scenario: Hewlett-Packard developed a new product aimed at a niche market for managers who require a portable device for financial calculations.

Hewlett-Packard is a well established vendor in both the computer and calculator businesses. In 1991 it launched a new product the HP 95LX or 'Jaguar' which is both computer and calculator.

The Jaguar is a 'palmtop' device weighing eleven ounces (300 grams), with a screen of 16 lines by 40 characters. It has Lotus 1-2-3 in ROM, together with HP Calc, a business calculator to work out cash flows, NPVs and so on. It also comes with the features of popular pocket organisers: appointment diary, telephone directory, memo-pad, file manager and communications program, allowing data to be exchanged with PC's and with other Jaguars. It has a range of plug-in cards for additional software. At the time of the launch, May 1991, the price was US$ 699.

The development of the HP 95LX involved not only design and ergonomic skills at HP, but drew in Intel Corporation and Phoenix Technologies for chips, and Microsoft and Lotus Development Corporation for software. Notwithstanding the need to collaborate across organisational boundaries, the whole project took 15 months from conception to market launch.

The Jaguar is clearly aimed at the Lotus 1-2-3 customer base, estimated at 10-15 million users worldwide. John Young, HP's CEO, believes that the Jaguar belongs to

... a whole new category of personal information products — less complex, less general-purpose, and more tailored to the way people work.

Sources: *Fortune*, 20 May 1991, pages 73-73 and *Byte*, May 1991, pages 44-46.

Given the technological convergence of computing and communications, competition has intensified in the complex and expensive area of network management. To the likely benefit of many organisations, two large suppliers of network management systems, the computer giant IBM and the communications giant AT&T, have made an agreement to develop software to enable their different (data and telecommunications) networks to communicate with each other.

The regulatory environment, including the strategic policy issue of standards for products and services, will also play a significant, often constraining, role in developments. For example, BT, formerly British Telecommunications PLC, was subjected to a major price review, in the light of profits earned at more than £100 per second.

Case: Microsoft

Scenario: In 1991, the US Federal Trade Commission launched an investigation into the activities of Microsoft in the markets for computer operating systems and software.

The world's leading producer of software for personal computers, Microsoft, is being investigated by the US Federal Trade Commission (FTC) because of allegations that the company has attempted to monopolise markets for operating systems and associated software. In addition, more general regulatory issues may be raised with regard to the marketing of software, particularly forthcoming products and the sharing of information about product design and development.

The dangers for Microsoft are twofold. In the short term the investigation may divert sufficient attention from top managers to cause them to loose their strategic position in the market. In the longer term, loss of revenue from MS-DOS could reduce the availability of cash for R&D, slowing or stopping the development of new products, leading to the demise of the corporation.

It is more than a little ironic that while the IBM PC was intended to give IBM dominance of the PC market, IBM has to fight hard for its relatively modest market share while, at the same time, handing Microsoft dominance of the operating system market and Intel dominance of the processor market. One industry commentator likened the payment for MS-DOS to a tax on using a PC and claimed it was the most hated tax since the British taxed tea in their North American colonies, leading up to the Boston Tea Party.

IBM as usual is playing several games, it is continuing to develop OS/2 as a direct competitor for MS-DOS and MS-Windows, while also developing its own flavour of Unix (AIX) and collaborating with Apple Computers on the Mac System 7. However, if, as seems increasingly likely, operating systems become commodities, then the whole argument could be irrelevant.

At the time of writing, the computer vendors are hoping to forget their bad year, 1991. Sales were down and, with intense price competition, profits were dismal and large-scale redundancies commonplace. While the world economic recession has had an adverse effect, there must be lingering doubts about the future because most organisations now have a reasonable amount of computing power. The effects of the economic recession in the early 1980's were hardly felt by computer manufacturers, because of a significant product development, the personal computer. If the price pressure is maintained, the manufacturers must look for major strategic innovations with new sources of added value, through software and specialist services. The new notepad type of personal computer with 'pens', which allow the use of handwriting, may extend the market to those people reluctant to use keyboards and may also be useful in activities which require the completion of a form.

There is no causal relationship between an industry's profitability and the 'success' of individual organisations. In the past, the information-based industries have been highly profitable, primarily because they were innovative. They are likely to continue to be profitable only if strategic innovation can be maintained (see, for example, James Womak et al.'s (1990) discussion of 'lean production' in the motor car industry). Indeed, the risks of a failure to innovate may be greater than the conventional risks of innovation. 'Maturity' has brought structural changes to the information-based industries, especially since there is so much excess capacity; medium-sized companies have been particularly vulnerable, especially those primarily in the minicomputer business. There may be a need to create new markets and it will probably be insufficient to develop new products and services; new ways of doing business, altering the competitive rules, will be essential. New players are unlikely to compete on traditional grounds. Organisational size is not a source of protection, as companies, such as Compaq Computers and Sun Microsystems, have demonstrated. Who will be next? Looking at the most rapidly growing companies in the USA, *Fortune* magazine identified the following ICT vendors amongst its 'Fast 100', with truly remarkable annual growth rates of sales (see Table 9.1). Growth is related to their ability to provide customers with better products and services.

Table 9.1   *Fastest growing ICT companies in the USA*

Company	Growth	Ranking
Zeos International	256%	1
Cisco Systems	228%	2
Exabyte	215%	3
Synoptics Communications	209%	4
Compucom Systems	203%	6
Sybase	167%	10
Cirrus Logic	135%	18
Intelligent Electronics	135%	19
LDDS Communications	130%	20
Xilink	123%	23
Conner Peripherals	121%	24
Advanced Logic Designs	121%	25

Source: *Fortune*, 7 October 1991.

The only certainty is that successful strategies will change. Andrew Rappaport and Shmuel Halevi (1991, page 69), for example, have argued recently that,

By the year 2000, the most successful computer companies will be those that buy computers rather than build them. The leaders will ... fabulously cheap and powerful hardware to create and deliver new applications, pioneer and control new computing paradigms, and assemble distribution and integration expertise that creates enduring influence with customers. So long as companies have reliable suppliers of adequate hardware — and this seldom means the most advanced hardware — there are fewer advantages to building it. The future belongs to the computerless computer company.

Both vendors and consultants in the information-based industries are focussing on providing full, customised business solutions. However, recognising that the vendors cannot do it all themselves, they are using collaborative alliances for products and services which they do not own. To this end, all major vendors have developed a 'channel strategy'; strategies which are sometimes elaborate and always designed to benefit the vendors' profit, their perceived differentiation and their control over their customers. Rappaport and Halevi certainly stirred up the industry with their article in *Harvard Business Review*, with a debate in the following issue of the journal, devoting over twenty pages to comments from leading figures in the industry and in academia. The strong case was made for continuing to manufacture in order:

- to ensure supply of new technologies;
- to learn about product innovation;
- to develop the symbiosis of hardware and software industries.

9.4 Concluding comment

Our future knowledge-based society and economy will be an exciting period in which to live and work. For organisations to be successful in the long-term, it is important to appreciate that:

- leadership will have to be different;
- management will have to be different;
- innovation will have to be increased.

The significance of new forces will have a growing effect, such as the concerns for sustainable development, given the growing damage to our planet, the increased labour mobility across national borders, the needs of the 'less developed' countries for technology transfer and, the changing geopolitical map of the world.

Moreover, with people who have grown up using information and communications technologies taking up managerial responsibilities, it is interesting to see the fundamental differences in their attitudes to these technologies. We cannot now live and work without ICTs.

Review questions

1 Highlight three important changes for people living and working in our future knowledge-based society and economy.

2 How does the idea of the knowledge platform help you to understand how a business might be redesigned?

3 Comment on the assertion that people are an organisation's key strategic assets.

4 What do you understand by the term 'electronic democracy'?

5 Explore the types of strategic innovation that may occur in the information-based industries over the next decades.

Study questions

1 Consider the assertion that, in the future, new skills and human capital will increasingly be the driving force behind organisational effectiveness, and information will increasingly be the driving force behind senior management's vision for their organisation.

2 Using the discussion in this book, particularly in Chapters 3 and 9, highlight areas of potential strategic innovation for the information-based industries.

3 Evaluate the Federal Trade Commission's case against Microsoft, how is it progressing and does it make sense?

4 Discuss the following criticism of Rappaport and Halevi's views of the ICT sector:

"On the contrary, if anything, the market axiom of the late twentieth century appears to be that the company that masters the manufacture of a product will eventually invent the next generation of that product — or if not actually invent it, make incremental improvements, obtain novel technology, and profit handsomely from new market applications." Daniel Burton, Council on Competitiveness, Washington, DC.

Further reading

Drucker, Peter "The New Realities" Heinemann, Oxford, 1989.

This is an important volume by an established management thinker. In a thought-provoking discussion across business, economics, politics, and society, Peter Drucker evaluates the limitations of existing management practices, especially the reliance on mechanistic analysis.

Lessem, Ronnie "Total Quality Learning" Blackwell, Oxford, 1991.

A volume on building a 'learning organisation' by the editor of a significant series on developmental management. Looking forward, Lessem (1991, page 58) argues,

"The nineteenth century was the age of the entrepreneur, the self-made man. In the twentieth century the rational executive took command. Thoughtful business administration took over from action-centred business entrepreneurship. The bureaucratic organisation took over from the pioneering enterprise. The twenty-first century, as I see it, will become the era of the learning organisation. Such a learning organisation will need to accommodate thoughts, feelings and actions."

Mangham, Iain and Annie Pye "The Doing of Managing" Blackwell, Oxford, 1991.

Founded on interviews with forty-seven senior executives, Iain Mangham and Annie Pye explore the basic force behind organisational performance — how managers manage. In a thoughtful and well-argued way, this book demonstrates clearly that management is an art, not a science, which has to be performed not prescribed. As the book's cover highlights:

"It is not a how-to-do-it text, nor a simple tale of heroic deeds; nor is it an attempt to prove and predict. It is a delightfully written very serious story about the doing of managing."

Serge, Peter M "The Fifth Discipline" Doubleday Currency, New York, 1990.

In considering the learning organisation, the art and practice of it, Peter Serge stresses the need to overcome learning difficulties:

"Learning disabilities are tragic in children, but they are fatal in organisations. Because of them, few corporations live even half as long as a person — most die before they reach the age of forty."

Womak, James P, Daniel T Jones and Daniel Roos "The Machine that changed the World" Rawson Associates, New York, 1990.

The global dynamics of the motor car industry are discussed. The concept of "lean production", doing more with less, is introduced. Probably, one of the best written management book of recent years.

Wurman, Richard S "Information Anxiety" Pan, London, 1991.

An interesting, indeed lively, book that provokes the reader to re-examine their use of information which is available from a range of sources in an array of different forms. Wurman (page 310) argues that,

"The ultra-sophistication and proliferation of the information delivery equipment has contributed to a strange phenomenon that is at the heart of information anxiety: we have lost the ability to control the flow of information. We used to have to make a conscious decision to go looking for information, to take action to find it. Now, the equipment of the information age permits the transmission of information without the desire, or even the permission, of the receiver. We are increasingly vulnerable to the invasion of information; it intrudes our lives, often uninvited, at inopportune times."

Bibliography

Andrews, Kenneth R (editor) "Ethics in Practice" Harvard Business School Press, Cambridge, 1989.

Ansoff, H Igor "Implementing Strategic Management" Prentice-Hall, Englewood Cliffs, 1984.

Anthony, Robert N "Planning and Control Systems" Harvard Business School Press, Boston, 1965.

Araskog, Rand "The ITT Wars: a CEO speaks out on takeovers" Henry Holt, New York, 1989.

Arms, Caroline (editor) "Campus Networking Strategies" Digital Press, Bedford, 1988.

Ashworth, Caroline & Mike Goodland "SSADM: a practical approach" McGraw-Hill, Maidenhead, 1990.

Badaracco, Joseph L "The Knowledge Link: how firms compete through strategic alliances" Harvard Business School Press, Cambridge, 1991.

Bartlett, Christopher and Sumantra Ghoshal "Managing across Borders: the transnational solution" Hutchison, London, 1989.

Beaumont, John R and David Walters "Information Management in Service Industries: towards a strategic framework" *Journal of Information Systems* **1** (3) pp 155-172, 1991.

Beer, Michael, Bert Spector, Paul Lawrence, Quinn Mills and Richard Walton "Managing Human Assets" Free Press, New York, 1984.

Belasco, James A "Teaching the Elephant to Dance: empowering change in your organisation" Hutchison Business Books, London, 1990.

Bell, Daniel "The Coming of the Post-Industrial Society: a venture in social forecasting" Penguin, Harmondsworth, 1976.

Bittlestone, Robert "Financial Control in the 1990's" *International Journal of Information Resource Management* **1** (1), pp 12-18, 1990.

Boehm, Eric H and Forest W Horton "Distance Learning Methodology and Information Resources Management" *International Journal of Information Resource Management* **2** (1) pp 5-10, 1991.

Brandt, Willy "North-South: a programme for survival" Pan Books Ltd, London, 1980.

Britcher, R N "Re-engineering Software: a case study" *IBM Systems Journal* **29** (4) pp 551-567, 1990.

Brooks, Fredrick P "The Mythical Man Month" Addison-Wesley, Wokingham, 1975.

Bruce-Gardyne, Jock (Lord) "Ministers and Mandarins: inside the Whitehall Village" Sidgwick and Jackson, London, 1986.

Buchanan, David A and James McCalman "High Performance Work Systems: the Digital experience" Routledge, London, 1989.

Burk, Cornelius F and Forest W Horton "InfoMap: a complete guide to discovering corporate information resources" Prentice-Hall, Englewood Cliffs, 1988.

Buzzell, Robert D and Bradley T Gale "The PIMS Principles: linking strategy to performance" Free Press, New York, 1987.

Campbell, J A "Expert Systems" *IUCC Bulletin* **5** pp 499-502, 1983.

Campbell-Kelly, Martin "ICL: a business and technical history" Oxford University Press, Oxford, 1989.

Carlzon, Jan "Moments of Truth: new strategies for today's customer-driven economy" Harper and Row, New York, 1987.

Cash, James I, F Warren McFarlan, James L McKenney and Michael R Vitale "Corporate Information Systems Management" Irwin, Homewood, 1988.

Central Computer and Telecommunications Agency "Managing Information as a Resource" HMSO, London, 1990.

Chandler, Alfred J "Strategy and Structure: chapters in the history of the American industrial enterprise" MIT Press, Cambirdge, 1962.

Chandler, Alfred J "Scale and Scope: the dynamics of industrial capitalism" Harvard University Press and Belknap, Cambridge, 1990.

Clutterbuck, David (editor) "Information 2000: insights into the coming decades in information technology" Pitman, London, 1989.

Cohen, Bernard, W T Harwood and M I Jackson "The Specification of Complex Systems" Addison-Wesley, Wokingham, 1986.

Collins, Harry M "Artifical Experts: social knowledge and intelligent machines" MIT Press, London, 1990.

Coopers and Lybrand "A Challenge to Complacency: changing attitudes to training" Manpower Services Commission, London, 1985.

Crozier, Michel "L'Organisation à l'Ecoute" Les Editions d'Organisation, Paris, 1990.

Date, Chris "An Introduction to Database Systems, Volume 1" Third Edition, Addison-Wesley, 1989.

Davidow, William H and Bro Uttal "Total Customer Service" Harper and Row, New York, 1989.

Digital Equipment Corporation "Guide to Information Systems" Digital Equipment Corporation, Bedford, MA, 1990. (EC-G0768-54/90)

Deal, Terrence E and Allen A Kennedy "Corporate Culture" Penguin Books, Harmondsworth, 1988.

Dearden, John and Richard L Nolan "How to Control the Computer Resource" *Harvard Business Review* 51 (6) pp 68-75, 1973

Delamarter, Richard "Big Blue: IBM's use and abuse of power" Pan, London, 1988.

Department of Trade and Industry "Competition and Choice: telecommunications policy for the 1990s: a consultative document" (Cm 1303) HMSO, London, 1990.

Department of Trade and Industry "Competition and Choice: telecommunications policy for the 1990s" (Cm 1461) HMSO, London, 1991.

Department of Trade and Industry: Vanguard "Electronic Trading Case Studies" HMSO, London, 1990.

Department of Trade and Industry "Expert System Opportunities; Guidelines for the introduction of expert systems technology" HMSO, London, 1990

Drucker, Peter F "The Practice of Management" New York, 1954.

Drucker, Peter F "The New Realities: in government and politics ... in economy and business ... in society ... and in world view" Heinemann, Oxford, 1989.

Drucker, Peter F "What Executives Need to Learn" *Prism* (Arthur D Little Inc) pp 73-84, fourth quarter 1990.

Drucker, Peter "The New Productivity Challenge" *Harvard Business Review* **69** (6) pp 69-79, 1991.

Earl, Michael J "Management Strategies for Information Technology" Prentice-Hall, Englewood Cliffs, 1989.

Earl, Michael J (editor) "Informaiton Management: the strategic dimension" Oxford Clarendon Press, Oxford, 1988.

Elam, Joyce J, Michael J Grinzberg, Peter G W Keen and Robert W Zmud "Transforming the IS Organisation" International Centre for Information Technologies, Washington, 1989.

Ellis, Clarence and Najah Naffah "Design of Office Information Systems" Springer-Verlag, 1987.

Emery, James C "Management Information Systems: the critical strategic resource" Oxford University Press, New York, 1987.

Farbey, Barbara, Frank Land, and David Targett "Evaluating Investments in IT" Working Paper, London Business School, London, 1990.

Feigenbaum, Ed, Pamela McCorduck and H P Nii "The Rise of the Expert Company" Macmillan, London, 1988.

Flamm, Kenneth "Creating the Computer: government, industry and high technology" Brookings Institution, Washington, 1988.

Friedman, Andrew and Cornford "Computer Systems Development: history, organisations and implementation" John Wiley and Sons, Chichester, 1989.

Galliers, Robert D (editor) "Information Analysis: selected readings" Addison-Wesley, Wokingham, 1987.

Galliers, Robert D and Sutherland Anthony R "Information systems management and strategy formulation: the 'stages of growth model' revisited" *Journal of Information Systems* **1** (2) pp 89-114, 1991.

Garvin, David "Quality Management" Free Press, New York, 1988.

Gerstein, Marc S "The Technology Connection: strategy and change in the information age" Addison-Wesley, Wokingham, 1987.

Gibson, Cyrus F and Richard L Nolan "Managing the Four Stages of EDP Growth" *Harvard Business Review* **52** (1) pp 76-88, 1974.

Goldsmith, Walter and David Clutterbuck "The Winning Streak: Britain's top companies reveal their formulas for success" Weidenfeld and Nicolson, London, 1984.

Goold, Michael and Andrew Campbell "Strategies and Styles: the role of the centre in managing diversified corporations" Blackwell, Oxford, 1987.

Grant, Robert M "Contemporary Strategy Analysis" Blackwell, Oxford, 1991.

Gray, Paul, William R King, Ephraim R McLean and Hugh J Watson "Management of Information Systems" Dryden Press, Chicago, 1989.

Gorry, G Anthony and Michael S Scott Morton "A Framework for Management Information Systems" *Sloan Management Review* **30** (3) pp 49-61, 1989.

Greenley, Gordon E "Strategic Management" Prentice-Hall, New Jersey, 1989.

Grohowski, Ron, Chris McGoff, Doug Vogel, Ben Martz and Jay Nunamaker "Implmenting Electronic Meeting Systems at IBM: lessons learned and success factors" *MIS Quarterly* **14** (4) pp 368-383, 1990.

Hafner, Katie and John Markoff "Cyberpunk" Fourth Estate, New York, 1991.

Hague, Sir Douglas "Beyond Universities" Institute of Economic Affairs, London, 1991.

Handy, Charles, Colin Gordon, Ian Gow and Colin Randlestone "The Making of Modern Managers" Pitman, London, 1988.

Handy, Charles "The Age of Unreason" Business Books, London, 1989.

Harrington, H James "Business Process Improvement: the breakthrough strategy for total quality, productivity and competitiveness" McGraw-Hill, New York, 1991.

Harris, Donald G and David Walters "Retail Operations Management" Prentice-Hall, New York, 1991.

Harris, Louis and Associates "New Strategies for Corporate Growth: information systems in the 1990s" Report for United Research Co Inc and the Business Week Newsletter for Information Executives, Morristown, New Jersey, 1989.

Hax, Arnoldo C and Nicolas S Majluf "Strategic Management: an integrative perspective" Prentice-Hall, International, New Jersey, 1984.

Heller, Joseph "Catch-22" Simon and Schuster, New York, 1961.

Hendry, John "Innovating for Failure: government policy and the early British Computer industry" MIT Press, London, 1989.

Hopper, Max D "Rattling the SABRE: new ways to compete on information" *Harvard Business Review* **68** (3) pp 118-125, 1990.

Huczynski, Andrzej A and David A Buchanan "Organisational Behaviour: an introductory text" Second Edition, Prentice-Hall, London, 1991.

Humphrey, Watt S & Marc Kellner "Software Process Modeling: principles of entity process models" pp 331-342 in *Proceedings of the 11th International Conference on Software Engineering, 15-18 May, 1989, Pittsburgh Pennsylvania*, IEEE Computer Society Press.

Hussey, David E (editor) "International Review of Strategic Management" John Wiley and Sons, London, 1990. (twice yearly.)

International Computers Limited "Product Guide" ICL, Bracknell, 1990.

Imai, Maasaki "Kaizen: the key to Japan's competitive success" McGraw-Hill, New York, 1986.

International Business Machines "Business Systems Planning: information systems planning guide" IBM, Atlanta, 1984 (GE20-0527-4).

Jacobsen, Gary and John Hillkirk "Xerox: an American Samurai" Macmillan, New York, 1986.

Jarke, Matthias (editor) "Managers, Micros and Mainframes: integrating systems for end-users" John Wiley and Sons, Chichester, 1986.

Johnson, H Thomas and Kaplan, Robert S "The Rise and Fall of Management Accounting" Harvard Business School Press, Cambridge, 1987.

Kanter, Rosabeth Moss "The Change Masters" Geore Allen and Unwin, London, 1983.

Kanter, Rosabeth Moss "When Giants Learn to Dance: mastering the challenge of strategy, management and careers in the 1990's" Simon and Schuster, New York, 1989.

Kanter, Rosabeth Moss, Barry A Stein and Todd D Jick "The Challenge of Organisational Change: how people experience it and manage it" Free Press, New York, 1991.

Kapp, Marco "IT Security in a Changing World" *International Journal of Information Resource Management* **1** (1) pp 19-27, 1990.

Kaye, David "GameChange: the impact of information technology on corporate strategies and structure: a boardroom agenda" Butterworth-Heinemann, Oxford, 1990.

Kearney, A T "The Barriers and the Opportunities of Information Technology: a management perspective" Department of Trade and Industry, London, 1984.

Keen, Peter G W "Shaping the Future: business design through information technology" Harvard Business School Press, Boston, 1991.

Kidder, Tracy "The Soul of a New Machine" Atlantic Monthly Press, Boston, 1981.

Kobayashi, Koji "The Rise of NEC" Blackwell, Oxford, 1991.

Konsynski, Benn R and F Warren McFarlan "Information Partnerships: shared data, shared scale" *Harvard Business Review* **68** (5) pp 114-120, September-October 1990.

Kotler, Philip "Marketing Management" Prentice-Hall, Englewood Cliffs, 1988.

Kumar, Kuldeep "Post implementation evaluation of computer-based IS: current practice" *Communications of the ACM* **33** (2), pp 203-212, 1990.

Lawrensen, John and Lionel Barber "The Price of Truth: the story of Reuters' millions" Mainstream, Edinburgh, 1985.

Leebaert, Derek (editor) "Technology 2001" MIT Press, Boston, 1991.

Lessem, Ronnie "Total Quality Learning: building a learning organisation" Blackwell, Oxford, 1991.

Lincoln, Tom (editor) "Managing Information Systems for Profit" John Wiley and Sons, Chichester, 1990.

Lodge, George "Perestroika in America: restructuring business-government relations for world competitiveness" Harvard Business School Press, Cambridge, 1990.

Macdonald, K Hugh "The Management in the 1990s Research Programme" *International Journal of Information Resource Management* **1** (1) pp 5-11, 1990.

McFarlan, F Warren "Portfolio Approach to Information Systems" *Harvard Business Review* **59** (5) pp 142-150, 1981.

MacGregor, Ian "The Enemies Within: the story of the miners' strike" Collins, Glasgow, 1986.

Macintosh, Norman B "The Social Software of Accounting and Information Systems" John Wiley and Sons, Chichester, 1985.

Mackintosh, Ian "Sunrise Europe: the dynamics of information technology" Basil Blackwell, Oxford, 1986.

McNamee, Patrick B "Strategic Management: a PC-based approach" Butterworth-Heinemann, Oxford, 1992.

McNurlin, Barbara C and Ralph H Sprague "Information Systems Management in Practice" Second Edition, Prentice-Hall, Englewood Cliffs, 1989.

Madnick, Stuart E (editor) "The Strategic Use of Information Technology" Oxford University Press, Oxford, 1988.

Majorcas-Cohen, P "The Translator as Information User" pp 61-88 in C Picken (editor) *Translating and the Computer* Aslib, London, 1986.

Mangham, Iain and Annie Pye "The Doing of Managing" Blackwell, Oxford, 1991.

Marchand, D A and Forest W Horton "Infotrends" John Wiley and Sons, New York, 1986.

Marciniak, John and Donald Reifer "Software Acquisition Management" John Wiley and Sons, Chichester, 1990.

Methé, David T "Technological Competition in Global Industries: marketing and planning strategies for American industry" Quorum Books, London, 1991

Meyer, N Dean and Mary E Boone "The Information Edge" McGraw-Hill, New York, 1987.

Miles, Ian Tim Brady, Andy Davies, Leslie Haddon, Nicole Jagger, Mark Matthews, Howard Rush and Sally Wyatt "Mapping the Information Economy" British Library Research Report 77, London, 1990.

Mills, D Quinn "Rebirth of the Corporation" John Wiley and Sons, New York, 1991.

Mintzberg, Henry "Mintzberg on Management; inside our strange world of organizations" Free Press, New York, 1989.

Mintzberg, Henry "Strategy Formation: schools of thought" pp 105-236 in *Perspectives on Strategic Management* James W Fredrickson (editor) Harper and Row, New York, 1990.

Morgan, James C and J Jeffrey "Creating the Japanese Market" Free Press, New York, 1991.

Mortensen, Erik "Office Automation: agenda for organisational change" pp 197-199 in *Productivity in the Information Age: proceedings of the 46th ASIS annual meeting 1983*, Volume 20, Edited by A S Caputo, R A V Diener, R F Vondran and C I Wasserman. ASIS, 1983.

Mumford, Enid and W Bruce MacDonald "XSEL's Progress: the continuing journey of an expert system" John Wiley and Sons, Chichester, 1989.

Nairn, G "Going for IT" *Infomatics* July 1988, pp 34-37.

Naisbitt, John and Patricia Aburdene "Megatrends 2000" Sidgwick & Jackson, London, 1990.

National Economic Development Office "IT Futures Surveyed" NEDO, London, 1986.

Nolan, Richard L "Managing the Crises in Data Processing" *Harvard Business Review* **57** (2) pp 115-126, 1979.

Nonaka, Ikujiro "The Knowledge-creating Company" *Harvard Business Review* **69** (6) pp 96-104.

Northmore, D "Freedom of Information Handbook" Bloomsbury, London, 1990.

Ohmae, Kenichi "The Borderless World" Collins, Glasgow, 1990.

Olle, T William, Jacques Hagelstein, Ian Macdonald, Colette Rolland, Henk Sol, Franc van Assche and Alexander Verrijn-Stuart "Information Systems Methodologies: a framework for understanding" Second Edition, Addison-Wesley, Wokingham, 1991.

Orna, Elizabeth "Practical Information Policies" Gower, Aldershot, 1991.

Palmer, Colin and S Ottley "From potential to reality: hybrids: critical force in the application of information technology in the 1990s" Report by the BCS Task Group on Hybrids, British Computer Society, London, 1990.

Parker, Marilyn M and Robert J Benson "Information Economics: linking business performance to information technology" Prentice-Hall, Englewood Cliffs, 1988.

Parker, Marilyn M, H Edgar Trainer and Robert J Benson "Information Strategy and Economics" Prentice-Hall, Eaglewood Cliffs, 1989.

Parkinson, Lynn K and Stephen T Parkinson "Using the Microcomputer in Marketing" McGraw-Hill, London, 1987.

Parsons, Gregory "Strategic Information Technology" pp 182-189 reprinted in E K Somogyi and R D Galliers (editors) *Towards Strategic Information Systems* Abacus Press, Tunbridge Wells, 1983.

Pascale, Richard T and Anthony G Athos "The Art of Japanese Management" Simon and Schuster, New York, 1981.

Peters, G "Evaluating your Computer Investment Strategy" *Journal of Information Technology* **3** (3) pp 178-188, 1988.

Peters, Thomas J and Robert H Waterman "In Search of Excellence: lessons from America's best-run companies." Harper and Row, New York, 1982.

Peters, Thomas J "Thriving on Chaos: a handbook for a management revolution" Alfred A Knopf, New York, 1987.

Pettigrew, Andrew M and Richard Whipp "Managing Change for Competitive Success" Blackwell, Oxford, 1991.

Porter, Michael E "Competitive Strategy: techniques for analyzing industries and competitors" Free Press, New York, 1980.

Porter, Michael E "Cases in Competitive Strategy" Free Press, New York, 1983.

Porter, Michael E "Competitive Advantage: creating and sustaining superior performance" Free Press, New York, 1985.

Porter, Michael E "The Competitive Advantage of Nations" Free Press, New York, 1991.

Prahalad, C K and Gary Hamel "The Core Competence of the Corporation" *Harvard Business Review* **68** (3) pp 79-91, 1990.

Prestowitz, C V "Trading Places" Basic Books, New York, 1988.

Pugh, Emerson W "IBM's 360 and Early 370 Systems" MIT Press, Boston, 1991.

Rappaport, Andrew S and Shmuel Halevi "The Computerless Computer Company" *Harvard Business Review* **69** (4), pp 69-80, 1991.

Ray, M "Information Resource Management: four cornerstones for implementing IRM" *Information Management Review* **2** (2) pp 9-15, 1986.

Reich, Robert "The World of Work: preparing for 21st century capitalism" Alfred A Knopf, New York, 1991.

Rheingold, Howard "Virtual Reality" Secker and Warburg, New York, 1991.

Rockart, John F "Chief Executives Define Their Own Data Needs" *Harvard Business Review* **57** (2) pp 81-93, 1979

Rockart, John F "The Line Takes the Leadership: IS management in a wired society" *Sloan Management Review* **29** (4) pp 57-64, 1988.

Rodgers, Buck "The IBM Way: insights into the World's most successful marketing organisation" Harper & Row, New York, 1986.

Russell, Fred "The Case for CASE" *ICL Technical Journal* **6** (3) pp 479-495, 1989.

Salomon, Jean-Jacques "Le Gaulois, Le Cow-boy et Le Samouraï: la politique française de la technologie" Economica, Paris, 1986.

Schein, Ed "Process Consulting" Two volumes. Addison-Wesley, Reading, 1987.

Schein, Ed "Organisational Culture and Leadership" Jossey-Bass, San Francisco, 1989.

Scott-Morton, Michael S (editor) "The Corporation of the 1990's: information technology and organisational transformation" Oxford University Press, Oxford, 1991.

Sculley, John "Odyssey: Pepsi to Apple" Fontana, London, 1987.

Shearer, Cheryl "Vision Statement" *International Journal of Information Resource Management* **2** (1) pp vi-vii, 1991.

Simmons, J R M "LEO and the Managers" Macdonald, London, 1962.

Simon, Herbert A "The New Science of Managment Decision-Making" Prentice-Hall, Englewood Cliffs, 1977.

Sommerville, Ian "Software Engineering" Third Edition, Addison-Wesley, Wokingham, 1989.

Sprague, Ralph H and Hugh J Watson "Decision Support Systems: putting theory into practice" Prentice-Hall, Englewood Cliffs, 1989.

Smith, Adam "An Inquiry into the Nature and Causes of the Wealth of Nations" Strahan and Cadell, London, 1776. (Reprinted Oxford University Press, Oxford, 1976.)

Spurr, Kathy and Paul Layzell (editors) "CASE on Trial" John Wiley and Sons, Chichester, 1990.

Stacey, Ralph D "Dynamic Strategic Management" Kogan Page, London, 1990.

Stacey, Ralph D "The Chaos Frontier: creative strategic control for business" Butterworth Heinemann, Oxford, 1991.

Stalk, George and Thomas M Hout "Competing Against Time" Free Press, New York, 1990.

Stoll, Clifford "Stalking the Wily Hacker" *Communications of the ACM* **31** (5) pp 484-497, 1988.

Strassmann, Paul A "Information Payoff: the transformation of work in the electronic age" Free Press, New York, 1985.

Strassmann, Paul A "The Business Value of Computers: an executive's guide" The Information Press, New Canaan, 1990.

Sveiby, Karl E and Tom Lloyd "Managing Knowhow: add value ... by valuing creativity" Bloomsbury, London, 1987.

Swanson, E Burton and Cynthia M Beath "Maintaining Information Systems in Organisations" John Wiley and Sons, Chichester, 1989.

Synnott, William R "The Information Weapon" John Wiley and Sons, London, 1987.

Synnott, W R and W H Gruber "Information Resource Management: opportunities and strategies for the 1980's" John Wiley and Sons, New York, 1981.

Thimbleby, Harold "User Interface Design" Addison-Wesley, Wokingham, 1990.

Trevor, Malcolm "Toshiba's New British Company: competitiveness through innovation in industry" Policy Studies Institute, London, 1988.

van der Erve, Marc "The Power of Tomorow's Management" Heinemann, Oxford, 1989.

van Tulder, Rob and Gerd Junne "European Multinationals in Core Technologies" John Wiley and Sons, Chichester, 1988.

Wang, An "Lessons: an autobiography" Addison-Wesley, Wokingham, 1986.

Ward, John, Pat Griffiths and Paul Whitmore "Strategic Planning for Information Systems" John Wiley and Sons, London, 1990

Weber, Ron "EDP Audit" McGraw-Hill, New York, 1989.

Whitehead, Alfred North "Science and the Modern World" Macmillan, New York, 1925.

Wiseman, Charles "Strategy and Computers: information systems as competitive weapons" Dow-Jones Irwin, Homewood, 1985.

Wood-Harper, A T and S W Corder "Information Resource Management: towards a web-based methodology for end user computing" *Journal of Applied Systems Analysis* **15** pp 83-101, 1988.

Womak, James P, Daniel T Jones and David Roos "The Machine that changed the World" Rawson Associates, New York, 1990.

Wurman, Richard S "Information Anxiety: what to do when information doesn't tell you what you want to know" Pan, London, 1991.

Yeates, Don "Project Management for Information Systems" Pitman, 1991.

Zachman, J A "A Framework for Information Systems Architecture" *IBM Systems Journal* **26** (3), pp 276-292.

Zuboff, Shoshana "In the Age of the Smart Machine: the future of work and power" Basic Books, New York, 1988.

Glossary

4GL
　　See Fourth Generation Language.

Anti-trust
　　Action by government or by civil litigation to break up monopolies, oligopolies and cartels.

Application software
　　Software for a user-defined task or group of tasks, as distinct from system software.

Application Specific Integrated Circuit (ASIC)
　　Integrated circuits designed for specific purposes, as distinct from general purpose microprocessors.

Architecture
　　The principles of design used in a computer or an integrated circuit.

Artificial Intelligence (AI)
　　Computer programs which perform tasks going beyond procedural tasks, into areas normally associated with human intelligence. For example, expert systems, natural language processing, theorem proving and visual perception.

Assembly language
　　A mnemonic language notation for machine code. A low-level language, very closely related to the hardware of a specific computer.

Batch processing
　　A method of processing transactions in which they are sorted into batches and the transactions in each batch are processed sequentially. Usually associated with files held on magnetic tape.

Big Blue
　　A colloquial term for International Business Machines (IBM), so-called because of the size of the corporation and the colour of the cabinets containing the computers.

Binary
　　A number system comprising only the digits one and zero, which is represented inside computers by switches in on and off positions. Sometimes used to refer to compiled programs, which are in binary form.

Bit
　　An abbreviation for a single binary digit.

Bottom line
　　A colloquial term for net profit.

Buffer
　　An area of memory used to facilitate the flow of data between two devices by holding data for a brief period. It is used to allow transfer of data between devices operating at different speeds and where the basic blocks of data are different. For example, between a disc drive (slow) and RAM (fast).

Business strategy
　　A pattern of decisions in an organisation that indicates its objectives, goals and purposes, usually made explicit in a document.

Byte

A single character, usually comprising eight continuous bits of data.

C

A high-level programming language, usually associated with Unix.

Cartel

A group of business organisations combining together to exercise control over a market, usually to the detriment of consumers and/or competitors.

Central Processing Unit (CPU)

The principal operating component of a computer.

Chip

An integrated circuit. So-called because it is one small piece broken off a much larger wafer of semiconductor material. Used in computers for memory and to process data. (See also semiconductor.)

Clone

An accurate and detailed copy which performs, or is claimed to perform, exactly the same functions as the original. For example, clones of Lotus 1-2-3 and IBM PCs.

COBOL

An acronym for Common Business Language. An early computer language used to develop business data processing applications.

Competition

The rivalry between businesses trying to win the same market.

Compiler

A computer program which converts computer programs of a particular language, for example, COBOL, into a form which the computer can execute.

Critical mass

The smallest mass of fissile material which can support a chain reaction (used to determine the minimum size of nuclear reactors and nuclear bombs). By analogy, it is extended to refer to the minimum size of a community of users required to sustain a shared computer application.

Cross-subsidy

The use of profits from one line of business to subsidise another.

Data base

A file of data that is defined and accessed by means of a data base management system. Sometimes extended to include any data file.

Data Base Administrator (DBA)

The person in charge of a data base management system, including design, implementation, specification and maintenance.

Data Base Management System (DBMS)

A suite of programs providing access to and control over databases, usually including interactive queries, report generator and systems for the maintenance of the integrity of the data.

Data dictionary

Data describing the data contained in a Data Base Management System (see also Metadata).

Decision Support System (DSS)

> Modelling and simulation software to help answer 'what if...?' questions, with facilities to allow tailoring for individual decision-making styles.

Desk Top Publishing (DTP)

> A suite of computer programs for the design and manipulation of page layouts of text and diagrams.

Disc drive

> A peripheral device connected to a computer for the storage and retrieval of data, either magnetic or optical. (See also hard disc and floppy disc.)

Distributed database

> A data base in which different parts are stored at different locations, but which operates as a single system.

Distributed processing

> The organisation of the processing of data in a distributed system.

Distributed system

> A system in which number of components at different locations are operated together as a single system.

Distribution channel

> The means by which products and services are taken to market, for example, a network of dealers.

Dumping

> The selling of goods or services at prices less than the costs of production and distribution. Usually undertaken with a view to establishing a large market share and, in the longer term, to increasing the price to make profits.

Dynamic Random Access Memory (DRAM)

> At type of computer memory chip used in personal computers and workstations. Dynamic refers to the volatility of the memory which requires it to be 'refreshed' at regular intervals.

Editor

> A computer program used to edit computer programs and text files of, for example, data.

Electronic Data Interchange (EDI)

> The exchange of formatted data between computers, for example, invoices and statements.

Electronic mail

> The exchange of unstructured data between named individuals, through the use of electronic mailboxes on computers.

Encryption

> The process of encoding data in order to make it readable only to those authorised to do so.

Execute

> To carry out an instruction or program.

Exporting

> Converting data held in the format of one computer program into the format of another program, making it readable by the other program. For example, exporting a chart from Lotus 1-2-3 in order to read it into Microsoft Word.

Facsimile (fax)

A means of scanning images then transmitting the image over a telecommunications network and reproducing the image.

Fault-tolerant

A device or system that can continue to operate after the failure of one or more parts, made possible because it contains redundant components which can take over the functions of the failed parts. For example, an integrated circuit, computer or network.

Fifth generation

A generation of computer systems currently under development which display characteristics of intelligence. Originally announced in Japan in the early 1980's.

Floppy disc

A mass storage medium with magnetic material on a flimsy plastic sheet, in sizes of 8, 5.25 and 3.5 inch diameter. Some confusion is caused by their often being in hard plastic cases. (c.f. hard disc.)

Fortune 500

A list published annually by *Fortune* magazine detailing the five hundred largest companies in the world.

Fourth Generation

The current generation of computers, based on architectures developed in the 1970's.

Fourth Generation Language (4GL)

A high-level language designed for non-specialist end-users, to allow them to query data bases and to generate reports.

Gateway

The point at which two networks meet. If the networks operate different protocols then the necessary conversion is undertaken.

Giga

One billion units. For example, 1 Gigahertz is 1,000,000,000 Hertz.

Half-life

The time in which half the atoms of a given quantity of a radioactive isotope take to undergo at least one disintegration. Used by analogy to describe anything which decays rapidly or exponentially (c.f. critical mass).

Hard copy

Printed or plotted output from a computer system.

Hard disc

A mass storage device in which the magnetic material is on fixed or 'hard' metal discs. Also known as a Winchester disc, after the IBM research centre at which the disc drives were invented.

Hardware

Those parts of computer systems which are physical, for example, electronic and electro-mechanical components.

High-level language

A category of programming language which is only loosely related to the physical architecture of the computer, for example, C and COBOL.

Icon

An image used on a computer screen to represent a process, program or document. For example, a waste-bin is commonly used to represent somewhere files can be disposed of.

Image processing

The processing of an image or picture which has been converted into a digital array of data.

Integrated circuit

See chip.

Integrated Services Digital Network (ISDN)

A telecommunications system in which voice, data and images can be transmitted as a single data stream.

Integrity

The maintenance of the accuracy of a database by the testing of changes and updates before they are implemented.

Interpreter

A computer program which executes programs one line at a time. (c.f. Compiler.)

Kilo

A thousands units. For example, 4 kilobytes is 4,000 bytes.

Knowledge-based system

A category of information system which covers a wide range of systems which display 'knowledge' or 'intelligence', including: expert systems and machine translation. (See also Artificial intelligence.)

Laptop computer

A lightweight personal computer, typically around three kilograms, usually operating with battery power.

Large Scale Integration (LSI)

The combination of many components (transistors, resistors and capacitors on a single small piece of semiconductor).

Local Area Network (LAN)

A communications network linking devices within a confined area, for example, a university campus or office block.

Local loop

The telephone link between an exchange and a subscriber.

Machine code

The code used by a particular computer to control and execute operations.

Mega

A million units. For example, 1 Megabyte is 1,000,000 bytes.

Menu

A list displayed on a computer screen from which the user can select one of a number of options. Usually appearing as 'pop-up' or 'drop-down' menus.

Metadata

Data about data, i.e., the structure, syntax and semantics of data held in a database. (see also Data Dictionary)

Micro

One thousandth of a unit. For example, 1 micrometre is 0.001 of a metre.

Microcomputer

A computer with a single microprocessor.

Microprocessor

A 'computer on a chip', i.e., all the major components of a central processor unit in a single integrated circuit.

MIPS

Millions of Instructions per Second. A means of measuring the power of a computer.

Modem

Modulator-demodulator for use in connection of computers and other digital devices using analogue telephone networks.

Monitors

Visual display units for computers and terminals, based on the cathode ray tubes used in television sets.

Monopoly

The exclusive right or privilege to deal in a product or commodity, sometimes granted by government or achieved by dominance of the market.

Monopsony

A market in which only one buyer exists, for whose business a number of suppliers compete, or where one buyer is so large as to exercise undue influence over suppliers.

Nano

One millionth of a unit. For example, 1 nanometre is 0.000001 of a metre.

National champion

A company supported by its government through preferential purchasing by the public sector and, sometimes, by the private sector.

Nationalisation

To make something, usually land or business organisations, the property of the nation or state.

Natural language

A spoken or written language such as English or German, as distinct from a programming language.

Network

A loosely defined term for a collection of devices linked together using metal cables, optical fibre cables and radio links. (See local area networks and wide area networks.)

Niche

A small, distinct part of a market which can be directly addressed by a supplier.

Notepad computer

A very lightweight personal computer, approximately the size of an A4 notepad (294mm by 207 mm) and, perhaps, 25mm thick. Often using a pen or scribe to allow the use of handwriting.

Office Information System (OIS)

A toolbox of facilities for a community of users including: word processing, electronic mail, 'reach through' access to a variety of databases and other information systems.

Oligopoly
> A market where a small number of suppliers have undue influence or control.

Open System
> A system in which the devices are connected in a network using non-proprietary standards and protocols.

Open Systems Interconnection (OSI)
> A framework for the specification of standards for open system protocols.

Operating system
> The suite of computer programs which control the use of the system resources, for example, IBM VM or MS-DOS.

Optical fibre
> A thinly drawn strand of glass which transmits light very efficiently. The cables are flexible, light and carry enormous quantities of data.

Original Equipment Manufacturer (OEM)
> A company which resells equipment, purchased from another supplier, integrated into more comprehensive systems.

Packet switching
> A technique for the transmission of data by its division into small units or 'packets' using store-and-forward.

Palmtop
> A very compact personal computer, little more than the size of an electronic calculator.

Peripheral
> A device connected to a computer.

Plotter
> A pen-based output device, allowing the drawing of maps, graphs and diagrams.

Plug Compatible Manufacturer (PCM)
> A company which manufactures computer components and sub-systems which are compatible with the computer systems of another manufacturer, usually IBM. (PCM is also used to mean pulse code modulation.)

Pointer
> A device such as a mouse, joy-stick or tracker ball used to control the position of a cursor on a screen and thus to control computer programs.

Port
> (Verb) To transfer a program from one computer system to another (see Portability).
>
> (Noun) An output connection from a computer. For example, for connection of a computer to a printer or modem.

Portability
> (personal computers) A computer that can be carried (see also laptop and palmtop).
>
> (software) A measure of the ease with which a computer program can be transferred from one computer to another.

Printed Circuit Board (PCB)
> A plastic board with copper strips on the surface as conductors on which are mounted electronic components.

Printer

An output device that converts text or a chart into characters or lines and areas on paper. The usual types of printers are: dot-matrix, ink-jet, thermal and laser.

Privatisation

The selling into private ownership of companies which once belonged to the state (see also Nationalisation).

Profit Centre

An organisational division or unit which is divided for the purpose of allocation of profits and losses. Such a unit is expected to make profits and must trade as a company within a company.

Proprietary

Technology which is owned by a company and is protected by patent.

Protocol

A statement or agreement governing the exchange of data between two or more entities.

Prototype

A model from which something is developed.

Reduced Instruction Set Chip (RISC)

A chip which is specifically designed to have a small number of basic instructions which it can execute rapidly.

Reverse engineer

The task of taking apart a system in order to build a replica. Often undertaken illegally in order to develop similar products or clones.

Run

See execute.

Semiconductor

Originally the description of certain chemical substances which are neither conductors nor insulators. These materials, usually silicon, germanium or germanium arsenide, have been used to manufacture transistors and integrated circuits and the name is also used for those components.

Shrink-wrapped

A reference to certain types of software which are sold by dealers in packages which are wrapped in plastic at the point of manufacture. The implication being that they can be used without any modification or customisation.

Silicon Valley

An area of California, south of San Fransisco, centred on San Jose and Palo Alto where there is a considerable concentration of information-based industries.

Software

A term for the intangible parts of a computer, notably the software.

Structured Query Language (SQL)

An international standard for the interrogation and maintenance of relational databases.

Systems integrator

An information-based company supplying customers with information systems including hardware and software from a number of vendors.

Telecommunications

A network for the transmission of analogue or digital information.

Turnkey system

A system supplied by a vendor or value-added reseller or similar, which can be switched on and run without any further technical work on the part of the customer.

Unix

A leading computer operating system, developed at AT&T Bell Labs and originally used only in research labs and the universities. In the late 1980's it became a leading commercial system.

Value-Added Reseller (VAR)

A supplier of computer systems comprising systems (usually hardware) to which it has added value, usually by the provision of software for a particular application.

Very Large Scale Integration (VLSI)

The combination of more than 100,000 components (transistors, resistors and capacitors) on a single small piece of semiconductor.

Virtual

In effect, but not in fact. For example, a single hard disc on a file server can be made to appear as a number of virtual floppy disc drives to users of a network.

Visual Display Unit (VDU)

See Monitor.

Wide Area Network (WAN)

A communications network extending over a large area, usually beyond a single site and often requiring the use of services provided by a telecommunications operator.

WIMPs

Windows, Icons, Menus and Pointers.

Window

A portion of a screen within which a particular function or piece of software is operated. A computer screen can be divided into many windows, which can overlap and can operate simultaneously.

Word

A unit of computer memory, usually 16 or 32 bits, determining the maximum length of an instruction and the size of an integer.

Workstation

A category of computer which usually has a powerful processor with a keyboard and screen attached to a network. Many workstations are 'discless', relying on network servers to provide access to disc drives.

WYSIWYG

'What You See Is What You Get'. A term used to refer to word processing and desktop publishing software, where the screen appearance of the text is identical (or nearly so) to that which will appear on the printed page.

Index